BOB DORIAN'S
CLASSIC MOVIES

BOB DORIAN'S
CLASSIC
MOVIES

BOB DORIAN
HOST, AMERICAN MOVIE CLASSICS^{sm}
WITH DOROTHY CURLEY

BOB ADAMS, INC.
PUBLISHERS
Holbrook, Massachusetts

Published by
Bob Adams, Inc.
260 Center Street
Holbrook, MA 02343

Printed in the United States of America

ISBN: 1-55850-859-7

A   B   C   D   E   F   G   H   I   J

For Jane: my childhood sweetheart,
my wife, and my very best friend.

Contents

Acknowledgments

Many heartfelt thanks to our researcher, John Cocchi, whose knowledge of classic movies could fill many volumes. Welcome encouragement and suggestions from Rosemarie Spera, Pat Davis, George Callahan, Marino Amoruso, and Lewis Bogach. Special thanks to Norm Blumenthal and Richard Ballinger for putting the team together.

For my husband, John C. Tecklenburg II, for his gentle critique; and my parents, Helen and J. Clifford Curley, for all those dinners we ate on tray tables while watching the Sunday Afternoon Movie.

Most of all we thank the stars of Hollywood's Golden Age (whose lives off-screen were as fascinating as those of the characters they played), the producers, directors, writers, designers, composers, and technicians who brought the fantasies to life.

— *Bob Dorian* and *Dorothy Curley*

Introduction

I'm not a movie expert. I'm a fan. I happen to love good films, and I know a lot of great stories.

A movie expert "experiences a film"; I go to the movies. A movie expert watches for deep symbolism; I try to pick Betty Grable out of the chorus. And I don't care if Cary Grant always played himself. I happen to like watching him.

The experts will analyze why I have chosen this rather eclectic group of pictures. I'll be honest: one way or another, they're my favorites. I wouldn't argue that *Charlie Chan at Treasure Island* is one of the greatest films ever made, but I do like the stories associated with it, and I think you will, too.

The pictures included here do have one thing in common. They're the kind of movies you can watch over and over again, and each time you watch them they touch something within you. If you have a favorite I've missed, I apologize. Maybe I can include it in the next book.

—Bob Dorian

Alice Adams

1935, RKO Radio
Produced by Pandro Berman
Directed by George Stevens

S·Y·N·O·P·S·I·S

An unsophisticated small town girl (Katharine Hepburn), who yearns to be accepted by society, wins the love of an unpretentious man (Fred MacMurray).
Academy Award nominations: Best Picture; Katherine Hepburn, Best Actress.

How does a producer decide who should direct a movie? Sometimes it's a matter of fate. Other times fate gets a helping hand.

Katharine Hepburn had a clause in her contract giving her final approval of the director, so she and producer Pan Berman met to discuss who would be assigned to *Alice Adams.* They narrowed it down to two men. The most logical choice was William Wyler, who had just finished a hit film called *The Good Fairy*, and the unlikely one was thirty-one year old George Stevens, who had only one feature film to his credit. Wyler was a proven commodity but was often difficult to work with, and Hepburn knew that making a picture with Wyler could be an unpleasant experience. He also came with a high price tag. Stevens, on the other hand, was under contract to Berman and received a relatively low weekly salary. His style was quieter than Wyler's, and besides, Katharine Hepburn found the young director quite attractive.

After arguing the pros and cons of each man, they decided to let fate make the decision. Berman flipped a coin: heads it's Wyler, tails it's Stevens. The coin came down heads. William Wyler would direct *Alice Adams.* Berman took one look at Hepburn's face and said, "Let's flip again." They did, it came up tails, and they both cheered. So much for fate!

Although Hepburn wanted Stevens on the picture, it did not mean that director and leading lady worked together in perfect harmony. In fact, on the first day of shooting she was afraid she had made a serious mistake. She and Stevens disagreed so violently about the opening shot that she left the set and spent most of the afternoon in her dressing room. Total footage in the can for an entire day's shooting: thirty seconds.

The tension between director and leading lady was evident; for the next several weeks they addressed each other as "Mr. Stevens" and "Miss Hepburn." When they rehearsed the porch scene with Fred MacMurray, she wanted to play it her way; Stevens wanted her to tone down her actions and reactions. On the day they were scheduled to shoot, they still hadn't resolved their differences. Throughout the morning Hepburn did the scene her way and Stevens told her to do it again his way. They broke for lunch, came back, and did the scene again and again and then again. It was a battle of wills, but after seventy-nine takes, Hepburn gave in and toned down her actions.

On another

occasion, it didn't take seventy-nine takes for Hepburn to concede. After spending hours rehearsing a scene in which Hepburn ran into her room, threw herself on a bed and cried, Stevens decided he wanted it to

have a totally different feel. He told her to walk slowly to the window, stare out, and begin to weep. When she refused, saying she wanted to cry on the bed, the way they had rehearsed it, he told her if she wasn't a good enough actress to cry, he would have someone else dub in the sobs. Hepburn was so annoyed that he would question her acting ability that she did the scene as he had instructed, and at the proper moment, she broke down and wept. After Stevens gently said, "Cut," she turned to him and, using his given name for the first time, said, "How was that, George?"

In another scene Hepburn cried on cue at the end of a long speech delivered by Fred Stone. The first time they filmed it there was something wrong with the lighting, the next time, a problem with the microphones.

Stevens was amazed when, time after time, Hepburn was able to cry exactly on cue. She explained that she was so moved by Stone's performance, she could have cried fifty times when she heard him say the word "home."

Despite their differences on the set, Hepburn recognized that George Stevens was able to bring out her simpler, softer side as few other directors have ever done. Stevens' three films with Hepburn show a vulnerable side of the usually tough Katherine Hepburn that has rarely been captured on film.

Alice Adams was one of over six films in which Hedda Hopper appeared during the 1930s. She gave up acting after she began her gossip column in 1938.

All About Eve

1950, 20th Century-Fox
Produced by Darryl F. Zanuck
Directed by Joseph Mankiewicz

S·Y·N·O·P·S·I·S

An established stage actress (Bette Davis) finds her position threatened by an ambitious newcomer (Anne Baxter).

Academy Awards: Best Picture; Joseph Mankiewicz, Best Director; George Sanders, Supporting Actor; Joseph Mankiewicz, Screenplay; Edith Head, Charles LeMaire, Costume Design; Fox Sound Department, Sound Recording.

Academy Award nominations: Bette Davis, Anne Baxter, Best Actress; Celeste Holm, Thelma Ritter, Supporting Actress; Milton Krasner, Black and White Cinematography; Lyle Wheeler and George Davis, Art Direction; Alfred Newman, Score; Barbara McLean, Film Editing.

Fate often takes a hand in determining who gets cast in major motion pictures. In 1950 Claudette Colbert was in the hospital suffering from a cracked vertebra received in a skiing accident. Darryl Zanuck sent her a most unusual get-well present: a bouquet of flowers tied to a pogo stick, his not-so-subtle way of telling her to come back to work. He delayed filming *All About Eve* for two months because he wanted Colbert for the role of Margo Channing. But he couldn't hold the production forever, and Claudette Colbert's misfortune became Bette Davis' lucky break. Davis had been cast in so many mediocre pictures in the late forties that she said director Joseph Mankiewicz's decision to cast her in *All About Eve* "resurrected her from the dead."

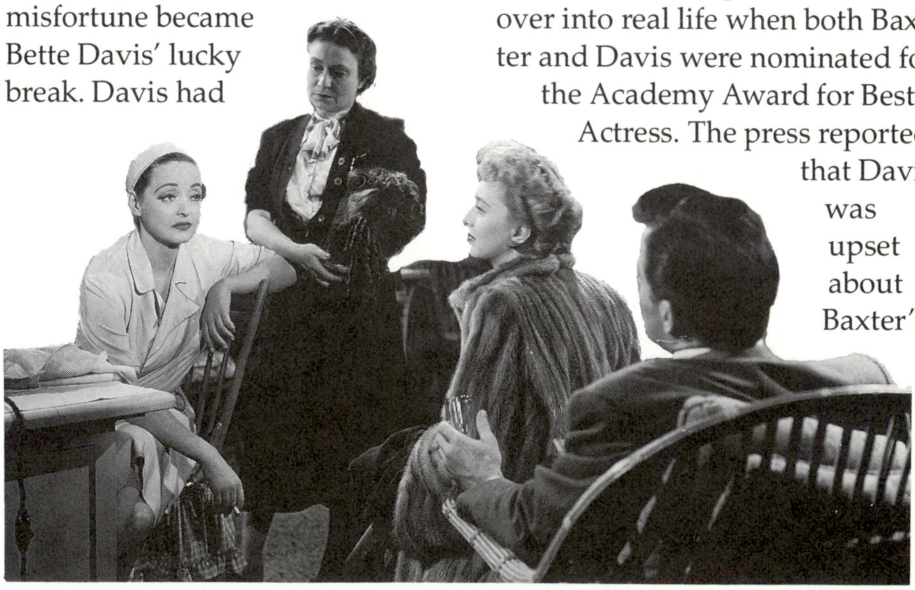

This picture is about the competition between Eve, a younger actress played by Anne Baxter, and Margo, the older woman whose star is beginning to fade. That competition carried over into real life when both Baxter and Davis were nominated for the Academy Award for Best Actress. The press reported that Davis was upset about Baxter's nomination in the Best Actress category, rather than as Best Supporting Actress. Baxter replied, "The movie's called *All About Eve*, not *All About Margo*." Neither Baxter nor Davis won the coveted award that year. The only performer to win an Oscar for *All About Eve* was George Sanders, in the Supporting Actor category. When his name was called, Sanders went up on stage, bowed to the audience, walked off, and began to cry.

All About Eve received a record fourteen Oscar nominations and beat out *Sunset Boulevard, Born Yesterday,* and *Father of the Bride* for Best Picture. When Mankiewicz walked away with Oscars for Best Director and Best Screenplay, he became the first person to win four Academy Awards in two years. The previous year he had won for writing and directing *A Letter to Three Wives.*

With all the attention given to the Oscar nominees, it was easy to overlook the performance turned in by an insecure newcomer named Marilyn Monroe. She was signed by 20th Century-Fox for $500 a week and a guarantee of one week's work. During location filming in San Francisco, Mankiewicz recalled that, even when invited to join the others at breaks or for meals, Marilyn stayed by herself. One of Marilyn's greatest insecurities was her lack of formal education, and she was afraid that in such literate company her ignorance would be exposed.

Hollywood legend holds that this film was based on an incident from Tallulah Bankhead's life, but that's not true. *All About Eve* was based on a short story called "The Wisdom of Eve," written by actress Mary Orr for the May, 1946, issue of Hearst's *International Cosmopolitan* magazine. It was the true story of German actress Elisabeth Bergner and her husband, director Paul Czinner, who had befriended a young actress, only to have her turn on them. As for the Tallulah

Bankhead connection, Bette Davis supposedly based her portrayal of Margo Channing on Bankhead. Tallulah later played Margo in a television version of *All About Eve* in 1952.

"Minor awards are for such as the writer and director—since their function is merely to construct a tower so that the world can applaud a light which flashes on top of it."

—Addison in *All About Eve*, speaking of writers and directors in the theater. Written by Joseph Mankiewicz, who won Academy Awards for writing and directing the film.

Anna and the King of Siam

1946, 20th Century-Fox
Produced by Louis D. Lighton
Directed by John Cromwell

S·Y·N·O·P·S·I·S

In 1862, an Englishwoman goes to Siam to tutor the wives and children of the King.

Academy Awards: Arthur Miller, Black and White Cinematography; Lyle Wheeler and William Darling, Black and White Interior Decoration.

Academy Award nominations: Gale Sondergaard, Supporting Actress; Bernard Hermann, Score of Comedy or Drama.

The story of Rex Harrison's first trip to Hollywood almost qualifies as an outline for a mini-series. His adventures began when he, his wife, Lilli Palmer, and their infant son, Carey, sold their home, packed up their belongings, and sailed for America. Their crossing was unusual because in 1945 they were the only civilians on a ship filled with American soldiers returning home after World War II. What a wild trip that must have been!

Harrison and his wife understood that the crowds welcoming the ship in the New York harbor were there to greet the soldiers, not one relatively unknown British actor and his family. After three more days crossing the continent on the Superchief, a representative of the studio met the Harrison family at the train station. The man was amazed that Rex Harrison so closely resembled the real King of Siam, the character he had come to play. Harrison took this as a compliment until he saw a picture of the king, who was about twenty years older, two feet shorter, and, in Harrison's opinion, extremely ugly.

After he and his family settled into a house they had rented from Clifton Webb, he was ready to jump into the part. That's when he discovered another fact of life in Hollywood. The sets weren't ready, so the studio was willing to pay Rex Harrison $4,000 a week to do absolutely nothing. He used the time to good advantage, researching the King's life and preparing for the role. Once they began filming, however, director John Cromwell was so annoyed that Harrison had worked on the character without his direction that throughout the five months of filming, he ignored Harrison and limited his critique to leading lady Irene Dunne and the supporting cast. Harrison also found it odd that the actors he socialized with, including Ronald Colman, Tyrone Power, Clark Gable, and producer Sam Goldwyn, never talked about acting or asked for advice. American filmmaking certainly seemed different from the English variety. For Rex Harrison, working in Hollywood was like being a stranger in a strange land.

For the role of the king, Harrison's eyes were fitted with small rubber attachments to give him an Oriental look, and he and Linda Darnell wore body make-up to color their skin a light brown. Gale Sondergaard, who played the first wife, was allergic to the make-up, so she spent weeks in the sun getting a dark tan. During the filming, she also came down with a condition the doctors called "housewife's knees" as a result of spending so much time bowing and kneeling.

The terror of housewife's knees was mild compared with what Linda Darnell and Neyle Morrow experienced, however. For the scene in which they were burned at the stake, they were chained to two huge piles of eucalyptus logs, which were set on fire. The pungent odor of burning eucalyptus permeated the entire back lot. After they finished the scene, Darnell found that her Panung, that sarong-like dress Siamese women wore, was severely scorched in several places. That was as close to method acting as she cared to come.

Don't go looking for Siam on a contemporary map; it no longer exists as an independent kingdom. It's now the country of Thailand, with its capitol at Bangkok. Just north of the city, preserved as an historical monument, is the summer palace of the King, where the real Anna Owens actually taught

the royal family. If you ever visit there, watch the movie before you go, because you'll recognize many of the rooms and locations, duplicated for the film. In fact, when Rex Harrison visited the palace in the 1970s, he felt as if he were back on the Fox sound stage. By the way, if you do visit, wear dark socks. You'll have to take off your shoes before entering, and if you wear light socks, they'll be black by the time you come out.

"The status I have achieved has been achieved through tears. So for my career, I cry."
—Irene Dunne

Arsenic and Old Lace

1944, Warner Bros.
Produced by Howard Lindsay and Russell Crouse
Directed by Frank Capra

S·Y·N·O·P·S·I·S

A newly married man (Cary Grant) is horrified to learn his maiden aunts (Josephine Hull, Jean Adair) have been serving poisoned elderberry wine to lonely men.

In 1922 a teenager named Archie Leach was a member of the Pender Giants, a traveling troupe of stilt walkers and acrobats featured in circuses and on the vaudeville circuit. The troupe was booked into the Temple Theater in Rochester, New York, when Archie came down with rheumatic fever. He was much too sick to perform and spent several weeks confined to his room in a boarding house. One of the headliners at the Temple was a comedienne named Jean Adair. She recognized the boy's loneliness and visited him daily, bringing him candy, fruit, and most importantly, companionship.

Fast-forward almost twenty years to the fall of 1941. Director Frank Capra volunteered for the U.S. Signal Corps but knew he wouldn't be called up for several months. His family couldn't maintain their standard of living on his army paycheck, and he wanted to make enough money to see them through his absence. He saw *Arsenic and Old Lace* on Broadway and knew that with its one set and limited characters it could quickly and easily be made into a film. However, Jack Warner owned the rights, with the stipulation that the picture couldn't be released until after the Broadway run was over. At the rate tickets were selling, that could be three or four years in the future.

Capra contacted the cast and found out that Josephine Hull, Jean Adair, and John Alexander were all owed four weeks' vacation, and would be willing to appear in the film version. Next he approached Cary Grant promising that if the actor accepted the role, he'd rework the script so that Mortimer Brewster was a starring role.

Grant accepted. Capra then approached Jack Warner. He convinced the studio executive of the wisdom of making the picture while Cary Grant and the original Broadway performers were available. Warner surprised the industry by hiring Capra to make a film that would spend several years in the Warner storage vaults.

The first day on the set Jean Adair was introduced to Cary Grant. Grant told her that they had met before; Adair said that, while she was certainly familiar with Grant's work, she couldn't recall ever having been introduced. He said, "I'm Archie Leach," and smiled as recognition dawned on her face. As they reminisced about the time she spent nursing him in that Rochester boarding house, she said, "You were a very nice boy, and so grateful!" Grant kissed her gently on the cheek and said, "He's still grateful, Miss Adair."

Cary Grant's gratitude did not end with his feelings for the lady who had helped him so

many years earlier. He was also grateful for the success he enjoyed, both in his adopted country and in his native England. He wanted to give something back, so he donated his entire after-tax salary from *Arsenic and Old Lace* to the American Red Cross, the United Service Organization, and British War Relief.

The fact that he was essentially working without pay didn't mean he was any less committed to the quality of the picture. As always he was involved in every detail of his work, even changing lamps, curtains, and furniture he felt were inappropriate in the Brewster house.

Grant was surprised to find another old friend of Archie Leach at work on *Arsenic and Old Lace*. Grant, when he was still a teenager named Archie, had once shared a New York apartment with an aspiring costume designer named Jack Kelly, who was now designing the costumes for the *Arsenic* cast. Grant decided it was time to put Archie Leach officially to rest, and he arranged to have that name appear in the film on one of the tombstones in the graveyard next door to the Brewster house.

Filming was still underway when the Japanese bombed Pearl Harbor. The days following the attack were grim, and it took all the combined comedic talent of its stars to keep the picture on a

light note. The day after the attack, a representative of the Signal Corps contacted Capra about his impending active duty, but the Corps gave Capra an additional six weeks to edit his picture before reporting for duty.

After just four weeks of filming, *Arsenic and Old Lace* was in the can. The three Broadway performers went back to New York, where the stage version ran for more than 1,300 performances. Because of the play's overwhelming success, Warner Bros. could not release the film version until the fall of 1944.

P·L·A·Y·E·R·S

Cary Grant .... Mortimer Brewster
Raymond Massey
.... Jonathan Brewster
Priscilla Lane............. Elaine Harper
Josephine Hull .... Abby Brewster
Jean Adair .... Martha Brewster
Featuring:
    Jack Carson
    Edward Everett Horton
    Peter Lorre
    James Gleason
    John Alexander
    Grant Mitchell

"People can find enough misery and hardship in the world without going to the movies to find it. That thought influences me more than anything else in picking a script."
—Cary Grant.

Ball of Fire

1941, RKO Radio
Produced by Samuel Goldwyn
Directed by Howard Hawks

S·Y·N·O·P·S·I·S

While researching an encyclopedia, a linguistics professor (Gary Cooper) falls in love with a stripper (Barbara Stanwyck).

Academy Award nominations:
Barbara Stanwyck, Best Actress; Billy Wilder and Thomas Monroe, Original Story; Alfred Newman, Score; Thomas Moulton, Sound.

How do you write off bar bills and gambling losses as legitimate business expenses? People in the movie business call it "research." Billy Wilder and his partner, Charles Brackett, got away with it in 1940, and they sold the results of their research to Sam Goldwyn for $10,000. At least, that's what Billy Wilder thought they would get. Goldwyn agreed to give him $7,500 up front and the additional $2,500 if *Ball of Fire* was a hit. Despite good returns at the box office, Wilder had considerable trouble getting the additional $2,500 out of the producer.

The story they sold was a take-off of *Snow White and the Seven Dwarfs*, with Snow White a stripper and the Dwarfs a group of aging professors working on an encyclopedia. Gary Cooper plays the only youthful professor who, while working on an entry for "Slang," realizes his life had been far too sheltered and goes about correcting his educational deficiencies with a crash course in moral corruption tutored by Sugarpuss O'Shea. Of course, Wilder and Brackett had to do the same kind of research, but in their case they had the

carte blanche of a Hollywood expense account.

There is one scene in *Ball of Fire* that had all of Hollywood talking. Director Howard Hawks told cinematographer Gregg Toland what he wanted, and Toland got it—

though it had originally sounded impossible. When Gary Cooper walks into Barbara Stanwyck's bedroom, only her eyes are visible, shining in the darkness. It had seemed like an impossible request, because if Toland threw enough light on her eyes to make the shot work, the light would also illuminate the rest of her face.

How was it done? Toland told Stanwyck not to report to the make-up department; he had something different in mind. To create the effect the director wanted, he applied a light coat of black greasepaint to Stanwyck's face. When they shot the scene, all the camera captured were her tempting, come-hither eyes glowing in the blackness.

While Hollywood was talking about Toland's impossible shot, the rest of the country was learning to talk to the younger generation. In the course of studying the latest slang, Gary Cooper was taught that "dig me" means "understand," a "lambie pie" is a charming person, the "screaming mimis" refers to a nervous condition, a person who's "off the beam" is functioning poorly, and "get chicken" means to become cowardly. For most of the country, these definitions were on the cutting edge of cool. Once *Ball of Fire* hit the theaters, the older generation was able to communicate with the younger generation, at least temporarily.

One of the highlights of *Ball of Fire* is the cabaret scene in which Barbara Stanwyck sings "The Drum Boogie" to the music of Gene Krupa and his band. During a

break, Krupa started playing the song on a matchbox, using the wooden matches as drumsticks. Director Howard Hawks loved it, Krupa loved it, Stanwyck loved it, and so did the rest of the world. The tiny matchbox variation was such a contrast to Krupa's usual outrageous style, Hawks used it in the final film.

While Krupa's inspiration was a welcome addition to the picture, Irving Fein's brainstorm bombed. Fein was Sam Goldwyn's publicity chief, and he wanted to get as much sensational press as possible out of the striptease aspects of Stanwyck's character. He hired some extras to picket the Goldwyn studios with signs like, "Goldwyn unfair to strippers" and "Why don't you use a real stripper?" It worked, but Fein wanted Goldwyn to go one step further. There was a

stripper in Los Angeles named Betty Rowland who actually called herself "Ball of Fire." Wouldn't it be great publicity if she sued the studio? Before he could put his plan into effect, Goldwyn received a little surprise. That "Ball of Fire" had already filed suit for half a million dollars in damages. Sam Goldwyn settled out of court, but he could never be convinced that it was only a coincidence.

One of the books used as a prop in *Ball of Fire* had the title "The Life and Times of Irving Sindler." Irving Sindler was the prop master on *Ball of Fire*.

Bedlam

1946, RKO Radio
Produced by Val Lewton
Directed by Mark Robson

S·Y·N·O·P·S·I·S

A woman (Anna Lee), wrongly imprisoned in an insane asylum, leads the inmates to revolt against inhumane treatment.

Look up the word "bedlam" in the dictionary, and you'll find it has come to mean, "a scene of uproar or confusion." That wasn't the original meaning of the word. "Bedlam" was a nickname for St. Mary's of Bethlehem, an eighteenth century London hospital. Say "Bethlehem" quickly and you can see the derivation of the word: Bethlehem... bethlem... bedlam. Why would the name of a hospital become synonymous with mass confusion? Today we'd call St. Mary's a hospital for the mentally ill. In the eighteenth century it was called an insane asylum. Because doctors of those days were not prepared to deal with diseases of the mind, patients were locked up, chained, or even tortured in the name of medicine. What better setting for a horror film than a place of utter despair, a place where human minds are held captive?

Although Bedlam was a real place where inmates were not treated but rather mistreated, the specific events and characters in the film were fictitious. That didn't matter to the British censors, who banned the film for its attack on the integrity of a great British institution.

Horror impresario Val Lewton was inspired to write the script for *Bedlam* after he saw a painting called "The Rake's Progress" by eighteenth century artist William Hogarth. A depiction of life in an asylum, it's the eighth in a series that details the rise and fall of a young man who inherits wealth. The picture imparts the general confusion of the place and the abject despair of inmates, who roam freely within its walls. Many of the figures inspired characters in the film, including two fashionably dressed women who are seen whispering together. They had escaped the tedium of their daily routine by paying admission to the hospital to laugh at the antics of the inmates. In this macabre film Boris Karloff directs the inmates to perform for the wealthy spectators. The painting was also used as a transition between scenes, an element that's often cut when *Bedlam* is shown on broadcast television.

Bedlam was the last of the eleven horror pictures Val Lewton produced for RKO between 1942 and 1946. Lewton's horror films are considered classics because they were more literate than the average horror entry. Instead of dinosaurs from the deep or creatures from Transylvanian forests, Lewton's monsters were often found in the minds of human beings. His poetic themes almost always centered on the fear

of the unknown.

Lewton was a former script editor for David O. Selznick and, like the best Hollywood producers, he left his own recognizable mark on all his movies. His work for the RKO horror unit included *Cat People, The Seventh Victim, The Body Snatcher,* and *Bedlam.* He started out producing low-budget movies, but the critical acclaim he received influenced RKO's decision to assign him larger budgets. A higher budget for Lewton was still minor compared with most Hollywood productions, however, and he was forced to scrounge whatever he could from the RKO back lot. The interior of the asylum was actually the church where Bing Crosby preached in *The Bells of St. Mary's,* and many of the costumes were recycled from other projects.

I've often wondered if Lewton's fascination with man's destruction of himself and

P·L·A·Y·E·R·S

Boris Karloff ....Master George Sims
Anna Lee .... Nell Bowen
Billy House .... Lord Mortimer
Richard Fraser ....Hannay
Featuring:
Glenn Vernon
Ian Wolfe
Jason Robards Sr.
Leyland Hodgson
Joan Newton
Elizabeth Russell
Victor Holbrook
Robert Clarke
Larry Wheat
Bruce Edwards
John Beck
Ellen Corby
John Ince
Skelton Knaggs
John Goldsworthy
Foster Phinney
Tommy Noonan
Harry Harvey

the fear of premature death he exhibited in his movies was prophetic. He died unexpectedly in 1951 at the age of forty-six.

One of Anna Lee's costumes in *Bedlam* had previously been worn by Vivien Leigh in *Gone With the Wind*.

The Best Years of Our Lives

1946, RKO Radio
Produced by Samuel Goldwyn
Directed by William Wyler

S·Y·N·O·P·S·I·S

Three veterans (Fredric March, Dana Andrews, Harold Russell) face different crises when they return home from World War II.

Academy Awards: Best Picture; William Wyler, Best Director; Fredric March, Best Actor; Harold Russell, Supporting Actor; Robert E. Sherwood, Screenplay; Hugo Friedhofer, Scoring of a Dramatic or Comedy Picture; Daniel Mandell, Film Editing.

Academy Award nominations: Gordon Sawyer, Sound Recording.

What movies do best is to show people whose lives have changed, radically, unalterably, permanently. In 1946, World War II was over and millions of American servicemen returned home. After seeing the violence and destructive power of war, it was difficult for these veterans to pick up their civilian lives. Producer Sam Goldwyn read an article in *Time* that detailed the unique problems of the returning GIs, problems faced not only by the men themselves but also by their families and friends. Goldwyn assigned war correspondent MacKinlay Kantor to write a story dealing with the issue and Pulitzer Prize-winning playwright Robert Sherwood to turn the story into a screenplay. The result, *The Best Years of Our Lives*, is one of the most meaningful and moving films ever made in Hollywood.

It's the story of three servicemen coming home to the same small Midwestern community. In announcing his decision to make the film, Sam Goldwyn declared that the public was bored with all the old formulas: they wanted real stories about real people. Goldwyn went on to criticize Hollywood, saying the in-

dustry must find "honest stories with something important to say, stories that reflect these disturbing times in which we live." This raised the ire of fellow producer (and chief competitor) Darryl Zanuck, who accused Goldwyn of being a master of self-promotion. According to Zanuck, if Goldwyn had just produced a musical, he'd be saying Hollywood's job was to brighten the lives of the people and not worry them with serious issues.

Director William Wyler had no problem casting Fredric March and Dana Andrews as two of the principals, but finding an actor to play the third veteran wasn't as simple. The character was a man who had lost both his hands in the war, and Wyler knew that no mere actor, no matter how good, could play the part. He cast a man with no acting experience: Harold Russell, who had lost both hands in a training accident and had stain-

less steel hooks on the ends of his arms. In his first commercial film Russell won an Oscar for Best Supporting Actor, as well as a special Oscar for "bringing hope and courage to his fellow veterans." If the Academy Board of Governors had known Russell would win for Best Supporting Actor, they would probably not have made the special award. The Board, which considered him a long shot at best, inadvertently made him the only person ever awarded two Oscars for the same performance.

Despite the good feelings brought on by winning seven Oscars, bad feelings between Sam Goldwyn and William Wyler continued. Wyler claimed that Goldwyn had promised to bill *The Best Years of Our Lives* as a "William Wyler Production." When Goldwyn refused, Wyler ended their thirteen-year association. Wyler and Goldwyn not only refused to work together for many years, but also refused to even speak to one another.

Eleven years after their triumphant night at the Oscars, Wyler sued Goldwyn for $400,000, which he claimed was his share of the profits from *The Best Years Of Our Lives*. Goldwyn settled out of court for an undisclosed sum.

Over the years the wars have changed, the issues have changed, the men have changed,

but the emotions will never change. Because it deals with universal issues faced by men returning home from war, *The Best Years of Our Lives* survives the test of time.

Fredric March's daughter, Penny, wasn't impressed with her father's Oscar win. She was more concerned with the terminal embarrassment only a teenager can feel when her classmates actually saw her father on the screen clad only in pajamas.

A Bill of Divorcement

1932, RKO Radio
Produced by David O. Selznick
Directed by George Cukor

S·Y·N·O·P·S·I·S

A man's (John Barrymore) bout with mental illness affects his daughter's (Katharine Hepburn) happiness.

In Hollywood, legends grow on every tree and bush, so it was natural that a few myths grew up around the stars of *A Bill of Divorcement*. Why? Because it was the meeting of two legends, one waning, one just beginning.

When John Barrymore was signed to make *A Bill of Divorcement*, his contract guaranteed he would be finished filming in just one month. This gave David Selznick very little time to find a leading lady. He and director George Cukor agreed to use a virtually unknown New York actress named Katharine Hepburn. While neither man predicted stardom for this unusual, outspoken New Englander, they both agreed she had a special quality.

Many of the stories frequently told about *A Bill of Divorcement* are apocryphal. There's one that says Barrymore once invited Hepburn into his dressing room, threw off all his clothes and attempted to seduce her. In one telling of the story, she ran out of the room saying, "My father doesn't want me to have babies." In another version of the same story, he did invite the young actress to his dressing room for a little private coaching, but instead of disrobing, confessed, "I think I've made a mistake," upon which Hepburn left.

Friction between the leading man and lady was allegedly so great that Hepburn was supposed to have said, "I'll never act with you again," to which Barrymore replied, "But my dear, I wasn't aware you had begun." Although it's an incident that has become part of the Barrymore legend, it never happened. Once filming began, Barrymore developed a deep respect for Hepburn's talent. He said she reminded him of his mother, Georgiana Drew, whom he considered the best actress of all time. Barrymore went out of his way to help Hepburn and coached her in every one of their scenes together. Because she had a tendency to turn away from the camera, for example, he would position himself with his back to the camera, forcing her to face it. She admitted her debt to him: "He never criticized me. He just shoved me into what I ought to do. He taught me all he could pour into a greenhorn in that short time . . . I learned a tremendous lot from Barrymore."

It was Katharine Hepburn's burning desire to excel in this role that inspired Barrymore's own performance. In one emotional scene between the two, Barrymore finished a take and saw that Hepburn was disappointed with him. In that moment, she made him realize

he had walked through the scene without putting anything of himself into his performance. He turned to director George Cukor and requested another take, a take Hepburn later recalled as the most shattering acting she had ever seen. Years later, Hepburn remembered John Barrymore as "a gentle, thoughtful human being," an image very much at odds with the acerbic, self-centered Barrymore reputation.

Playing a man who was struggling with mental illness had a special meaning for John Barrymore. His father, Maurice Barrymore, who had also been one of the premiere actors of his day, began to lose touch with reality as he grew older. He'd forget where he was, or even who he was. He experienced delusions and slipped into homicidal rages. Several times he awoke to find himself in what they called "the insane pavilion" at Bellveue Hospital. Unable to cope with his illness, his family was

forced to send him to the Long Island Home at Amityville, New York, where Maurice Barrymore spent the last four years of his life.

Throughout those years, John stood by, helpless, as his father slowly lost all contact with reality. John Barrymore was also afraid that he would inherit his father's madness. He brought a special quality to his role in *A Bill of Divorcement* because he had experienced first-hand a man's horror at the thought of passing his insanity on to his children.

"Katharine Hepburn . . . seems definitely established for an important cinema career."

—Film critic Richard Watts' review of *A Bill of Divorcement* for the *New York Herald Tribune*

The Bishop's Wife

1947, RKO Radio
Produced by Samuel Goldwyn
Directed by Henry Koster

S·Y·N·O·P·S·I·S

An angel (Cary Grant) helps a Bishop (David Niven) straighten out his financial and marital problems.

Academy Award: Goldwyn Sound Department, Sound Recording.

Academy Award nominations: Best Picture; Henry Koster, Best Director; Hugo Friedhofer, Scoring of a Dramatic or Comedy Picture; Monica Collingwood, Film Editing.

When they started filming *The Bishop's Wife* in 1947, David Niven was cast as the angel, Cary Grant was the bishop, and Teresa Wright was to play the bishop's wife. William Seiter was the director. Try to remember those assignments; beginning with the director, they are about to change faster than a Chinese fire drill. William Seiter had been a director since the silent days and had moved up from one-reelers to Abbott and Costello films. Somehow, his agent had talked Sam Goldwyn into hiring him at two-and-a-half times the salary of the highest paid directors of that time. After weeks of filming at a cost of $900,000, Goldwyn saw the rushes and was horrified. He paid Seiter half his outrageous fee to leave the project. Goldwyn then hired Henry Koster and told him to scrap everything and start from scratch.

Here's where the story gets interesting. According to Goldwyn's biographer, Goldwyn told Koster he had a brilliant idea. He wanted Grant and Niven to swap characters: Grant would play the Angel and Niven the Bishop. According to this version of the story, Grant was furious. He thought the Bishop was the better character and

sulked throughout the rest of the filming.

According to Cary Grant's biographer, however, it was Grant who went to Sam Goldwyn and begged for the switch. Goldwyn resisted at first and then gave in. It really doesn't matter who convinced whom; it was a good decision and that's the way Koster did the film.

Meanwhile, Teresa Wright became pregnant, so Goldwyn called Koster into his office to talk about a replacement. "How would you like to work with Laurette Taylor?" Goldwyn asked the director. "I'd love to," Koster replied, "but she's dead." Goldwyn became angry and swore that she had been sitting in his office just two hours earlier. He pressed the intercom on his desk and asked his secretary the name of the actress he interviewed. "Loretta Young," came the reply. "See," said Goldwyn, "she is *not* dead!"

When Koster began production, he ran into a dilemma. Cary Grant and Loretta Young, who both had the same best side, refused to allow him to shoot their right profiles. It was difficult to do a love scene with two actors facing the same direction, but Koster came up with a solution. He filmed the scene with Young looking out a window, talking about how beautiful the stars are. Grant came up from behind and put his hands on her shoulders. They were both facing the same direction, and both showed their left profiles to the camera.

When Goldwyn saw the rushes, he demanded to know why Koster chose such unusual staging for the scene. Koster told him, and Goldwyn stormed into Loretta Young's dressing room, saying, "If I only get half your face, you only get half your salary."

After filming was finished, Goldwyn was faced with another problem. He didn't like the way the film played for a preview audience, so he offered Billy Wilder and Charles Brackett a substantial amount of money to write several additional scenes over the weekend. Wilder and Brackett wrote the material, but they told Goldwyn they had decided to forget about billing him. "That was providential," Goldwyn replied, "because

P·L·A·Y·E·R·S

Cary Grant .... Dudley
David Niven......... Henry Brougham
Loretta Young......... Julia Brougham
Monty Woolley ..... Prof. Wutheridge
Featuring:
    James Gleason
    Gladys Cooper
    Elsa Lanchester
    Sara Haden
    Karolyn Grimes
    Tito Vuolo
    Regis Toomey
    Sarah Edwards
    Margaret McWade
    Anne O'Neal
    Ben Erway
    Erville Alderson
    Bobby Anderson
    Teddy Infuhr
    Eugene Borden
    Almira Sessions
    Claire DuBrey
    Margaret Wells
    Kitty O'Neill
    Isabel Jewell
    David Leonard
    Dorothy Vaughn
    Edgar Dearing
    The Mitchell Boys Choir

I've already forgotten about paying you!"

While filming a snow scene for *The Bishop's Wife*, Cary Grant stopped the action, saying that the windows would have frosted over. Grant refused to continue until prop men coated the windows with artificial frost.

The Boy with Green Hair

1948, RKO Radio
Produced by Dore Schary
Co-producers Adrian Scott and Stephen Ames
Directed by Joseph Losey

S·Y·N·O·P·S·I·S

When a child's hair turns green, he warns the world about the effects of war on children.

In the thirties and forties, movies that had a message were considered box office poison. When asked why he didn't include messages in his pictures, Sam Goldwyn gave his classic reply, "If you want a message, call Western Union." When *Crossfire* became RKO's biggest hit of 1947, the studio thought times were changing. *Crossfire* was one of the first major motion pictures to address problems of anti-Semitism, and with the picture's success, studio executives began looking for a cause that would top racial bigotry. It couldn't be anything too controversial, like politics or religion. It had to be something worth crusading for, but not anything that would make a lot of people angry. They settled on the perfect cause, one that would generate controversy without generating opposition. They decided to make *The Boy With Green Hair*, a movie about the effects of war on children. After all, who could take a stand against war orphans?

One man could, and unfortunately he bought the studio. When Howard Hughes bought RKO, he examined all of the movies that were in production. Hughes was so radically anti-communist that he disagreed with this film's pacifist message. He canceled its Thanksgiving release and put it back in production. Hughes didn't want to lose the investment he had in the initial work, but he demanded that several new scenes be shot and the whole picture reedited with a more conservative slant. After several months' work, he realized that diluting the film took away its power, so he changed his mind and released it in its original form.

One thing Hughes didn't delete from *The Boy With Green Hair* was a song called "Nature Boy," written by eden ahbez. All his life he was known as eden (with a small "e") ahbez (with a small "a"). He was a very religious man and felt the only name that should be capitalized was the name of God. While *The Boy with Green Hair* didn't make "Nature Boy" a hit, Nat King Cole's later recording of the song was one of his earliest hits.

Audiences liked the film, in which Pat O'Brien was allowed to show off his seldom-seen singing and dancing talents. Dean Stockwell was believable as the

boy even Miss Clairol couldn't help. He was the son of Broadway performers and made his stage debut at he age of seven alongside his brother, Guy Stockwell. Dean was one of Hollywood's most successful juveniles in the late forties, and his popularity, as well as the movie's timely message, helped bring people into the theaters.

While the movie and its stars attracted audiences, the advertising slogan also helped make this movie a hit. The publicity department was under strict orders from Howard Hughes to downplay the film's anti-war message, so the publicists came up with a classic ad line: "Please don't tell why his hair turned green." Hughes was satisfied that the print ads didn't say anything about the anti-war message the film delivered, and audiences were sufficiently intrigued to go to the theaters.

While Hughes' attitude may seem extreme, you must remember what was happening in the film industry at that time. The word "liberal" was considered synonymous with "communist." Anyone without a strong commitment to fight communism with whatever weapons it required was suspected of being a red, including two of the people who worked on this production.

Producer Adrian Scott, who was replaced when he was named as one of the original Hollywood Ten, was later blacklisted. Director Joseph Losey moved to England and worked under a pseudonym rather than live the life of a blacklisted director. Ironically, the movie that showcased the unfairness of war on children couldn't help two men who were caught in an unjust political war.

The Boy With Green Hair was the eighth film for fourteen-year-old Dwayne Hickman, years before he became television's Dobie Gillis.

Bringing Up Baby

1938, RKO
Produced and Directed by Howard Hawks

S·Y·N·O·P·S·I·S

Screwball comedy about a wacky heiress (Katharine Hepburn) and an anthropologist (Cary Grant), who search the Connecticut countryside for a lost dinosaur bone and Baby, a pet leopard.

It's not unusual for actors to experience stage fright when they walk on the set. Nervousness can put added energy into a performance. However, it is unusual for an actor to be frightened that a costar might suddenly take a bite out of an arm or leg. The unpredictable costar in this instance was an eight-year-old leopard named Nissa. Nissa wasn't your basic pet leopard. She was more than a little wild, even when she was under the control of her handler, Madame Polga Celeste.

Everyone on the set was afraid of Nissa. Everyone, that is, except Katharine Hepburn, who's never been afraid of anything.

Mme. Celeste gave Hepburn a few hints: wear a certain brand of perfume that Nissa liked, and put resin on the bottom of your shoes so you won't slip and upset her. Leading lady and leading leopard got along fine, except when Hepburn turned too quickly and swirled her skirt. Nissa didn't like swirling skirts. Hepburn, who knew when to give in, turned more slowly.

Katharine Hepburn was so good with Nissa that the trainer said if the actress ever gave up acting, she could find a new career as an animal trainer.

While Nissa stole the show, there was another famous animal actor who stole the bones. George, who buried Cary Grant's brontosaurus clavicle, was played by Asta, the dog who belonged to Nick and Nora Charles in the *Thin Man* series.

Cary Grant and Katharine Hepburn often improvised their dialogue. When Hepburn unexpectedly broke the heel of her shoe, they wove it

electrician who was working with a light directly overhead. "Eddie, if you had a choice of dropping that lamp on Miss Hepburn or me, whom would you choose?" Eddie called

into the dialogue so cleverly that Howard Hawks kept it in. Overall, Hawks was pleased with the chemistry that developed between them, but Hepburn had one habit he couldn't stand. She never stopped talking. One day an assistant director yelled "Quiet on the set!" Everyone instantly complied with the order and there was dead silence, except for Katharine Hepburn, whose ongoing conversation never lost a beat. Hawks instructed an assistant to tell everyone to sit down and stare at her until she stopped. She finally realized what was going on and asked, "Well, what are we waiting for?" Hawks replied, "I wondered when the parrot was going to stop talking." Hepburn led him aside and told him that the cast and crew were friends of hers, and he'd have trouble if he kept talking to her like that. Hawks called up to an

back, "Would you step aside, Mr. Hawks? I wouldnt want you to get hurt." Howard Hawks had at least one friend of his own.

Neither Katharine Hepburn nor Cary Grant had done enough screwball comedy to feel entirely comfortable with the style. At first Katharine Hepburn kept overacting, trying too hard to get laughs. Hawks brought in a wonderful comic named Walter Catlett, who read all of Hepburn's scenes sincerely, not with comedy in mind. The result was hilarious. Suddenly Katharine Hepburn understood how her character should be played, and she was so pleased with Catlett she insisted he be written into the picture.

With Hepburn's problems solved, Hawks turned to Cary Grant. The director thought Grant sounded stuffy when he

was supposed to be angry. Hawks told him about a friend who expressed his frustration by whinnying like a horse. Grant took the suggestion, toned it down a bit, and created the perfect mannerism to express David Huxley's frustration.

While *Bringing Up Baby* was not a hit at the box office, it is now considered one of the finest of the screwball comedies of the Thirties.

Cary Grant's fiancée in *Bringing Up Baby* was played by Virginia Walker, the wife of the film's director, Howard Hawks. This was her only screen credit.

Casablanca

1942, Warner Bros.
Produced by Hal Wallis
Directed by Michael Curtiz

S·Y·N·O·P·S·I·S

A Casablanca cafe owner (Humphrey Bogart) helps his former lover (Ingrid Bergman), and her husband (Paul Henreid) escape from the Nazis.

Academy Awards: Best Picture; Michael Curtiz, Director; Julius J. Epstein, Philip G. Epstein, and Howard Koch, Screenplay.

Academy Award nominations: Humphrey Bogart, Best Actor; Claude Rains, Supporting Actor; Arthur Edeson, Cinematography; Max Steiner, Score; Owen Marks, Editing.

Geraldine Fitzgerald was having lunch with Humphrey Bogart and Ingrid Bergman in the Warner Bros. commissary, listening to her friends complain bitterly about the movie they were making. According to Fitzgerald, Bogart was so upset about the unbelievability of the script, he had asked his lawyer to get him out of his contract. Bergman was unhappy because one line in the script referred to her as "the most beautiful woman in Europe," and she thought it was absurd. New script pages were rewritten every night, so each morning Bergman and Bogart would arrive on the set to find themselves unprepared for the day's work. To add to the confusion, no one could tell them how the story was going to end. The film they both so desperately wanted to get out of was *Casablanca*.

Finding a leading lady for *Casablanca* wasn't simple. The character of Ilsa was originally intended to be an American woman named Lois Meredith. Ann Sheridan was announced for the part, but other actresses were being tested. One of the writers was in love with a Russian ballet dancer named Tamara Toumanova, and he proposed that the woman should be a European. Toumanova tested for the part and didn't get it, but All-American Lois became the European Ilsa. Hedy Lamarr, Michele Morgan, and Edwige Fuillere were all considered for the female lead before Hal Wallis decided on a relative newcomer, Ingrid Bergman.

Wallis seriously considered casting Sam, piano player extraordinaire and Rick's closest friend, with a woman. The female Sam would be portrayed either by Hazel Scott, who played piano in New York clubs, or a relatively unknown Los Angeles night club performer named Elena Horn (Lena Horne). The decision was made to keep Sam male, with Clarence Muse and Dooley Wilson under consideration. Wallis, who preferred Muse, sent a memo to director Michael Curtiz, saying Dooley Wilson "isn't ideal for the part but if we get stuck and can't do any better I suppose he could play it." Wilson played Sam just fine. What he couldn't play was the piano, which was dubbed by Elliott Carpenter.

During the scripting process, Hal Wallis received directives from Joseph Breen, director of the Production Code Administration, also known as the Hollywood censor. Breen said his office could not possibly approve of the suggestion that Capt. Renault (Claude Rains) seduces women in exchange for visas. Wallis agreed to change the line "The girl will be released in the morning" to "...will be released later." And

Renault's line "At least your work keeps you outdoors" became "...gets you plenty of fresh air." With those changes, the morals of the American public were once more protected from overzealous Hollywood scriptwriters.

The biggest problem faced by producer, director, and leading players was finding the right ending. Should Ilsa stay with Rick? Should Rick die helping her escape? Should Rick spend the rest of his life in jail for helping her? Director Curtiz and the cast and crew had finished the rest of the picture when

they finally agreed that Ilsa would leave with Victor as Louis covers for Rick. The end line was scripted, "Louis, I might have known you'd mix your patriotism with a little larceny." Bogart delivered it that way, but Wallis also instructed Curtiz to shoot an alternate line: "Louis, I think this is the beginning of a beautiful friendship." It was also the ending of a beautiful movie.

"It will be a tough job to get a satisfactory picture out of this material, but I believe it can be done."
—Memo from screenwriter Wally Kline to Hal Wallis regarding *Casablanca.*

Charlie Chan at Treasure Island

1939, 20th Century-Fox
Produced by Sol Wurtzel
Directed by Norman Foster

S·Y·N·O·P·S·I·S

Charlie Chan's (Sidney Toler) investigation of a friend's reported suicide takes him to the Treasure Island exhibit at the San Francisco World's Fair.

A group of people are gathered in a room, their attention focused on one man. One person is particularly nervous but doesn't show it. The man in charge

addresses each in turn, then pulls a piece of evidence out of his pocket, linking one of them to a murder. The murderer admits his or her crime and tries to escape before learning that the piece of paper the detective brandished was his laundry list. Who else could it be but Charlie Chan?

When Charlie Chan, the pride of the Honolulu police force, was created in 1925 by Earl Derr Biggers, the idea of an Oriental hero was unique. At that time Asians were more likely to be presented as the villains on film or in literature. Chan first appeared on film as a supporting character, played by Japanese actor George Kuwa, in a 1926 ten-chapter serial called *House Without a Key*. All prints of that silent Chan have

been lost, as has his first talkie appearance in *Behind That Curtain*, a 1929 movie in which Warner Baxter tried to clear himself of a murder charge. Again Chan had a supporting role and appeared like the Seventh Cavalry at the end of the film with the evidence to clear Baxter's name.

Chan's first starring picture was *Charlie Chan Carries On*, made in 1931 with Swedish actor Warner Oland. Charlie Chan would never again be played on the screen by an actor of Asian descent.

Because Chan pictures all followed the same basic formula, producers had to try to make each one different. They sent Chan to Egypt, London, Monte Carlo, Panama, Reno, Rio, Shanghai, and the Berlin Olympics. He joined the circus and the secret service, appeared on Broadway and at the opera, went to the race track and the wax museum. Of course, the cast and crew

never actually traveled to these exotic places; all of Chan's adventures were filmed on sound stages and back lots.

The screenwriters looked for new and different ways of committing murder. Oland, who sat in on the story conferences discussing this grisly subject, once said, "There are only so many ways in which a man can be murdered, and many of them are unsuitable for screen purposes."

Chan pictures also provided opportunities for both aspiring actors (Ray Milland and Rita Hayworth) and established stars (Boris Karloff and Bela Lugosi).

Warner Oland made sixteen Chan pictures, and when he died in 1938, Sidney Toler took over for eleven more at Fox before continuing with a Monogram series. Curiously, both men had jade good luck charms that they carried with them at all times.

Oland's jade god, set in a silver ring, was given to him by his wife shortly before he was cast in his first screen role. He wore it at least once in all of his Chan films. Sidney Toler's jade ring proved he wasn't as good a detective as the man he played. According to family legend, his ring had been purchased by Toler's grandfather nearly one hundred years earlier and was made of the highest quality jade. When a display of rare jade came to Los Angeles, Toler sought out an expert, who told him he had a very nice piece of...agate. Would the real Charlie Chan have been fooled?

Charlie Chan at Treasure Island is generally considered the best of the many Chan pictures. Cesar Romero enjoyed learning the tricks he exhibited as Rhadini the illusionist; he said that, while any magician would consider them simplistic, they looked great on camera. Also in the cast was Loretta Young's older sister, Sally Blane, who just happened to be the wife of *Treasure Islands's* director, Norman Foster. Charlie Chan's number-two son was Victor Sen Yung, who had been employed as a houseboy for concert pianist Carmen de Obarrio

before he was cast in his first Chan picture. Chan's other sons had been played at various times by Benson Fong and Keye Luke.

In the 1960s distributors offered Chan pictures to television stations for as little as five dollars per showing. Possibly because of the bargain prices, stations ran the pictures and exposed a whole new generation to the inscrutable detective, who quickly became a cult hero. By the 1970s Chan pictures were in such demand that their rental rates were comparable to the major classics.

"Alibi, like dead fish, cannot stand test of time."
—Charlie Chan

Citizen Kane

1941, RKO/Mercury Theater
Produced and Directed by Orson Welles

S·Y·N·O·P·S·I·S

Upon the death of a notorious publisher (Orson Welles) , a newspaper reporter tries to uncover the hidden story of the man's life.

Academy Awards: Herman J. Mankiewicz and Orson Welles, Original Screenplay.

Academy Award nominations: Best Picture; Orson Welles, Best Actor; Orson Welles, Best Director; Gregg Toland, Black and White Cinematography; Perry Ferguson and Van Nest Polglase, Black and White Art Direction; Al Fields and Darrell Silvera, Black and White Interior Decoration; Robert Wise, Film Editing; John Aalberg, Sound Recording; Bernard Hermann, Score.

When Orson Welles landed a contract with RKO, he and Herman Mankiewicz tossed around ideas for their first film. Dillinger was discussed and rejected, as was Aimee Semple MacPherson. When William Randolph Hearst's name came up, Welles jumped on the idea. First, the publisher's life was full of scandal, and the publicity would be overwhelming. Second, Mankiewicz was a regular visitor at San Simeon, Hearst's California estate, and was familiar with many inside details. Third and most important, it was a character Welles could play himself.

Although his contract with RKO gave Welles complete artistic control over the picture, that freedom came with a string attached. RKO was in deep financial trouble, so the budget they offered him was incredibly limited. Many of the techniques cited as brilliant and innovative were actually invented because Welles couldn't afford to do the film the conventional way. For example, there are several crowd scenes in *Citizen Kane*, but no crowds. Welles drew on his radio experience to suggest crowds by using sound only. And then there

were the sets, or to be more accurate, there weren't the sets. Whenever they couldn't afford to complete a set, cinematographer Gregg Toland came up with innovative lighting plots in which the lack of furniture or walls wasn't immediately obvious.

In one of the most brilliant shots in the film, the camera seems to go right through a skylight in one continuous motion. It's actually two shots. The sign, the rooftops, and the skylight were all part of a model. As the shot zooms through the window, a lightning flash distracts the viewer and the cut is made to the full-sized interior of the club.

Before the film was finished, Welles began to realize he was wrong about how much publicity he'd generate by making a movie about one of the most powerful men in America. William Randolph Hearst was unhappy with reports about the film and used the power of his publishing empire to kill virtually all the film's publicity. Not one of the Hearst papers reviewed or

even mentioned the picture, and not one of the theatres owned by the other Hollywood studios ran it. When you look at *Citizen Kane* from Hearst's point of view, it's easy to understand his concern.

San Simeon was the meeting place for the richest, most powerful, most famous people in the world. One regular guest was screenwriter Herman Mankiewicz. Over the years the magnate made sure Mankiewicz received great press in all the Hearst papers. When rumors flew that Herman Mankiewicz was writing a script based upon the publisher's life, Hearst felt betrayed. The man who had been his guest on so many occasions, the man who had been privileged to witness so much of Hearst's private life, the man Hearst thought of as a friend was using his knowledge to publicly embarrass the publishing giant.

William Randolph Hearst's campaign to discredit *Citizen Kane* was a complete success. Despite ten Academy Award nominations, it lost $160,000 at

the box office. It took years before *Citizen Kane* was universally recognized as one of the greatest masterpieces of the American cinema.

Alan Ladd had a bit part as a reporter in *Citizen Kane.*

Come and Get It

1936, United Artists
Produced by Samuel Goldwyn
Directed by Howard Hawks and William Wyler

S·Y·N·O·P·S·I·S

In the latter part of the nineteenth century, the foreman of a Wisconsin lumber camp (Edward Arnold) becomes a timber tycoon.

Academy Award: Walter Brennan, Best Supporting Actor.

Academy Award nomination: Edward Curtiss, Film Editing.

Come and Get It , which was made by Samuel Goldwyn in 1936, could have been retitled *Come and Direct It*. Normally, every detail of a Sam Goldwyn production was personally supervised by Sam himself. This time, it didn't happen that way. Goldwyn was confined to the hospital for prostate and gall bladder surgery. In those days, following surgery, people stayed in the hospital a lot longer than they do today, so he was out of commission for quite a while. He demanded and received frequent briefings on *Come and Get It* and several other films that were in production, but nobody had the courage to tell him that director Howard Hawks had rewritten many of the scenes in Goldwyn's pet project.

Come and Get It was based on a novel by Edna Ferber, to whom Goldwyn had paid $100,000 for the rights and another $30,000 to act as script consultant. He also paid two of his regular scriptwriters to do the adaptation, so Goldwyn had a sizable sum of money invested in the script. When he viewed the rushes, he was horrified to learn that his director had taken the liberty of rewriting scenes he had approved and loved. Howard Hawks had even had the gall to change the ending of the picture without consulting the producer. While his doctor urged him not to get excited, he called Hawks to his bedside and demanded that the director reshoot the scenes in question. Hawks refused, choosing to quit and walk out on his contract with Goldwyn Studios.

Goldwyn called in William Wyler, who was making *Dodsworth* on an adjoining set, and told him to reshoot the scenes. Knowing that working on another man's film is a no-win situation, Wyler refused. Goldwyn became enraged and for the second time in one day, told a director, "You'll never work in this town again." Wyler checked his contract, realized Goldwyn could carry out his threat, and filmed the scenes at a cost of $900,000. Screen credit for *Come and Get It* reads, "Directed by Howard Hawks and William Wyler," but since neither man felt the picture was truly his, neither listed it on his official credits. To add to the confusion, a third man was also listed as a director on the picture. Second unit director Richard Rosson was credited for the logging scenes, with Walter Mayo as his assistant.

At Academy Award time, *Come and Get It* was nominated in two categories, Edward Curtiss for film editing and Walter Brennan as Best Supporting Actor. 1936 was the year the Academy added the award for supporting actor, and for a while it looked like it would be Brennan's exclusive property. In the first five years of the award's history, Brennan won it three times, for *Come and Get It*, *Kentucky*, and *The*

Westerner. Walter Brennen didn't get three Oscar statuettes for his mantle, however. That first year of the award, they only gave plaques for Best Supporting Actor and Actress. For the publicity pictures traditionally taken after the ceremony, Brennan and Gale Sondergaard, who won for Best Supporting Actress, were given prop Oscars to hold. As soon as the pictures were taken, so were the statuettes.

The real award should go to a husband and wife team appear-

ing in *Come and Get It*. With over fifty years of marital bliss, Joel McCrea and his wife, Frances Dee, have had one of the longest of the traditionally brief Hollywood marriages. While she didn't rate the star billing her husband received, she can be seen as an extra in the dining sequence.

Come and Get It was reissued in 1960 as *Roaring Timber*.

Crossfire

1947, RKO Radio
Produced by Adrian Scott
Directed by Edward Dmytryk

S·Y·N·O·P·S·I·S

While investigating a murder, a police detective (Robert Young) uncovers the murderer's (Robert Ryan) anti-Semitic motive.

Academy Award nominations:
Best Picture; Edward Dmytryk, Director; Robert Ryan, Supporting Actor; Gloria Grahame, Supporting Actress; John Paxton, Screenplay.

Veteran actors often complain that their costars try to upstage them by making exaggerated gestures or facial expressions that draw attention to themselves. Director Edward Dmytryk faced an unusual variation on that problem in *Crossfire*. He was working with three totally professional, intelligent actors, all of whom knew that in a film that features a lot of shouting, it's the low-key performance that has the most impact. When the three Roberts, Robert Ryan, Robert Mitchum, and Robert Young, were in the same scene, instead of trying to outdo one another, each tried to be *quieter* than the other two. Dmytryk finally had to put a stop to it, because the actors were soon speaking so softly that they couldn't be heard!

Robert Mitchum was definitely the winner in the Low Key Actor of the Month Club. Although his part was smaller than the others, he managed to make the bigger impact. Dmytryk admitted he had requested Mitchum for the picture solely because of the star's drawing power at the box office. After working with him, Dmytryk became a Mitchum fan. He was so impressed with the strength of Mitchum's performance that he padded Mitchum's part whenever possible. Dmytryk said that on the surface Mitchum was irresponsible and vague, but underneath was a true professional who knew the score better than most Hollywood veterans.

Dmytryk completed shooting in just twenty-two days and brought the picture in for less than $500,000. When *Crossfire* earned $1,270,000 on its first release, the profit margins made it a studio executive's dream.

Crossfire had the distinction of being one of Hollywood's first direct attacks on the viciousness of anti-Semitism. The novel it was based on, however, did not contain any Jewish characters. Richard Brooks wrote *The Brick Foxhole* about the murder of a homosexual, but that was a taboo subject in Hollywood in the forties, so *Crossfire's* theme was an exploration of another kind of prejudice. *The New York Times* named it one of the ten best films of 1947.

In addition to their costarring work on *Crossfire*, Mitchum and Ryan found themselves working together three more times over the next two decades in *The Racket* (1951) , *The Longest Day* (1962) and *Anzio* (1968).

Ironically, *Crossfire*, which contains a plea for tolerance, was the final film of producer Adrian Scott's career, and it would be Dmytryk's last Hollywood film for several years. They were two of the people known as the Hollywood Ten, and when they

refused to testify before the House Un-American Activities Committee, they were blacklisted. Many Hollywood insiders felt that *Crossfire's* nomination as Best Picture was as much a public show of support for the Hollywood Ten as a statement about the quality of the picture. Scott was sentenced to one year in prison and never produced another Hollywood movie. Dmytryk directed films in England before he returned in 1951 and voluntarily testified before the Committee. His blacklist was lifted when he named other members of the Communist party, including producer Adrian Scott.

Crossfire marked a more pleasant milestone in the career of Dore Schary. After he assumed responsibilities as head of production for RKO in early 1947, *Crossfire* was the first film on which he received executive producer credit.

Don't confuse this *Crossfire* with a 1933 Western by the same name, which starred Tom Keene. While there was no connection between the two films, Tom Keene, working under the name Richard Powers, also played a detective in the 1947 *Crossfire*.

A year after playing a minor role in *Crossfire*, Lex Barker became the screen's tenth Tarzan.

The Day the Earth Stood Still

1951, 20th Century-Fox
Produced by Julian Blaustein
Directed by Robert Wise

S·Y·N·O·P·S·I·S

A being from another planet (Michael Rennie) lands on Earth to warn that humans must learn peaceful coexistence.

Mention *The Day the Earth Stood Still* to science fiction fans and they'll probably answer, "Klaatu barada nikto." It's a key phrase in the plot's development. Roughly translated, it means "Klaatu said it's O.K," not one of the most meaningful concepts from one of the premiere science fiction films of all time. I'm sure some of you will say, "Science fiction, ho hum." Although it does feature a flying saucer, this is *not* a film where a thawed-out Tyrannosaurus Rex walks the streets of Tokyo. It's a sensitive, beautifully acted story that addressed the fears of the American public in the early fifties. And some of those fears are still relevant today.

Remember what was going on in the world in 1951. For six years the United States had had a monopoly on atomic weapons, but that was over. The Russians had just exploded their first atomic bomb, and Americans were scared. They knew that, for the first time in history, a war between superpowers could annihilate the human race. It was also a time when the human race was realizing the technology of space travel, so there was anxiety about a potential threat from without as well as from within. Early in the film these issues are put on the table, in a dinner scene in which each character expresses an opinion—opinions representing a cross-section of beliefs held by the American public at that time.

Darryl Zanuck didn't want to make this film: he thought

there had been too many invasion pictures and the public wouldn't be interested in another one. Robert Wise disagreed. Up to this point, all of the invasion films cast the extraterrestrials as villains who were trying to take over the earth. This movie was about hope, and made the visitor—who came to earth to help us solve our problems and avert a nuclear war—the hero. Wise convinced Zanuck to go ahead with the project and fought for the opportunity to direct *The Day the Earth Stood Still*. Not only did he want to make an important anti-nuclear statement, he also believed in UFO's! He said the people of the earth must have the biggest egos imaginable to think we are the only intelligent beings in the universe. Despite his misgivings, Zanuck gave Wise the support he needed by assembling a team of talented people, including Michael Rennie, Patricia Neal, and one of Hollywood's greatest composers, Bernard Herrmann, whose haunting score is one of the highlights

of the film.

One of the central characters is Gort, a tall, mysterious, robot-like figure. Talk about Hollywood casting... they hired the doorman from Grauman's Chinese Theater because he was almost seven feet tall. His metallic-looking suit had very little ventilation, so he could only remain in it for a few hours at a time. Costume makers actually constructed two of the foam-rubber suits, one with a zipper up the back for the front shots, and one with the zipper down the front for the back shots. Every time Gort turned around, the cameras stopped while he changed suits. When you watch the film, you'll notice you never see him turn completely around on camera. There's always a cutaway shot to break it up.

The Day the Earth Stood Still was based on "Farewell to the Master," a short story originally published in the science fiction magazine *Astounding* . In the film, after Klaatu is killed and temporarily resuscitated by Gort, he tells Patricia Neal that he doesn't know how long the temporary resurrection will last. The original story ends with the death of Klaatu, with one important addition. Someone apologizes to Gort for killing his master, and Gort turns at the entrance of the spaceship and speaks for the first

time. "You misunderstand. I am the master." That one sentence throws a chilling light on the possibilities, and I'm sorry they cut it from the film version.

The Day the Earth Stood Still remains one of the premiere cult movies of the fifties. Although the special effects pale beside modern computer animation, and its message is a little heavy handed, it remains a powerful statement about humanity's need to live in peace.

The opening song of the cult film *The Rocky Horror Picture Show* begins with the words, "Michael Rennie was ill *The Day the Earth Stood Still*... but he told us where we stand."

Dinner at Eight

1933, MGM
Produced by David O. Selznick
Directed by George Cukor

S·Y·N·O·P·S·I·S

A flighty society woman (Billie Burke) prepares a dinner party for an aristocratic British couple.

When Irving Thalberg went on sick leave from MGM, Louis B. Mayer brought in David O. Selznick to take up the slack. While he had produced many fine films at RKO, including *Symphony of Six Million, What Price Hollywood?*, and *A Bill of Divorcement*, Selznick wasn't yet the legendary producer of Hollywood's most successful movies. Studio personnel resented him and attributed his success to the fact that he was Mayer's son-in-law. One Hollywood periodical even headlined its story about Selznick, "The Son-In-Law Also Rises."

For his first MGM picture, Selznick knew he had to impress everyone in the industry. He arranged to borrow his favorite director, George Cukor, from Merian Cooper at RKO. In exchange, RKO would get the services of Lionel Barrymore, Myrna Loy, and Karen Morley. However, there was a catch. Cukor had to be back at RKO in early May to direct *Little Women*, and it was already the end of February. In a little more than two months, Selznick and Cukor had to agree on what picture they were making, get a script written, and cast it. All the costumes and sets had to be designed and constructed. And they had to have the entire picture in the can.

Selznick had seen a play called *Dinner at Eight* and liked the premise, but felt the script needed a lot of work before it could be translated to film. He bought the rights, and screenwriters Herman J. Mankiewicz and Frances Marion tailored roles for Wallace Beery, Marie Dressler, John Barrymore, and Clark Gable. Louis B. Mayer refused to allow Selznick to cast Gable in the picture, however, saying the role was much too sophisticated, and the part went to Edmund Lowe. Cukor suggested Jean Harlow, who had just made her starring debut in Howard Hughes' *Hell's Angels*, and the cast was set. Cukor was asked how he coped with so many stars on one set, but he didn't have any problems. They

were screen legends but they were also true professionals and worked with the director, not against him.

John Barrymore admitted his character was a combination of his father-

in-law Maurice Costello, silent star Lowell Sherman, and himself. He often asked Cukor if he could add a line, a word, or a piece of business, which inevitably added the right nuance for the character. Cukor also found that Barrymore listened to the director's suggestions and incorporated them into his multidimensional portrayal of a fading, second-rate actor. Cukor told Barrymore that the character shouldn't be allowed to die with dignity: he wanted something awful to happen to him. For his big death scene, Cukor asked the actor to do a "very ugly, middle-aged-awkward sprawl," which Barrymore pulled off to perfection, with one little addition. Just before expiring, Barrymore made sure the character died showing

his best profile. It was the kind of detail only a great actor brings to a role.

One of the most heroic performances in *Dinner at Eight* was turned in by Billie Burke. When production began, her husband, the legendary Florenz Ziegfeld, was critically ill, and died before the picture was finished. Burke, who knew the tight deadline Selznick was under, postponed her grief until her work was done. It's a tribute to her acting ability that the overwhelming grief she was experiencing doesn't come through on the screen.

They were well into the shooting schedule when Selznick decided that the ending of *Dinner at Eight* was weak. Under the pressure of a tight deadline, writer Donald Ogden Stewart came up with one of the most memorable closing lines in Hollywood history. Jean Harlow says she was reading a "nutty kind of book...This guy says that machinery is going to take the place of every profession." To which Marie Dressler replies, "Oh my dear, that's something you need never worry about."

Selznick's first feature for MGM, which was shot in just twenty-four days at a cost of

$387,000, made ten times its investment on its initial run. The boss's son-in-law proved he knew what he was doing.

P·L·A·Y·E·R·S

Marie Dressler	Carlotta Vance
John Barrymore	Larry Renault
Wallace Beery	Dan Packard
Jean Harlow	Kitty Packard

Featuring:
- Lionel Barrymore
- Lee Tracy
- Edmund Lowe
- Billie Burke
- Madge Evans
- Jean Hersholt
- Karen Morley
- Phillips Holmes
- May Robson
- Louise Closser Hale
- Grant Mitchell
- Elizabeth Patterson

To promote MGM's *Tarzan and His Mate*, the name of Marie Dressler's dog in *Dinner at Eight* was changed from "Mussolini" to "Tarzan."

The Dolly Sisters

1945, 20th Century-Fox
Produced by George Jessel
Directed by: Irving Cummings

S·Y·N·O·P·S·I·S

Hungarian immigrants Jenny and Rosie Dolly (Betty Grable and June Haver) become successful performers in New York City. Jenny falls in love with a composer (John Payne), and Rosie marries a wealthy man (Frank Latimore).

Academy Award nomination: Best Song "I Can't Begin to Tell You," Mack Gordon, James V. Monaco.

On October 25, 1892, a Hungarian woman named Mrs. Deutsch gave birth to twin girls, Janszicka and Roszika. The girls grew up to be the world-famous vaudeville act known as the Dolly Sisters. When George Jessel took over production of the movie version of the lives of the Dolly Sisters in 1945, he wanted to cast Betty Grable and Alice Faye as the siblings who took New York by storm. Grable accepted the role, but Alice Faye had retired from the screen and was quite happy with her chosen role of wife and mother. In her place, Jessel chose a nineteen-year-old actress named June Haver. No one seemed to notice that the brunette Dolly sisters were being played by two stunning blondes, or that Betty Grable was ten years older than the actress playing her twin sister.

Their leading man was John Payne. If Alice Faye had agreed to play Rosie, Payne would have been bumped down to third billing, but June Haver didn't have enough clout to get her name listed above his. She didn't remain at the bottom of the credits for long. Haver's performance in *The Dolly Sisters* was received so favorably that she was able to command top billing on her very next film, *Three Little Girls in Blue*, with George Montgomery.

The Dolly Sisters was filled with memorable performances by some of Hollywood's best character actors. Uncle Latsie was played by S.Z. Sakall, affectionately known to his friends as "Cuddles." It was appropriate that he play the uncle of two Hungarian sisters; he was born Eugene Gero Szakall in Budapest. He was a successful actor in Central Europe and was very popular in German talkies. When the Nazis invaded, he fled the country and spent the next fifteen years charming American audiences with his fractured English and endearing smile.

Another well-known face belonged to Sig Rumann, who came to the United States from Germany in the 1920s and made his film debut in '29. He built his reputation as the pompous Prussian or the excitable German, appearing in more than a hundred films in his four-decade career.

Reginald Gardiner was at the other end of the character spectrum. He was born in Wimbledon, England, and attended the prestigious Royal Acadamy of Dramatic Art. A popular fixture in Hollywood musicals of the thirties and forties, he invariably played the polished and urbane continental type.

The Dolly Sisters was produced by that jack-of-all-trades George Jessel, who, in addition to producing motion pictures, was a nightclub entertainer, actor, singer, songwriter, comedian, and America's unofficial "Toastmaster General." While he made his acting debut in film in Widow at the Races in 1911, it was 1945 before he made his producing debut with The Dolly Sisters.

The Dolly Sisters is one of those old-fashioned musicals in which every element of the plot is really just an excuse to break into song. Since it was a period piece, it showcased many of the songs that were popular just after the turn of the century, such as "Sidewalks of New York," "Pack Up Your Troubles," and "Carolina in the Morning"; songs you can't hear without humming along. For older audiences, watching this picture was a welcome trip down memory lane. Songwriters Joseph McCarthy (no relation to the senator) and Harry Carroll took a melody by Chopin and wrote, "I'm Always Chasing Rainbows." The song "I Can't Begin to Tell You" received an Oscar nomination as Best Song but lost to Rodgers and Hammerstein's "It Might As Well Be Spring" from State Fair.

P·L·A·Y·E·R·S

Betty Grable	Jenny Dolly
John Payne	Harry Fox
June Haver	Rosie Dolly
S.Z. Sakall	Uncle Latsie

Featuring:
Reginald Gardiner
Frank Latimore
Gene Sheldon
Sig Rumann
Trudy Marshall
Collette Lyons
Evan Thomas
Donna Jo Gribble
Robert Middlemass
Paul Hurst
Lester Allen
Frank Orth
Herbert Ashley
Trudy Berliner
Andre Charlot
Mae Marsh
Virginia Brissac
Frank Ferguson
J. Farrell MacDonald

The real Dolly Sisters made one starring film together, The Million Dollar Dollies, in 1918.

Dracula

1931, Universal
Produced by Carl Laemmle
Directed by Tod Browning

S·Y·N·O·P·S·I·S

A Transylvanian vampire (Bela Lugosi) moves to London and terrorizes a beautiful woman (Helen Chandler).

John Carradine, Louis Jourdan, Francis Lederer, Lon Chaney, Jr., Christopher Lee, and Frank Langella all did it, but only Bela Lugosi really lived it. They all played Dracula on the screen, but only Lugosi made it his life's work. Only Lugosi let Dracula consume the last twenty-five years of his life.

Lugosi was born in Hungary, not many miles from the real Transylvania. An actor in his native country, his work in organizing an actor's union made him a target for a new political regime. He fled to Germany, where he appeared in films before coming to the United States in 1921. With his Hungarian accent he would never be accepted as a leading man, but he was successful on the New York stage in character parts. In 1927 he was given the role that would change his life. He spent a year on Broadway in the title role of *Dracula* and another two years with the touring company. Since his English was not very good, he learned his lines phonetically, which helped shape the slow rhythms, the precise diction, and the odd inflections he brought to the role.

When Universal decided to make the film version in 1931, director Tod Browning wanted to cast an actor with whom he had made many films in the late twenties, horror impresario Lon Chaney. Before filming got underway, however, Chaney died of bronchial cancer. Lugosi was the obvious second choice. Browning and Lugosi teamed up to make one of the most frightening films of all time. The movie is full of beautiful photography and unexpected moments, such as when Lugosi passes through a series of cobwebs without breaking them. Instead of the traditional music score, *Dracula* is punctuated by creaking doors, howling wolves, eerie footsteps, and, occasionally, strains from *Swan Lake*. The fact that the viewer never actually saw the vampire suck the blood of his victims makes *Dracula* mild by today's standards, but in 1931 it was terrifying.

Universal had sufficient faith in the film, even before its release, to make a Spanish version with Carlos Villarias and an entirely different cast. The studio was afraid people might be disgusted by the film, however, so the publicity made no mention of fear or horror. Released on Valentine's Day and billed as "The Story of the Strangest Passion the World Has Ever Known," *Dracula* was an overwhelming success. In 1938 Universal released *Frankenstein* and *Dracula* on a double bill and made more on the reissue than on the original runs.

Bela Lugosi remained obsessed with Dracula for the rest of his life. He wore his cape in public and regularly repeated his famous line, "I . . . am . . . Dracula." For the rest of his career he played mainly Dracula, variations on the Dracula persona, or other evil monsters. Reporters were surprised to find that he gave interviews from a coffin.

As the years passed he began to lose touch with reality and was treated several times for drug addiction. In his will he left instructions that he wanted to be buried in his costume, a request his children honored. At the time of his death he was working on a low-budget movie called *Plan Nine from Outer Space*, now considered one of the worst movies ever made. When he died, the producers couldn't afford to reshoot his scenes, so they put an actor in a cape and filmed the stand-in from a distance.

When comedian Joey Bishop, who was playing poker with some friends, was told that Bela Lugosi had died, he said, "He'll be back."

"I never drink . . . wine."
—Bela Lugosi in *Dracula.*

Dragonwyck

1946, 20th Century-Fox
Produced by Darryl F. Zanuck
Directed by Joseph L. Mankiewicz

S·Y·N·O·P·S·I·S

A new bride (Gene Tierney) discovers that her wealthy husband (Vincent Price) is a murderer.

Joseph Mankiewicz was a top-rated Hollywood scriptwriter who wanted more out of his work. Being a writer wasn't enough; he felt that a writer could create the most magnificent work on paper, only to have a director alter it beyond recognition. He said that every good writer is already a director, that every script has been directed in the writer's mind before it ever goes on paper. When he told his boss, Louis B. Mayer, that he wanted a chance to take his work through the entire creative process, Mayer told him to become a producer, because "You have to crawl before you can walk." Despite Mankiewicz's success producing many fine pictures, including the first Spencer Tracy/Katharine Hepburn teaming, *Woman of the Year*, executives at MGM continually refused his request to direct his own work.

Everyone in Hollywood knew Mankiewicz was unhappy, and it wasn't long before he got an offer he couldn't refuse. Darryl Zanuck promised him the opportunity to produce, direct, and write his own films for 20th Century-Fox. But even then his first directing assignment was

several years in coming. In 1946 the great Ernst Lubitsch was assigned to produce and direct Gene Tierney and Walter Huston in *Dragonwyck*. Just before filming began, Lubitsch suffered a mild heart attack. Since Mankiewicz had written the screenplay, Lubitsch asked him to take over directoral duties. Leading lady Gene Tierney later said that Lubitsch was seized with the insecurity many people feel when faced with the overwhelming prospect that one's replacement might actually succeed. Lubitsch visited the set often, checking up on Mankiewicz's every move.

Eventually the visions of the two men clashed, and they argued so vehemently that Mankiewicz tried to bar Lubitsch from the set. When Darryl Zanuck insisted they cut a scene explaining the poisonous nature of a plant used as a murder weapon, Lubitsch asked to have his name removed from the picture, and Zanuck was listed as producer of record.

From the beginning, Mankiewicz exhibited many of the qualities shared by great directors. Naturally talented and creative, he was also smart enough to recognize areas in which he needed help. He sought out the opinions of Arthur Miller, the cinematographer on *Dragonwyck*, who helped him work out camera angles and shot sequences. He also had an unusual idea for Vincent Price. After asking the actor to lose a considerable amount of weight for the role, he added a corset-like brace to all of Price's costumes, forcing him to have perfectly erect, rigid posture.

In her autobiography, Gene Tierney wrote that filming *Dragonwyck* always remained fresh in her mind, but not for anything that happened in front of the

cameras. During a break in filming she was introduced to a guest on the set, a young naval lieutenant named John F. Kennedy. They met again at a party given by Sonja Henie; they began dating and Tierney found herself falling in love with this handsome young man who spoke with such certainty about being president. Their romance lasted many months and included trips to New England to meet the family. However, because she was a divorced woman and he was Catholic, Kennedy admitted they could never marry. Not wanting to get involved with a man who could never be hers, she ended the relationship. Several years later, when they met by chance in Paris, he asked if she would consider seeing him again. Once again she refused. Six months later she read about his engagement to Jacqueline Bouvier.

Tierney did not blame him

for his actions. At that time an aspiring Catholic politician could not afford to marry a divorced movie star. But Gene Tierney admitted that she remained in love with Jack Kennedy for many years.

Joseph Mankiewicz got back at his ex-mother-in-law by having one of the characters in *Dragonwyck* exclaim, "I've never even heard of Victoria Schermerhorn!"

Easter Parade

1948, MGM
Produced by Arthur Freed
Directed by Charles Walters

S·Y·N·O·P·S·I·S

A dancer (Fred Astaire) chooses a girl from the chorus (Judy Garland) to be his new partner.

Academy Award: Johnny Green and Roger Edens, Scoring of a Musical Picture.

When Irving Berlin wrote a song, it was never wasted. In 1917 he wrote "Smile and Show Your Dimple." Never heard of it? Don't be surprised; it wasn't a hit. Thirty years later, when Arthur Freed asked Berlin to write the music for a new Judy Garland/Gene Kelly musical, the composer dusted off the melody and called it "Easter Parade." In Berlin's words, it took a second marriage to bring happiness to his melody.

Freed had contracted with Berlin for eight songs, but when the producer didn't like "Let's Take an Old-Fashioned Walk,"

Berlin left and came back an hour later with "A Couple of Swells." Once again, nothing was wasted; Berlin used the rejected song in 1949 in a show called *Miss Liberty*.

Gene Kelly was well into rehearsals for *Easter Parade* when he did something foolish. Depending on whom you believe, it was either a football or a softball game that did him in. Whichever sport it was, the weekend warrior broke his ankle (he told the studio he had done it rehearsing a dance number). When producer Arthur Freed and writer Sidney Sheldon discussed possible replacements, Freed suggested Astaire. Sheldon was horrified, saying the public would never root for a twenty-five-year old girl to end up with a guy twice her age. Anyway, Fred Astaire had been in retirement for two years. Why would he want to do it?

As it turned out, Fred Astaire was more than ready to return to the screen. He had been spending his retirement racing his horses and setting up dance studios around the country, and now he was bored. A motion picture was exactly what he needed. However, he didn't want his acceptance of the role to interfere with a friendship, so he cleared it with Gene Kelly first. Kelly admitted that he'd be off his feet for at least six months and gave Astaire his blessing.

Fred Astaire was nervous on his first day back at work. He hadn't danced in two years and he wasn't sure if he could keep up with an energetic youngster like Judy Garland. Judy, who was worried about dancing with one of Hollywood's legitimate legends, was even more nervous. Once they settled into rehearsals, they overcame their apprehensions and became friends, with Astaire doing his Clark Gable/ Rhett Butler impression and Judy reciprocating with her own Scarlett O'Hara. Astaire said later that his numbers with Judy represented some of the high spots of his career.

Every Fred Astaire movie included a dance number that showcased a technique or special effect audiences had never seen before. *Easter Parade* was no exception. "Steppin' Out with my Baby" included a dramatic sequence that combined slow-motion dancing with regular-speed sound. It took Astaire and John Nichols, head of

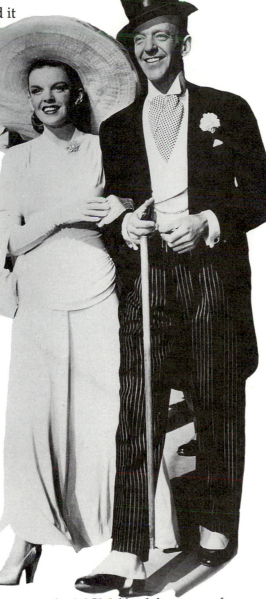

the MGM film laboratory, four weeks to work out the technical difficulties in synchronizing the dance movements with the music.

While Astaire was working on his big number, the technical crew was preparing for a spectacular *Easter Parade* on the back lot. They built two authentic blocks of Fifth Avenue looking north toward St. Patrick's, just as it was in New York in 1912. However, they only built the lower ten feet of the cathedral and one side of the street, which was filled with 700 extras and 100 period vehicles. After making the long tracking shots of the crowded avenue, the magicians in the film laboratory added the opposite side of the street.

After the film's first preview, Arthur Freed cut a number called "Mister Monotony," which Irving Berlin used several years later in *Call Me Madame*. When Irving Berlin wrote a song, it was never wasted.

"For a guy who had retired ostensibly, your comeback represents the greatest event since Satchel Paige."
—Bing Crosby to Fred Astaire.

The Farmer's Daughter

1947, RKO Radio
Produced by Dore Schary
Directed by H.C. Potter

S·Y·N·O·P·S·I·S

When she goes to work for a wealthy, political family, a naive Minnesota farm girl (Loretta Young) becomes involved in politics and runs for Congress.

Academy Award: Loretta Young, Best Actress.

Academy Award nomination: Charles Bickford, Supporting Actor.

David O. Selznick and producer Dore Schary just couldn't seem to agree on anything. They were working on a film Selznick wanted to call *Katie for Congress,* but Schary thought that was dull. He liked *The Farmer's Daughter;* Selznick thought it would remind people of those vulgar jokes about traveling salesmen. The casting discussions were also at an impasse. Selznick wanted Ingrid Bergman for the lead, but she turned it down, as did Olivia de Havilland and Rosalind Russell. Schary was on vacation in Arizona when he found out his boss was about to sign Sonja Henie. He immediately sent Selznick a memo, detailing why he thought they should go with Loretta Young. A day later Schary received a wire from Selznick: "OK, Forget Henie. But don't come around to me when you want skating

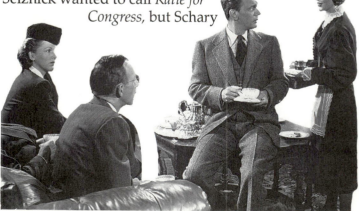

lessons!"

With Selznick on his side, Schary had to convince Loretta Young to accept the role. They met for lunch at Lucey's, a restaurant just across the street from Paramount Studios. Schary came away from the meeting totally in awe of Loretta Young, not because of her attitude; she was very willing to do the role. Schary was astonished by Loretta Young's appetite. She ate lamb chops, baked potatoes, green peas, stewed tomatoes, rolls and butter, two glasses of milk, a bowl of soup, and apple pie with ice cream for dessert. According to Schary, she ate like that every day of her life and never gained a pound. Now that's a talent!

The weeks before the Academy Awards ceremony, the Las Vegas oddsmakers were against Loretta Young. Rosalind Russell was the odds on favorite at 6–5, with Susan Hayward second at 6–1. The rest of the nominees—Loretta Young, Joan Crawford, and Dorothy McGuire, were considered long shots. An article in *Daily Variety* listed Loretta Young in fourth place for her performance in *The Bishop's Wife.* The writer obviously didn't know she was nominated for *The Farmer's Daughter*, not *The Bishop's Wife.*

On March 20, 1948, at the Shrine Auditorium, even presenter Fredric March couldn't believe his eyes. He ripped open the envelope, began to say "Rosalind.." did a double take and announced "Loretta Young." After she swept on to the stage in her green silk taffeta, she said, "Up to now, this occasion has been for me a spectator sport. But I dressed, just in case." As she walked off the stage, her heart was beating so fast the diamond necklace on her neck moved up and down in rhythm with her pulse. While Rosalind Russell didn't go home with an Oscar, she was given a copy of the *Los Angeles Times'* early edition, which came out with the headline, "ROZ RUSSELL WINS OSCAR." The next morning, Young said her only regret was

Russell's disappointment after being told she had won, and suggested that, in the future, newspapers discontinue the kinds of polls that led to the error.

No one wins an Oscar all by himself, or herself. With Joseph Cotten as her leading man and Ethel Barrymore as his mother, Loretta Young was surrounded by the best in the business. While filming a scene in which Cotten says goodbye to Barrymore before leaving for the capital, Barrymore decided to have some fun, so as he turned to go, she poked him with her cane. As he turned around in astonishment, she said, "Don't forget to tell the governor!" Cotten and director Hank Potter fell on the floor laughing. They had to postpone work on that scene because Cotton could not make his exit without cracking up.

The Farmer's Daughter, like *Mr. Smith Goes to Washington* and Goldie Hawn's *Protocol*, presents a myth we'd all like to believe. Honesty, integrity, and a commitment to truth and common sense will win out over political opportunism and special interests. More than four decades after *The Farmer's Daughter* was made, we could still use a Katie for Congress.

The Farmer's Daughter marked the screen debut of James Aurness, who later shortened his name to James Arness. He played one of Loretta Young's brothers.

42nd Street

1933, Warner Bros.
Produced by Darryl Zanuck
Directed by Lloyd Bacon

S·Y·N·O·P·S·I·S

When the star of a Broadway show (Bebe Daniels) breaks her ankle, an unknown member of the chorus (Ruby Keeler) goes on in her place.

Academy Award nominations: Best Picture; Nathan Levinson, Sound Recording.

In the early thirties, when Darryl Zanuck was making movies for Warner Bros., he was given one hard and fast rule: "No musicals!" Zanuck knew why Depression audiences were tired of musicals; the pictures were often just amalgamations of songs, with no plot to tie them together.

Zanuck wrote a script for a picture about a chorus girl who gets her big break when the star breaks her ankle. Actually, he wrote two versions of the script, one with musical numbers, one without. He showed one version to Jack and Harry Warner and the other to his co-conspirator, director Lloyd Bacon. During the day they shot the non-musical sequences on the Warner lot under the watchful eye of Jack Warner. Since Warner had recently purchased the Vitagraph studios, complete with their production facilities, Zanuck took the cast and crew to Vitagraph at night to film the musical numbers. Then Zanuck and Bacon put the dramatic and musical footage together and edited a rough cut of *42nd Street*. When Jack Warner saw it, he knew he had been had, but the film was so good, he didn't care. His first concern was how his brother Harry would react to it. Jack asked Zanuck to show Harry the non-musical version of the film, but Zanuck took the risk and sent Harry (who was in New York) the same version Jack had seen. Harry wired back, "This is the greatest picture you've sent me in five years."

Even when *42nd Street* was a runaway hit, the Warner brothers still couldn't grasp that the musical was back. After Zanuck's success, every studio geared up to make bigger, more lavish musicals. Fox made eight, Paramount made seven, MGM made six, and even RKO did five. Warner, the studio that began the run on musicals, had only one.

Part of the success of *42nd Street* can be attributed to the genius of Busby Berkeley, who single-handedly invented the extravagant production number. It was Berkeley who came up with images of hundreds of dancing girls in elaborate costumes twirling ribbons or hoops or forming human pianos or harps. In his chorus numbers, each dancer was one piece in a kaleidoscope of movement and grace. *42nd Street* includes a number performed on three huge turntables, grouped in a pyramid, which spin in opposite directions as girls tap dance. For another number a

Pullman car opens to reveal the travelers sleeping inside. The finale features the entire chorus forming a skyscraper, with Dick Powell and Ruby Keeler perched on top.

To cast the chorus, Berkeley interviewed 5,000 hopeful girls and chose the 300 with the prettiest faces. Of that number he picked the 200 with the most attractive ankles, then selected the 100 with the best knees. He said that at auditions he never needed to see the girls in bathing suits; he needed only to look into their eyes. During production he drew on his experience as an army drill instructor and put the chorines on a rigorous training program, including strict diets and prescribed sleeping hours. There is no record of who enforced the girls' required sleeping time.

Berkeley also invented the "Berkeley top shot," the technique of placing a camera on the ceiling of the studio and shooting dance numbers from above. He was also a genius at editing the scenes in the camera, which was proven by the fact that there are very few edits in a Busby Berkeley number. The camera is as carefully choreographed as the dancers, and it trucks and dollies along the chorus line in long unbroken sweeps. *42nd Street*, which contains three vintage Berkeley numbers, made him the most sought-after dance director in Hollywood.

"You're going out a youngster, but you've got to come back a star!"
—Warner Baxter to Ruby Keeler, in *42nd Street*.

Frankenstein

1931, Universal
Produced by Carl Laemmle Jr.
Directed by James Whale

S·Y·N·O·P·S·I·S

A scientist (Colin Clive) creates a man (Boris Karloff) from parts of corpses.

Let's clear up one thing. While people often refer to Boris Karloff as having played "Frankenstein," they're wrong. Karloff's character had no name in the film and was referred to only as "the monster." Frankenstein is the name of the monster's creator.

Bela Lugosi, who had just starred in the successful *Dracula*, originally agreed to play the diabolical Dr. Frankenstein, but Universal wanted him for the part of the monster. With his head built out to four times its normal size and his skin the consistency of polished clay, Lugosi made camera tests on the Dracula set. Universal's publicity department printed up posters touting him as the monster, but the monster wasn't a speaking role, and Lugosi wasn't interested.

When Boris Karloff was cast in the role that would make film history, director James Whale was concerned that the actor wasn't tall enough to play the part. His sleeves were shortened to make his arms look overly long, his jacket padded to add to his bulk. Forty-eight pounds of metal slowed him down, including a brace that kept his back straight and stiff and steel leg plates that kept his knees from bending. Boots weighing twelve-and-a-half pounds each raised his height to seven feet six inches and made walking an effort. While make-up artist Jack Pierce used the standard tools of putty and mortician's wax to create the monster's face, that gaunt look was not created totally by make up. Karloff had several false teeth, and he removed them to give his face that indented look. Since it took six hours to get him into the costume and the appliances, he couldn't eat in the studio commissary and had lunch each day in his dressing room. He couldn't smoke, either, because parts of his costume were flammable.

Preview audiences' negative reaction caused one scene to be cut from the release prints. Boris Karloff met a young girl who wasn't afraid of him. When she placed a flower in the lake, the monster was delighted to see that it floated. According to the script, Karloff was supposed to pick up the girl and gently place her in the water to see if she would also float. He didn't understand what happened when she drowned. When they filmed the scene, director James Whale insisted that instead of gently placing her in the water, Karloff should pick her up over his head and hurl her in. Karloff strenuously objected, saying the scene's impact was the contrast between the monster's innocence and the murder of a little girl. The director insisted, and Karloff did the scene as instructed. Some sources say Karloff was instrumental in getting the scene cut, while others maintain it was too distasteful to the audience at the previews. Whatever the reason, the scene was cut just after the monster reaches for the child. The next time she's seen, her father is carrying her corpse through the streets.

Preview audiences were not unanimously in favor of this film, and two patrons were particularly irate. One man threatened to sue the studio and the theater because he, his wife, and his child were upset by the film. Another man phoned the theater manager in the middle of the night, saying, "I can't sleep because of that picture and you aren't going to, either."

Another change was made for a later release. The way James Whale directed it, Colin Clive realizes his experiment worked and yelled, "It's alive! It's alive! In the name of God, now I know what it feels like to be God." The lines were included in the 1931 release prints. However, when it was re-released in 1938, the Production Code office demanded they delete the mention of God. After he yelled, "It's alive!" the following line was cut, leaving a jump cut to the next image.

While many of

the images in Frankenstein may not seem frightening today, to the thirties audience it was a new experience, one that opened their minds to the horrifying capabilities of science and technology.

There have been many imitations of this classic story, but it is safe to say that none has been able to capture the inherent honesty of Boris Karloff's original portrayal.

Visitors touring Universal Studios in Hollywood can still see a replica of the town the villagers marched through on their way to confront Dr. Frankenstein. The set was originally built for *All Quiet on the Western Front*.

From Here to Eternity

1953, Columbia
Produced by Buddy Adler
Directed by Fred Zinnemann

S•Y•N•O•P•S•I•S

Army life in Hawaii leading up to the attack on Pearl Harbor.

Academy Awards: Best Picture; Fred Zinnemann, Best Director; Frank Sinatra, Supporting Actor; Donna Reed, Supporting Actress; Daniel Taradash, Screenplay; Burnett Guffey, Black and White Cinematography; John P. Livadary, Sound Recording; William Lyon, Film Editing.

Academy Award nominations: Montgomery Clift, Best Actor; Deborah Kerr, Best Actress; Morris Stoloff and George Dunning, Musical Score; Jean Louis, Black and White Costume Design.

"*From Here to Eternity* is a dirty book." At least that's what people said in 1952 when Columbia paid $82,000 for the right to make it into a movie. It had nudity; it had sex; and (horrors!) it even had four-letter words. The joke around Hollywood went something like this: "Why would Harry Cohn buy a novel full of dirty words? Answer: Because he thinks everybody talks like that."

Censorship was definitely a problem in translating the novel into film. At that time the Production Code wouldn't allow a filmmaker to show a human navel, much less other body parts. In Hollywood all problems can eventually be worked out, even if it means compromising the original intent of the novel. In this case, it took twenty-seven scripts before everyone was happy, including the censors.

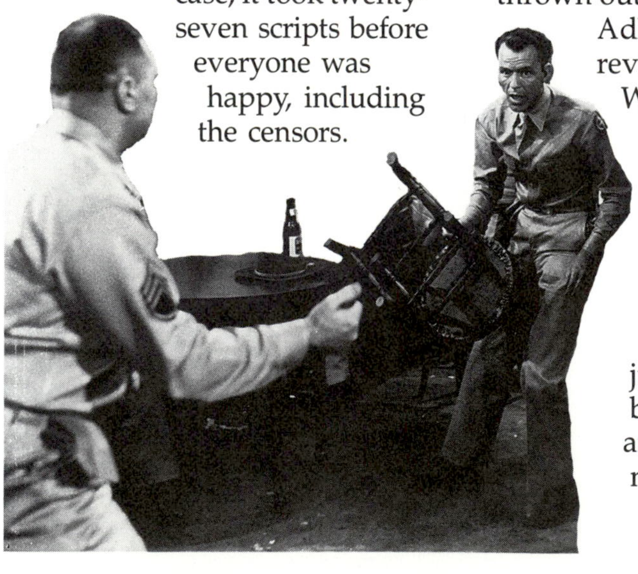

The censors weren't the only people producer Buddy Adler had to please with the script for *From Here to Eternity.* He needed the permission of the U.S. Army to film at the Schofield Barracks in Hawaii. The Army wasn't about to aid and abet anyone who might make them look bad, so their first demand was that the ending be changed. In the book Sergeant Warden was promoted; in the film he was thrown out of the Army. Buddy Adler personally took the revised script to Washington, and two days later he had the Army's full approval.

The studio's fight with the Army was over, but the casting wars were just beginning. Columbia head Harry Cohn and director Fred Zinnemann fought over each decision. Cohn wanted Aldo Ray for the part of Prewitt; Zinnemann wanted Montgomery Clift. Zinnemann finally ended the argument by threatening to quit if Clift wasn't given the role. Cohn lost the battle but not the war.

Cohn wanted Donna Reed for the part of the prostitute; Zinnemann wanted Julie Harris. Reed was screen-tested for the role, not once, not twice, but three times. Zinnemann finally gave in, and Reed proved herself by winning an Oscar for her performance.

Zinnemann resented Cohn's public announcement that Burt Lancaster and Joan Crawford were set for the leads, but the argument dissolved when Crawford quit over a costume dispute. Agent Bert Allenberg called and recomended his

Kerr spent three weeks with a voice coach to replace her English accent with an American one.

While all of these casting skirmishes are standard operating procedure in Hollywood, Frank Sinatra's casting as Sgt. Maggio was unique. Sinatra's career was floundering, he was having trouble filling the clubs, and movie offers were nonexistent. He was in Africa watching his wife, Ava Gardner, star in *Mogambo* and flew back at his own expense to read for the part. Sinatra told Harry Cohn he'd do the role for nothing, and Cohn all but took him up on it. Instead of his usual $150,000 fee, Sinatra did the part of Sgt. Maggio for $8,000. The bargain-basement actor turned in an Academy Award-winning performance, and his career was back on track.

When the film was finished, Harry Cohn made Fred Zinnemann

P·L·A·Y·E·R·S

Burt Lancaster... Sgt. Milton Warden
Montgomery Clift
.......................Robert E. Lee Prewitt
Deborah Kerr .... Karen Holmes
Frank Sinatra .... Angelo Maggio
Donna Reed..............(Alma) Lorene
Featuring:
  Ernest Borgnine
  Philip Ober
  Jack Warden
  Mickey Shaughnessy
  Harry Bellaver
  George Reeves
  John Dennis
  Tim Ryan
  Barbara Morrison
  Kristine Miller
  Jean Willes
  Merle Travis
  Arthur Keegan
  Claude Akins

and theater owners don't like long films because they can't schedule as many performances. To keep the theater owners happy, the scenes were edited out, reminding us once again that in show business, if you

client, Deborah Kerr, for the part. Cohn laughed at him. Later he met with his producer and director and told them of the absurd idea that British, cultured Deborah Kerr could play the part of the officer's wife who slept with enlisted men. Adler and Zinnemann looked at each other and said "Yes!" Cohn thought they were crazy, but agreed to the casting.

drop two scenes from the final cut. There was nothing wrong with the scenes; they were actually quite good. In one, Clift thought the planes attacking Pearl Harbor belonged to the Germans. The other was a musical interlude in which a few soldiers did a blues number. The scenes were cut because they made the film run more than two hours,

don't show a profit, you won't stay in business.

With its eight major Academy Awards, *From Here to Eternity* tied the record held by *Gone with the Wind*. The mark stood for six years, until *Ben-Hur* won eleven Oscars.

The Gay Divorcee

1934, RKO Radio
Produced by Pandro S. Berman
Directed by Mark Sandrich

S·Y·N·O·P·S·I·S

A typical Astaire/Rogers misadventure of mistaken identity—with delightful musical charm.

Academy Awards: "The Continental," Con Conrad and Herb Magidson, Best Musical Composition.

Academy Award Nominations: Best Picture; Van Nest Polglase and Carroll Clark, Interior Decoration; Carl Dreher, Sound Recording; Max Steiner, Musical Score.

Fred Astaire and Ginger Rogers made their debut as a dance team when they did "The Carioca" in *Flying Down to Rio*, a 1933 RKO film starring Dolores Del Rio and Gene Raymond. At the time, Astaire and Rogers had no idea their partnership would make cinema history. Astaire appeared in the film while on a break between the Broadway production of Cole Porter's *The Gay Divorce* and the musical's London run. He left for England without seeing the finished film and didn't know it was a success until he received a cable weeks later. The cable was followed by a personal visit from producer Pandro Berman, who wanted to make *The Gay Divorce* Astaire's first starring film.

The play's transition from stage to screen was made with few alterations. Enforcers of the newly instituted Production Code insisted the title be changed from *The Gay Divorce* to *The Gay Divorcee*. In the interests of protecting the moral fiber of the American public, it was all right for a divorcee to be gay, but not the divorce itself. Like many of the Hays Office judgments, this one didn't make much sense, but it was minor enough not to matter.

Astaire's character, who was a writer in the stage play, became a dancer, and "The Continental" was added. When it was first edited, this complicated musical number ran an unbelievable thirty-five minutes. It was eventually cut to just over sixteen. That made it the longest production number in any musical of that time. In 1951, Gene Kelly and Leslie Caron set the twenty-two minute record with their ballet sequence in *An American in Paris*.

Dance Director Dave Gould, (along with Astaire and Rogers), was conscious of making "The Continental" bigger and more spectacular than "The Carioca." They succeeded. While both songs were nominated for the Academy's first-ever award for Best Song, "The Continental" won.

Fred Astaire was pleased with the dance numbers in *The Gay Divorcee*. In his earlier Hollywood experience he had felt the dance routines suffered from being under-rehearsed. Since he was now a proven commodity, he was able to demand and get six weeks of rehearsal exclusively for the musical numbers. It's interesting to note that in 1934, microphones weren't sophisticated enough to pick up a clean recording of the taps as the dancers' feet hit the floor. Just as the singing voices were dubbed in later, so were the floor noises. Dancers watched the edited film as they redid the dances with the microphones at their feet.

One of my favorite numbers from this film is "Let's k-nock k-nees," performed by comedic great Edward Everett Horton and a young blonde named Betty Grable. Grable would later appear with Fred and Ginger in *Follow the Fleet*, but it would be ten years before she reached the height of her stardom. While Grable was on her way to

the top, the actress who played Aunt Hortense had been there and back. Alice Brady had been the beautiful leading lady of countless silent films and was one of the highest-paid stars of the era. As the movies changed, she changed with them, and played comedy roles throughout the thirties.

The Gay Divorcee set the standard for the Astaire/Rogers musicals to come, many of which were produced by Pandro Berman and directed by Mark Sandrich. Supporting casts often included Edward Everett Horton and Eric Blore.

P·L·A·Y·E·R·S

Fred Astaire.................. Guy Holden
Ginger Rogers...........Mimi Glossop
Alice Brady
.... Aunt Hortense Ditherwell
Edward Everett Horton
.... Egbert Fitzgerald
Featuring:
    Erik Rhodes
    Eric Blore
    Betty Grable
    Charles Coleman
    William Austin
    Lillian Miles

Charles Coleman, who played Fred Astaire's valet, was known as "Hollywood's Most Perfect Butler."

The Ghost and Mrs. Muir

1947, 20th Century-Fox
Produced by Fred Kohlmar
Directed by Joseph L. Mankiewicz

S·Y·N·O·P·S·I·S

A widow (Gene Tierney) moves into a cottage on the British coast and falls in love with the ghost of the former occupant, a salty sea captain (Rex Harrison).

Academy Award nomination: Charles Lang, Jr., Black and White Cinematography.

Studios live in fear that their stars will injure themselves, so they often forbid dangerous activities like skiing or auto racing. But they couldn't stop Gene Tierney from walking up the stairs.

Fanny Brice's daughter, Fran Stark, invited Gene Tierney over to her house to see her new baby. As Tierney ran up to the nursery, she twisted her ankle and pulled up short. She hadn't fallen or tripped; she just stood there, at the top of the stairs, unable to put any weight on her foot. Although she was in considerable pain, she stayed long enough to see the baby, then went right to her doctor for x-rays. Sure enough, she had broken a bone in her foot.

Executives at 20th Century-Fox were not pleased about her accident, because filming on *The Ghost and Mrs. Muir* was scheduled to begin the following day. Since she appeared in almost every scene, it was difficult to shoot around her. They held up filming as long as possible, then worked on the scenes in which she didn't have to walk. Her cast was cleverly hidden or eliminated from each shot. Tierney was especially anxious to get through the picture, because she wanted to go to New York to join her husband, Oleg Cassini. Over the objections of her doctor she had the cast removed two weeks early and finished her walking scenes in considerable pain.

The Ghost and Mrs. Muir was the second Hollywood film for Rex Harrison, following the successful Anna and the King of Siam. Harrison said playing Captain Gregg was difficult, because, as a ghost, he couldn't touch his co-star in any way, and yet the love story had to come across. As far as the censors were concerned, The Ghost and Mrs. Muir was the ideal love story, one that contained no language of love, no lingering kisses, and absolutely no bodily contact.

In support was a future star, eight-year-old Natalie Wood. She received her start in films when Irving Pichel was filming Happy Land in her home town of Santa Rosa, California. He needed a group of neighborhood children to fill out a scene, and she was chosen. Pichel was so impressed,

he cast her as Orson Welles's adopted daughter in Tomorrow is Forever, and a child star was born. Wood appeared in The Bride Wore Boots and Miracle on 34th Street before playing Anna in The Ghost and Mrs. Muir.

Vanessa Brown, who played Anna as a grown woman, was someone who could do it all. Born in Vienna in 1928, she moved with her family to New York, where she appeared on Broadway at the age of thirteen in Watch on the Rhine. She was intelligent enough to be chosen as one of radio's Quiz Kids and later attended UCLA. She broke into films, appearing in a string of "B" pictures, and played Jane to Lex Barker's Tarzan in Tarzan and the Slave Girl. She eventually retired from acting to marry film and TV director Mark Sandrich, but she didn't remain idle. While bringing up their family, she wrote magazine articles, a novel, and a nonfiction book and did on-air interviews for the Voice of America.

While Captain Gregg and Mrs. Muir seemed to have vanished together into the spirit world, they didn't stay there. They kept coming back, in sort of a show business version of reincarnation. They

were seen on television in 1955 on the 20th Century-Fox Hour, and in 1968 they came back in their own series played by Hope Lange and Edward Mulhare. That show was noteworthy because many episodes were directed by former actors, including Gene Reynolds, Ida Lupino, John Erman, and Lee Philips. It was dropped by NBC after one season and picked up by ABC. Five years later, after a brief incarnation as a Broadway musical, Lucy Muir and Captain Gregg were finally allowed to rest in peace.

Gene Tierney's husband, Oleg Cassini, designed all of her costumes in The Ghost and Mrs. Muir.

Grand Hotel

1932, MGM
Produced by Irving Thalberg
Directed by Edmund Goulding

S·Y·N·O·P·S·I·S

Intimate stories of guests who stay one night at the Grand Hotel.

Academy Award: Best Picture.

One of the most poignant stories in Hollywood history was the dramatic downfall of silent screen star John Gilbert, who could not adapt to the changes brought about by talking pictures. *Grand Hotel* was one of the nails in the coffin of his career.

He and Greta Garbo had been one of the silent screen's hottest teams, so when she was cast in *Grand Hotel*, she asked for John Gilbert as her co-star. In fact, Gilbert was promised the role by his close friend, Irving Thalberg. But when Gilbert's first three talkies failed, Thalberg had to tell Gilbert he had cast John Barrymore.

Garbo wasn't pleased to be playing opposite John Barrymore, whom she thought was an egomaniacal poseur. Barrymore, meanwhile, told his friends that he expected her to be cold and disdainful. Each was pleasantly surprised to find the other professional and hard working. At times Barrymore modified his performance to accentuate hers, and she once rearranged the furniture to feature his famous left profile.

As a measure of her respect for him, she posed with Barrymore for publicity pictures, something she rarely agreed to do. However, she would not loosen her restrictions and allow visitors on the set. After she asked one of Barrymore's friends to leave the sound stage, he supported her right to work on a closed set. Garbo on Barrymore: "...one of the very few who had that divine madness without which a great artist cannot work or live." Barrymore on Garbo: "She is a fine lady and a great actress and the rest is silence."

Twenty-eight-year-old Joan Crawford was determined to hold her own against her legendary costars. Garbo had always been one of her idols, and Crawford had often hidden on sound stages where Garbo was working in order to watch and learn. Although they were both cast in *Grand Hotel,* they had no scenes together, and Crawford still didn't get the chance to work with her idol. When her work is compared with the performances of Garbo and Barrymore, however, she more than held her own. Edmund Goulding said her work with Lionel Barrymore was the most genuinely touching scene he had ever watched.

It was director Edmund Goulding, hired because of his reputation for dealing with difficult talent, who deserves the most credit for *Grand Hotel.* He handled the raging egos of the stars by keeping them apart. He filmed master shots with all the performers in the scene, but for the close-ups he'd dismiss the others and work exclusively with one. His accomplishment in dealing with the diverse egos in *Grand Hotel* and other films earned him the nickname "Lion Tamer."

Grand Hotel was one of the earliest pictures released with a definite marketing strategy. After its triumphant premiere at Sid Grauman's Chinese Theater, MGM held it for two months while advance nationwide publicity built anticipation. The strategy worked. The day after *Grand Hotel* opened in New York, the Astor theater sold out for eight weeks. The picture cost $700,000 to make, almost half of which went to six salaries: Garbo, $68,000; Crawford, $60,000; John Barrymore, $55,750; Wallace Beery, $55,000; Lionel Barrymore, $25,000; director Edmund Goulding, $52,000. It returned more than $2.5 million in its initial release.

The closing line of *Grand Hotel* was the same as the opening line: "Grand Hotel. Always the same. People come, people go. Nothing ever happens." Nothing but a $1.8-million profit for MGM.

Greta Garbo, about to commit suicide, is startled by John Barrymore:
"Who are you?"
"Someone who loves you."
(Pause) "I want to be alone."

The Grapes of Wrath

1940, 20th Century-Fox
Produced by Darryl F. Zanuck
Directed by John Ford

S·Y·N·O·P·S·I·S

The trials of the Joad family's search for jobs during the Great Depression. Desertion, death, and hardship meet them on the road.

Academy Awards: John Ford, Best Director; Jane Darwell, Best Supporting Actress.

Academy Award Nominations: Best Picture; Henry Fonda, Best Actor; Nunnally Johnson, Screenplay; E.H. Hansen, Sound Recording; Robert E. Simpson, Editing.

In the late 1930s, up-and-coming young actor Henry Fonda was an ardent admirer of John Steinbeck's novels, and one of his favorites was *The Grapes of Wrath*. Fonda was a freelance actor who signed with individual studios to make one picture at a time. That way he could appear in pictures he liked and not be forced to accept roles he didn't care for. One day he got a call from his agent, Leland Hayward, who asked him if he'd like to star in *The Grapes of Wrath*. Fonda was excited and immediately agreed to do the part. However, there was a catch. Darryl Zanuck would cast him as Tom Joad only if Fonda would agree to sign a seven-year contract with 20th Century-Fox. If Fonda wouldn't sign the contract, the role would go to Tyrone Power or Don Ameche. That was the deal; take it or leave it. Fonda took it, and tied himself up for seven years and countless mediocre pictures, just to play Tom Joad. By the way, neither John Steinbeck nor director John Ford wanted Tyrone Power or Don Ameche for the lead. They both thought that Henry Fonda was the only man in Hollywood who could do it justice.

Standard operating procedure on a John Ford film called for very little rehearsal, and most scenes were in the can in one or two takes. Ford felt that the more the actors did the lines, the less

realistic they became. The final scene between Henry Fonda and Jane Darwell is a case in point. The only thing they rehearsed was one piece of technical business, where Fonda lit a match and the light was supposed to spill over Darwell's face. Cameraman Gregg Toland rigged a small light in the palm of Fonda's hand and ran the wires down his sleeve. They spent half an hour rehearsing Fonda's actions so that the light would hit Darwell properly. Then, without running over their lines even once, they called in John Ford and did the scene. The first time they heard each other say their lines was in front of the camera.

While the closing scene was not in John Steinbeck's novel, it was added with the author's full approval. When Steinbeck sold the rights to the book to Zanuck for a then-astronomical $100,000, the author included an unusual clause in the contract. It stipulated that Zanuck would maintain the main ingredients and intent of the literary work. Darryl Zanuck wrote the closing dialogue, which changed the unhappy ending to a more upbeat one. Then he called Steinbeck and Ford to his office to explain the new ending and obtain their approval. In the middle of the meeting, Zanuck was called away from his office by a terrible tragedy on the back lot. Shirley Temple had fallen down and might have chipped a tooth. As Zanuck left the room, Steinbeck told him not to worry, that the ending of *The Grapes of Wrath* was unimportant compared to Shirley Temple's tooth.

Henry Fonda was nominated for an Academy Award for his performance as Tom Joad, and many people still believe he should have won it. He was beaten out by his best friend and ex-roommate, James Stewart, for *The Philadelphia Story*.

Fonda's first and only Oscar was the one he received for *On Golden Pond*, his very last motion picture.

The Grapes of Wrath was nominated for seven Oscars, including Best Picture, but won only two. To this day I consider *The Grapes of Wrath* one of the top ten movies of all time.

James Stewart, who won the 1940 Best Actor Oscar over Henry Fonda, admitted that he had voted for Fonda.

Great Expectations

1946, British; Cineguild-Independent Producers Production
Produced by Anthony Havelock-Allen and Ronald Neame
Directed by David Lean

S·Y·N·O·P·S·I·S

Charles Dickens' classic tale of a young orphan boy who becomes a gentleman.

Academy Awards: Guy Green, Black and White Cinematography; John Bryan, Black and White Art Direction.

Academy Award nominations: Best Picture; David Lean, Best Director; Ronald Neame, David Lean, Anthony Havelock-Allan, Kay Walsh and Cecil McGivern, Screenplay.

For Valerie Hobson, *Great Expectations* wasn't just the title of a novel by Charles Dickens. It also described her feelings when she was cast in the role of Estella in a 1934 Hollywood production of the Dickens novel. Hobson was an aspiring starlet without any major film roles to her credit. Her great expectations would soon turn to dust. First Universal decided to replace her with Jane Wyatt, moving her to a secondary role. Then, to add insult to injury, her scenes were left on the cutting room floor. Her illusions shattered, Valerie Hobson returned to her native England, where she found success and quickly became one of Britain's leading actresses.

Let's jump forward twelve years to 1946. Director David Lean is preparing another version of *Great Expectations*. Whom did he cast as Estella? Valerie Hobson. It must have given her a great deal of satisfaction when

the critics said that Lean's *Great Expectations* was vastly superior to the earlier, American version.

While top-billed John Mills and Valerie Hobson were well known in England at the time, David Lean cast several newcomers in supporting roles. Hidden well down in the credits are Alec Guinness and Jean Simmons. When none of the juvenile British actors of the era seemed right for the role of Pip as a boy, the studio conducted a talent search. Seven hundred eager young boys auditioned, and thirteen-year-old Anthony Wager got the part. The son of a London plumber, he had never appeared on stage in any capacity. Veterans Mills and Hobson coached him, and their work paid off. He turned in a charming performance.

Supporting actor Bernard Miles, who played the blacksmith, surprised everyone with his knowledge of how his part should be played. He told the film's technical advisor that the tongs he had been given as a prop were from the wrong historical period. The technical advisor did further research and concluded Miles was right. The actor's grandfather had been a

blacksmith, and Miles had apprenticed under him for five years before he left the stables for the sound stages. He came full circle when he found himself cast as a blacksmith in *Great Expectations*.

Finlay Currie, who played Magwitch, did not look the part when he showed up on the first day of filming. First they shaved off his thick, iron-grey hair and attached a thin fringe around the side of his head that continued down to his collar. With a three-day growth of beard and a black eye patch, he was ready to strike terror into the hearts of the audience. The opening sequence where he grabs young Pip is still considered one of the greatest opening scenes of all time.

Great Expectations was good enough to win awards on both sides of the Atlantic. In addition to its five Academy Award

nominations it won the Picturegoer Annual Award, the Daily Express film award, and others. But none of these is as rare as one sentence from the *New York Times*. One of the toughest critics in the United States called Lean's *Great Expectations* "a perfect motion picture."

Swiss skating star Arnold Gerschweiler taught Valerie Hobson to ice skate for her role of Estella. His evaluation of his pupil? "She's no Sonja Henie, but she does have a fine style."

Gunga Din

1939, RKO Radio
Produced by Pandro S. Berman
Directed by George Stevens

S·Y·N·O·P·S·I·S

Two British sergeants in India (Cary Grant and Victor McLaglen), who are fighting off the revolt of the murderous Thuggees, try to convince their friend (Douglas Fairbanks, Jr.) not to marry and leave the military.
Academy Award nomination: Joseph H. August, Black and White Cinematography.

For many years Hollywood wanted to make a movie of Rudyard Kipling's classic poem, "Gunga Din." There were two problems. First, the poem wasn't very long and didn't contain many characters or a well-developed plot. The second problem was making *Gunga Din* different from other films about the British military in India.

Many writers were assigned to the project, but the scripts sat on various shelves for years. In 1936, Howard Hawks, Ben Hecht, and Charles MacArthur went to work on the latest version. A month later they sent a wire to the production head at RKO:

"Have finally figured out tale involving two sacrifices, one for love, the other for England, which neither resembles *Bengal Lancers* nor *The Charge of the Light Brigade* and contains something like two thousand deaths, thirty elephants and a peck of maharajahs — stop — We have this now in a cocktail shaker and have poured out some thirty-five pages of glittering prose."

RKO bought it and cast Cary Grant and Douglas Fairbanks, Jr., in the leading roles. Interestingly, producer Pandro Berman didn't care which role was played by which actor. Grant and Fairbanks were friends and didn't want to start any arguments, so they solved the problem like true gentlemen. They flipped a coin, and Grant took the role of Cutter while Fairbanks played Ballantine. Because he had a reputation for bringing in a project on time and within budget, George Stevens was brought in to direct. Unfortunately, Stevens had no control over Mother Nature. They went 220 miles northeast of Los Angeles to shoot on location in Lone Pine, where the temperature during the day peaked at 115°, while at night it dropped to near freezing. After several days of work, a freak snowstorm high in the mountains changed Mt. Whitney to a snow-capped peak. Filming came to a halt while they waited for the background to return to normal. The cast and crew also rode out a windstorm that damaged the sets, and were forced to dig themselves out after a three-day dust storm. The physical hazards were only part of the challenge of bringing *Gunga Din* to the screen. Since the script had never been

finalized, the stars and director found themselves writing their own material. Each night Cary Grant, Douglas Fairbanks, Jr., writer Joel Sayre, and George Stevens would gather in Stevens' tent, where they lit a fire to keep warm. They threw ideas around and walked through some possible dialogue, and the next day, that's what they'd shoot. When RKO became aware of the mounting costs, studio executives cancelled the production. Stevens and his cohorts decided to ignore the messages telling them to return to Hollywood. Instead, they sent back the rushes. RKO executives screened the rushes, realized the film's potential, and left them alone.

Gunga Din was finally finished and released to rave reviews. For years afterward

Douglas Fairbanks, Jr., would run into people who had served in India. Invariably they swore they knew the exact spot where the battle scenes had been filmed. When he told them the battles were recreated on location in California, they refused to believe him. For Douglas Fairbanks, Jr., and Cary Grant, those days they spent in the treacherous conditions at Lone Pine were fond memories. Over the years Fairbanks would receive long-distance calls from Cary Grant, who inevitably identified himself as "Sergeant Cutter." Fairbanks would pick up the phone and reply, "Sergeant Ballantine here."

An Indian critic called *Gunga Din* "imperialist propaganda of the crudest, most vulgar sort." Because of the way Indians were portrayed, the film was unconditionally banned by the Indian government.

Hell's Angels

1930, United Artists
Produced and Directed by Howard Hughes

S·Y·N·O·P·S·I·S

Two brothers (Ben Lyon and James Hall), members of the Royal Flying Corps during World War I, fall in love with the same woman (Jean Harlow), who betrays them both.

Academy Award nomination: Gaetano Gaudio and Harry Perry, Cinematography.

In the spring of 1927 the word went out in aviation circles: Hollywood producer Howard Hughes wants you and your plane for his personal air force. Hughes supervised a worldwide search for authentic World War I aircraft and the pilots to fly them. By the time the cameras rolled on *Hell's Angels*, Hughes' 137 pilots and as many mechanics constituted the largest air fleet ever assembled for a film. Inglewood Field, which became Los Angeles International Airport, was the site of the British flying school, while nearby Chatsworth became the home base for the infamous Baron von Richtofen.

Hughes' intention was to spare no expense making the *Top Gun* of his day. The sky battles alone cost two million dollars, an astronomical figure in those days. During filming the aircraft covered 227,000 miles, years before the advent of frequent flier programs. With more than 20,000 extras, Howard Hughes literally had a cast of thousands for his aviation epic.

Hughes, who had earned his pilot's license only two months before shooting, came to respect his flyers' judgement the hard way. He told one of his pilots to take off sharply and then roll into a steep climbing turn. The pilot refused, saying the maneuver would surely result in a stall and spin. Hughes said he'd never ask a pilot to do something he wouldn't do himself, so he jumped into the plane and took it up. Just as the pilot predicted, Hughes got up around 400 feet, and the plane came crashing back to earth. No one could have predicted that Howard Hughes would pick himself out of the wreckage, totally unhurt.

Two years and three million dollars later, Hughes previewed his silent film to a less than enthusiastic audience. The only thing *Hell's Angels* lacked, he decided, was sound. Hughes recalled the cast and, after shooting two million feet of silent film, some of it in color, he decided to make a talkie.

He fired his star, Greta Nissen, who spoke with a heavy Scandinavian accent, and replaced her with an unknown eighteen-year-old named Jean Harlow, who signed with Hughes for $150 a week.

All of the scenes with actors were re-shot to accommodate the new dialogue, but Hughes decided not to re-stage the air battles. Sound for individual and formation flying was recorded separately by a number of pilots, and then added to the aerial sequences.

Hell's Angels gave the public everything a movie could give in 1930. It had sound, it had a few color scenes, and it had a few scenes shot in an early wide screen process. Last but by no means least, the film had Jean Harlow, the original blonde bombshell! (Prior to this time all the bombshells had been brunettes, like Theda Bara and Pola Negri.)

When Hell's Angels hit the theaters, Harlow was the proverbial overnight success.

Howard Hughes had her under personal contract, but instead of making more films with her, he sold her contract to MGM for $60,000. Over the next seven years she starred in Iron Man, Public Enemy, and Platinum Blonde, among others.

Being associated with Hell's Angels wasn't healthy for Howard Hughes—or for several others. Although the picture was one of the ten biggest moneymakers of 1930, Hughes never did recoup the $4 million production cost. But he lost only money on the motion picture.

Others lost their lives. Pilot Al Johnson was killed when his plane hit high-tension wires on take-off and exploded. Mechanic Phil Jones was lost in the crash of the giant German

Gotha Bomber (actually a Sikorsky S-29A transport). Cameraman E. Burton Steene suffered a fatal stroke while on the set of Hell's Angels.

P·L·A·Y·E·R·S

Ben Lyon .... Monte Rutledge
James Hall .... Roy Rutledge
Jean Harlow .... Helen
John Darrow .... Karl Arnstedt
Featuring:
Lucien Prival
Frank Clarke
Roy Wilson
Douglas Gilmore
Jane Winton
Evelyn Hall
William B. Davidson
Wyndham Standing
Carl von Haartman
F. Schumann-Heink
Stephen Carr
Pat Somerset
William von Brincken
Hans Joby
Lena Malena
Harry Semels
Marilyn Morgan

"Life is short. I want to live while I'm alive."

—Jean Harlow to Ben Lyon in Hell's Angels. Seven years later, Harlow would die unexpectedly at the age of 26.

His Girl Friday

1940, Columbia
Produced and Directed by Howard Hawks

S·Y·N·O·P·S·I·S

Romantic comedy about a man (Cary Grant) and his ex-wife (Rosalind Russell), who work together on a newspaper. While covering a murder case, she decides to forsake her fiancee and go back to her ex-husband.

The year was 1939, and a man named Frederick Brisson was involved in a shipboard romance while crossing the Atlantic Ocean from England to America. Unfortunately, the woman he fell in love with was in Los Angeles at the time.

There was only one movie on board ship, which was shown over and over and over again. It was *The Women*, starring Rosalind Russell. Freddie had never met Rosalind but he fell in love with her and told his companions he would marry her some day. Were these the delusions of a deranged man? Not at all.

When he arrived in Los Angeles, he stayed at a friend's house in Santa Monica. That friend was Cary Grant, and as luck, or fate, would have it, Grant was working on a picture called *His Girl Friday*. His costar? The love of Freddie Brisson's fantasy

life, Rosalind Russell. Freddie continually asked for an introduction, and Grant tried to arrange the meeting, but Rosalind was simply not interested in a blind date. Considering the circumstances, I can't say I blame her! Freddie kept up the pressure, Cary kept asking, and Rosalind finally relented. In October of 1941 Cary Grant was the best man at the wedding of Frederick Brisson

and Rosalind Russell.

His Girl Friday was based on *The Front Page*, a 1928 play by Ben Hecht and Charles MacArthur. It detailed some of the newspapermen's own exploits from their long careers in journalism. When Howard Hawks was assigned to direct the 1940 Columbia version, the studio wanted Cary Grant and Walter Winchell for the leading roles. Before he cast the picture, Hawks wanted a feel for the dialogue. While he read one of the parts, he had a script girl read the other. He was struck by the new meanings that sprang up when the roles were read by a man and a woman, so the Walter Winchell role went to Rosalind Russell.

Both Cary Grant and Rosalind Russell were famous for their ad libs, so Hawks rehearsed their scenes and then turned them loose. Russell unexpectedly threw her handbag at Grant, and Grant ducked and then picked up the scripted dialogue. Hawks

left it in. Grant forgot Ralph Bellamy's character's name and referred to "that fellow who looks like Ralph Bellamy." Once again, Hawks left it in.

Hawks was credited as inventing the technique of "overlapping dialogue" for *His Girl Friday*, but the actors said the script just seemed to play better that way. Overlapping is most effective in fast-paced romantic comedies in which the hero and heroine are adversaries. At one point Rosalind Russell expressed the fear that she and Grant were talking so fast, no one in the audience would understand a word they said! Hawks assured her it was just perfect. He was right.

Hawks was also right about the scene in which Cary Grant shoves Rosalind Russell on to the couch. The first time they tried it, Grant gave her a tentative little push. Hawks stopped the scene and told Grant to push her a lot harder. Grant replied that he didn't want to kill his costar.

Hawks thought it over for a moment, considered how he wanted the scene to play, and replied, "Go ahead and kill her!" There is no one quite as compassionate as a Hollywood director who knows what he wants.

Carole Lombard, Jean Arthur, Irene Dunne, Claudette Colbert and Ginger Rogers all turned down the role of Hildy Johnson in *His Girl Friday.*

The Hound of the Baskervilles

1939, 20th Century-Fox
Produced by Gene Markey
Directed by Sidney Lanfield

S·Y·N·O·P·S·I·S

Sherlock Holmes (Basil Rathbone) and Dr. Watson (Nigel Bruce) investigate a murder tied to a legend of an animal that attacks only the members of one family.

Before *The Hound of the Baskervilles* was made, no one would have believed that Basil Rathbone would ever play a hero. He was much too effective as one of Hollywood's greatest villains. He had crossed swords with Tyrone Power and Errol Flynn, threatened the most beautiful women in Hollywood, and performed every dastardly deed that villains are known for. But once he donned a Deerstalker hat and a Meerscham pipe, he changed his image from villain to hero.

Many actors have played Sir Arthur Conan Doyle's analytical detective, but no one was as successful as Basil Rathbone. Conan

Doyle created Sherlock Holmes in 1887, modeling his creation after one of his own teachers. Perhaps Holmes was a man of his time. 1887 was the year Jack the Ripper terrorized London and baffled the authorities, and the British public needed to believe

in an infallible crimestopper who inevitably made criminals pay for their heinous crimes.

Early filmmakers in America, Scandinavia, France, and Germany featured Sherlock Holmes in countless films, but most of those prints have been lost. While Basil Rathbone became the most famous Sherlock, he wasn't the most filmed. Britisher Eille Norwood played the master sleuth in fifty silent movies, but Holmes' analytical style didn't lend itself to the silent screen, where action was more readily understood than logic.

Another early Holmes film, painstakingly restored by British historian Kevin Brownlon, is the 1922 Sam Goldwyn prduction with John Barrymore as the master detective and Roland Young (before he was Topper) as Dr. Watson. William Powell is in support. In 1931, Raymond Massey made his screen debut as

Sherlock Holmes in *The Speckled Band*.

Then, in 1939, the perfect Holmes emerged, accompanied by the appropriate Watson. *The Hound of the Baskervilles* was chosen as a screen vehicle, but unlike earlier adaptations, the screenwriters stuck closely to the original Conan Doyle story. To avoid confusion with the actor, the name of the butler, played by John Carradine, was changed from Barrymore to Barryman. Censors demanded that the villain's wife became the villain's sister to legitimize her romance with Richard Greene, and a seance was added that was not in the original story. They also changed the ending slightly. In Conan Doyle's version, the villain is definitely killed in the Grimpen Mire, while the film leaves it open.

Only the stature of Sherlock Holmes could have made acceptable his most startling closing speech, which begins with an innocent line: "I've had a rather strenuous day, I think I'll turn in." Holmes then starts for the door, turns, and completely takes us by surprise as he adds: "Oh Watson, the needle!" Rhett Butler was having trouble with the censors that year for using the word "damn," but Holmes was getting away with drug addiction! The problem was not mentioned on screen again for 37 years, when Holmes was painfully cured in *The Seven Percent Solution*.

Because Basil Rathbone took Holmes seriously without sacrificing the character's wry wit, *The Hound of the Baskervilles* was the best of the fourteen films featuring the Rathbone/Bruce combination. Director Sidney Lanfield added his own creative touches by forgoing the usual backgrund music in favor of eerie sound effects. The sound track is full of doors creaking and wolves howling on the moors. Although the film was shot entirely on the Fox lot, the London scenes are believable, and the shots on the moors were enhanced by mist made from dry ice and a barely perceptible covering of gauze over the camera lens.

"Of all the adventures," said Basil Rathbone, "*The Hound* is my favorite story: and it was in this picture that I had the stimulating experience of creating within my own limited framework, a character that has intrigued me as much as any I have ever played."

For me, always, Basil Rathbone was the man who *was* Sherlock Holmes.

P·L·A·Y·E·R·S

Richard Greene
.... Sir Henry Baskerville
Basil Rathbone..... Sherlock Holmes
Wendy Barrie .... Beryl Stapleton
Nigel Bruce ....Dr. Watson
Featuring:
    Lionel Atwell
    John Carradine
    Barlowe Borland
    Beryl Mercer
    Morton Lowry
    Ralph Forbes
    E.E. Clive
    Eily Maylon
    Nigel de Brulier
    Mary Gordon
    Peter Willes
    Ivan Simpson
    Ian MacLaren
    John Burton
    Dennis Green
    Evan Thomas

With a total of 176 films played by 76 different actors, Sherlock Holmes remains the most often depicted fictional character on film.

The House On 92nd Street

1945, 20th Century-Fox
Produced by Louis de Rochemont
Directed by Henry Hathaway

S·Y·N·O·P·S·I·S

The FBI tracks a Nazi spy ring plotting to steal information on the atomic bomb.

It's not unusual for a sound stage to be completely closed to visitors and the actors and crew pledged to secrecy. Usually it's a publicity gimmick, or it's done to keep a surprise en-ding from being publicized before the picture is finished. When 20th Century-Fox was making *The House on 92nd Street*, security was the tightest it had ever been on the studio lot. Most of the filming was done in absolute secrecy, and certain pages of the script were withheld until the film was almost finished. It wasn't a surprise ending they were trying to conceal; it was our government's secret weapon for ending World War II.

The script pages kept from the cast and crew referred to Process 97 but they were actually references to the atomic bomb. The F.B.I. had made a deal with documentary filmmaker Louis de Rochemont. If he would cooperate with their requirements for security, the Bureau would break precedent and cooperate with him to make a docudrama dealing with the new atomic bomb technology. Up to this point the F.B.I. had never given its full cooperation to any Hollywood producer.

Once the White House had officially announced the dropping of the bomb on Japan, the cast and crew were given the remaining script pages and the movie was completed.

As part of the deal, the F.B.I. allowed Fox the unprecedented opportunity to take cameras into Bureau headquarters in Washington, D.C. Lloyd Nolan was invited to spend time at the F.B.I. training school, learning how to portray a federal inspector. He learned everything, from the serious way an agent carries himself when dealing with the public, to the proper way to look at evidence through a microscope. The F.B.I. also loaned the studio a specially camouflaged van containing a hidden camera, which was used to make candid shots on the streets of New York City. De Rochemont, who was primarily a documentary filmmaker, was thrilled with the van. He said it allowed him to eliminate obvious, self-conscious extras and the unreality of standard movie sets.

Why would the F.B.I. go to all this trouble? Most Americans in 1945 knew we had dropped something called an atomic bomb on Japan but were not sure what this mysterious new weapon was all about. The F.B.I. knew that movies were one of the most powerful influences on public opinion, so it encouraged Hollywood to present the weapon as

necessary to the defense and security of the country.

William Eythe did the honors as the federal agent who went undercover to infiltrate the spy ring. As one of the few handsome young men who did not go off to fight in World War II, he was given many of the roles that would have gone to Tyrone Power. When the war ended and Power returned to claim his place at Fox, Eythe freelanced, starring in many action pictures. We'll never know how good an actor he could have become, because he died of hepatitis at the age of thirty-eight. He was married only once, to Buff Cobb, who later wed CBS newsman Mike Wallace.

The House on 92nd Street was without a doubt the best Hollywood role for Signe Hasso, who became an actress by the flip of a coin. Her mother once took her and her sister to an audition at the Swedish Royal Theater. The director liked both girls equally, so he flipped a coin, and Signe got the part. She was one of the lucky few able to make the transition from little-girl roles to mature leading lady. She starred in pictures in

her native Sweden for almost ten years before making her way to Hollywood, where she quickly graduated from supporting roles to leads. She played opposite Dick Powell in *To the Ends of the Earth* and Ronald Colman in *A Double Life.*

E.G. Marshall played the morgue attendant in *The House on 92nd Street.* This was his first speaking part.

How Green Was My Valley

1941 20th Century-Fox
Produced by Darryl F. Zanuck
Directed by John Ford

Drama about a close-knit family in a Welsh mining town.

Academy Awards: Best Picture; John Ford, Best Director; Donald Crisp, Supporting Actor; Richard Day and Nathan Juran, Art Direction; Thomas Little, Interior Decoration; Arthur Miller, Black and White Cinematography.

Academy Award Nominations: Sara Allgood, Supporting Actress; Philip Dunne, Screenplay; E.H. Hansen, Sound Recording; Alfred Newman, Score; James B. Clark, Film Editing.

When Darryl Zanuck bought the rights to Richard Llewellyn's novel, *How Green was my Valley*, he wanted to portray life in a Welsh mining town as accurately as possible. He considered filming the entire picture in the Thondda Valley in Wales, but World War II made it impractical, if not impossible, to take an entire production company to Britain. If they couldn't go to Wales, Wales would have to come to them. Twentieth Century-Fox construction superintendent Ben Wurtzel was given one hundred men and eighty acres near Bernt's Crags in the Ventura Hills of the San Fernando Valley, thirty miles north of Hollywood. It took six weeks to build an authentic Welsh mining town, complete right down to the veins of coal running underground. In wartime, coal was a valuable commodity. The studio discouraged poachers by placing a twenty-four hour guard over the several hundred tons of coal that were shipped to the location.

How Green Was My Valley was directed by one of the great directors of Hollywood, John Ford. But he wasn't originally signed to the project. William Wyler supervised the pre-production, collaborated with Philip Dunne to fine-tune the script, and cast the picture, spending weeks looking for a little boy to play Huw Morgan.

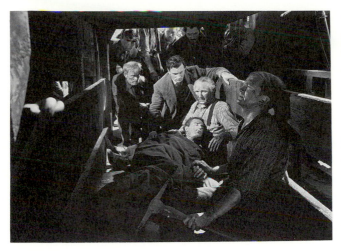

Many British parents had sent their children abroad to escape the blitz, so there were a great many English children in the United States at that time. Wyler finally found him: Roddy McDowall, veteran of twenty British films but unknown in the United States.

Wyler was ready to begin filming in the summer of 1940, but the studio ran into several delays. By the time Fox was ready, Wyler wasn't available. Rather than wait for him, Zanuck hired John Ford, who accepted all of Wyler's casting decisions and pre-production work but also gave the film the small touches that distinguish a John Ford picture.

To keep the actors in character on the set, Ford hired the Welsh Eisteddfod Chorus to sing Welsh hymns in four-part harmony. The songs, which were taught to the cast by Welsh baritone Tudor Williams and actor Rhys Williams, were used as transitional elements throughout the film.

One unfortunate incident on the set illustrates how dangerous even simple stunts can be. John Ford wanted to use a stunt double for a scene in which Anna Lee falls down a staircase, but Lee insisted she could do the scene herself. If she had known she was pregnant at the time, she probably would not have attempted it. She did the stunt, landed very hard, and was rushed to a hospital, where she had a miscarriage. For the rest of his life John Ford blamed himself for the loss of her baby.

How Green Was My Valley was universally recognized as one of John Ford's best and beat out *Citizen Kane, The Little Foxes, The Maltese Falcon, Sergeant York,* and *Suspicion* for the Academy Award for Best Picture of 1941.

This would be the last John Ford picture the American public would enjoy for many years. After wrapping up work on *How Green was My Valley,* John Ford became chief of the field photographic branch of the Office of Strategic Services. The films he made as a lieutenant commander in the U.S. Navy exhibited his high standards for excellence. His first military film, *The Battle of Midway,* won an Oscar for excellence in documentary work.

Because she was English, Anna Lee was afraid John Ford would replace her in *How Green Was My Valley.* Knowing he was proud of his Irish heritage, she told him she had an Irish grandfather named Thomas Michael O'Connell.

The Hunchback of Notre Dame

1939, RKO Radio
Produced by Pandro S. Berman
Directed by William Dieterle

S·Y·N·O·P·S·I·S

A hunchbacked bellringer (Charles Laughton) falls in love with a beautiful woman (Maureen O'Hara) and sacrifices his life for her.
Academy Award nominations: Alfred Newman, Score; John Aalberg, Sound.

Film crews are a tough breed. The men and women who do the makeup and the lighting, record the sound, arrange the props, and handle thousands of technical details rarely get caught up in the emotion of a scene. If they did, they wouldn't be doing their jobs properly.

That's one of the reasons the filming of the bell-ringing scene in *The Hunchback of Notre Dame* was so incredible.

It was 1939. As Charles Laughton was playing out scenes of man's inhumanity to man, Adolph Hitler was invading Poland. According to director William Dieterle, the tension on the sound stage was unbearable. England and France had just declared war on the Third Reich. It was hard for even seasoned professionals to forget what was happening in the real world and concentrate on their work.

Dieterle called for "action," Laughton began ringing the bell, and something happened. The sound of the bell touched each person present on that sound stage, touched something so deep within them that everybody, including the director, forgot that they were shooting a film. Dieterle later wrote, "Something super-dimensional happened at that moment, and I forgot to call 'cut' as the scene ended. Laughton went on ringing the bells after the scene was over. Finally, completely exhausted, he stopped. No one was able to speak, nobody moved. Finally, in his dressing room, Charles could only say, 'I couldn't think of Esmerelda in that scene at all. I could only think of the poor people out there, going to fight that bloody, bloody war! To arouse the world, to stop that terrible butchery! Awake! Awake! That's what I felt when I was ringing the bells!'"

P·L·A·Y·E·R·S

Charles Laughton..........Quasimodo
Sir Cedric Hardwicke..............Frollo
Thomas Mitchell....................Clopin
Maureen O'Hara ....Esmerelda
Edmond O'Brien.............. Gringoire
Featuring:
    Alan Marshall
    Walter Hampden
    Katharine Alexander
    Harry Davenport
    George Zucco
    Fritz Leiber
    Etienne Girradot
    Helene Whitney
    Minna Gombell
    Arthur Hohl
    George Tobias
    Rod La Rocque

To say Charles Laughton's performance was "brilliant" or "unforgettable" diminishes its magnitude. The physical hardships he suffered were enough to break most actors, but he managed to persevere and put in a performance that transcends the story.

The Paris cathedral was recreated on a San Fernando Valley ranch, where the daytime temperature rarely went below 100 degrees. Laughton's costume included a four-pound hump, rubber makeup that pushed one side of his face up and the other side down, and special contact lenses that gave his eyes a milky look and were agonizing to wear. In the bell-ringing scenes he fought the sweltering heat as he pulled ropes attached to hundred-pound bells. Often the sweat would ruin his makeup and they'd have to do a scene again. His wife said that he would come home and break down from the physical agony of five hours of makeup followed by the all-day shooting schedule. He had welts on his arms, hips, and back from the whipping scenes and tears in his eyes from the prospect of doing it all again the next day.

On the last day of filming, one of the crew members asked Laughton to do the scene from *Ruggles of Red Gap*, in which Laughton recited the Gettysburg address. Laughton did it in his hunchback makeup. Imagine, this misshapen man who had been tormented all his life speaking Lincoln's words about liberty and justice and all men being created equal. Unfortunately, they didn't roll the cameras. It's a performance that exists today only in the hearts of those who witnessed it.

The 1939 version of The *Hunchback of Notre Dame* was the film debut of Edmund O'Brien, and the first American film for 18-year-old Maureen O'Hara.

I Remember Mama

1948, RKO Radio
Produced by Harriet Parsons
Directed by George Stevens

S·Y·N·O·P·S·I·S

Sentimental drama about a Norwegian family in San Francisco in 1910.

Academy Award Nominations: Irene Dunne, Best Actress; Oscar Homolka, Supporting Actor; Barbara Bel Geddes, Ellen Corby, Supporting Actress; Nicholas Musuruca, Black and White Cinematography.

If ever there was an unlikely subject for a major motion picture, it's the trials and tribulations of a Norwegian family living in San Francisco in 1910. While *I Remember Mama* may have been different from any of the standard Hollywood formulas, it didn't take a studio visionary to predict the movie would be a hit. It was based on Kathryn Forbes's best-selling novel, *Mama's Bank Account,* which detailed her remembrances of her very colorful family. Then John Van Druten turned it into a play, which was produced on Broadway by Richard Rodgers and Oscar Hammerstein.

The film version was produced by Harriet Parsons, one of the few women working in that capacity. Harriet's mother was Louella Parsons, whose gossip column controlled the fate of every Merton who wanted to make it in the movies.

When casting *I Remember Mama,* Parsons' biggest concern was finding a convincing actress for the role of Mama. Her first choice, believe it or not, was Greta Garbo. After all, she did have a great European accent! Around the same time, Alfred Hitchcock asked Garbo to star in *The Paradine Case.* She turned them both down with one comment: "No mamas, no murderesses."

Parsons finally cast Irene Dunne as the head of the family. Ironically, two of the women she cast in supporting roles would later play two of the best-known matriarchs on television. Barbara Bel Geddes, who played Katrin, the narrator of the film, is better known for her role as Miss Ellie, the only woman who could tell J.R. what to do on television's *Dallas.* Aunt Trina was played by Ellen Corby, who was beloved for her role as Grandma Walton on *The Waltons. I Remember Mama* also features a rare appearance by Edgar Bergen without his dummy, Charlie McCarthy.

I Remember Mama became *Mama,* one of the first hit television shows based on a movie. Every week it opened with the off-screen narration of daughter Katrin, who said she remembered many incidents from her adolescence, "but most of all, I remember Mama." Peggy Wood played Mama in the series, with Robin Morgan as the daughter. You may remember the young actor who played the son. He was Dick van Patten, who grew up to become the father on television's *Eight is Enough.*

I Remember Mama survives as an icon of a simpler era, one without television news, home computers, or mind-boggling budget deficits. It recalls a time when passage to adulthood was marked by something as simple

as your first cup of coffee. While it would be impossible to turn back the clock and live the way our forebears did, it's comforting to know that we can watch a film like *I Remember Mama* and hearken back to those kinder, simpler times.

Rudy Vallee, who plays a supporting role in *I Remember Mama*, was unsuccessful in his efforts to get the City of Los Angeles to change the name of his street to Rue de Vallee.

In Old Chicago

1937, 20th Century-Fox
Produced by Darryl F. Zanuck
Directed by Henry King

S·Y·N·O·P·S·I·S

The story of two brothers (Tyrone Power, Don Ameche) whose rivalry culminates in a fight that starts the Great Chicago Fire.

Academy Awards: Alice Brady, Supporting Actress; Robert Webb, Assistant Director.

Academy Award Nominations: Best Picture; Niven Busch, Original Story; E.H. Hansen, Sound Recording; Louis Silvers, Score.

In Hollywood everyone copies success, even if it means disaster. When MGM scored a big hit with Clark Gable in a picture about the San Francisco earthquake, 20th Century-Fox started looking for a disaster they could call their own. After considering many disasters, both natural and man made, the big winner was the Great Chicago Fire.

Since Darryl Zanuck wanted his cataclysm to be as good as MGM's, he wanted Clark Gable for the lead. At the time, MGM wanted Shirley Temple for *The Wizard of Oz*, so the studios agreed to an even trade: Temple for Gable.

A script about the Chicago fire was written for Clark Gable and Jean Harlow. However, Fox director Henry King convinced Darryl Zanuck that, at thirty-six, Gable was too old for the part. Zanuck canceled the deal with MGM and told them they'd have to find someone else to star in *The Wizard of Oz*.

It was rumored around Hollywood that aspects of Dion and Jack O'Leary, the main characters in *In Old Chicago*, were modeled after Darryl Zanuck. The brash, pushy young man who achieves success on his own terms, as well as his kinder, idealistic brother, reflected the dual nature Zanuck often exhibited. When Henry King suggested Tyrone Power and Don Ameche for the roles, Zanuck was satisfied his image was safe.

For the female lead, Jean Harlow was replaced by another blonde, 20th Century-Fox star Alice Faye. Although Faye usually received top billing, when she costarred with Tyrone Power, she was content with second. The way she looked at it, it was all in the family. She, Tyrone Power, and Don Ameche had made so many pictures together, she thought of them more as brothers than as rivals for press and attention.

In fact, their antics on the set resembled the high-spirited tricks brothers and sisters might play on each other. One of Alice Faye's deepest secrets was that she wore false nails to hide her habit of biting her fingernails. When Tyrone Power found out, he

waited until they were in the middle of a love scene, tenderly took her hand and surreptitiously pulled one of the nails off. As he found out, what goes around, comes around. Power always wore a cap that covered a gap between his front teeth. After a particularly passionate love scene, the cap dislodged and fell to the floor, whereupon Faye "accidentally" stepped on it.

Since the movie climaxes with the Great Chicago Fire, almost ten percent of the $1,800,000 budget was spent on spectacular pyrotechnic effects. The studio decided it was much too dangerous for women to be on the set during the fire scenes, so all the female roles were played by stuntmen wearing dresses or skirts. The fire they set on the Fox lot took three days to put out.

For Alice Faye the Great Dress Fire was a lot more memorable than the Great Chicago Fire. A musical number took place on stage with candles instead of electrical footlights.

Faye's voluminous costume, which featured feathers waving in the breeze, came too close to the candles and caught fire. As Alice Faye raced off the set, she caught one of her high heels and tumbled down the stairs, injuring her back. While the dress fire didn't cause her permanent injury, she wasn't as fortunate with the fall. For the rest of her life she had lower back problems caused by her accident.

Alice Faye's memories of this movie weren't all painful. More than fifty years after making *In Old Chicago*, she still sighs and recalls, "Kissing Tyrone Power was like dying and going to Heaven."

An Oscar for work on *In Old Chicago* went to Robert Webb, as Best Assistant Director, who handled directing duties on the spectacular fire scenes. Webb was the last man to get that particular award, because the following year the assistant director category was eliminated. He was later promoted, and directed

Elvis Presley in *Love Me Tender,* as well as second unit footage in *The Agony And The Ecstasy.*

Alice Brady broke her ankle and was unable to attend the Academy Award ceremony. When her name was announced, a gentleman stepped forward and accepted the award on her behalf. Unfortunately, Brady hadn't sent him: the man pulled off the perfect crime.

The Informer

1935, RKO Radio
Produced by Cliff Reid
Directed by John Ford

S·Y·N·O·P·S·I·S

An Irishman (Victor McLaglen) turns his friend over to the British Police for a reward of twenty pounds. Irish rebels track him down and get revenge.

Academy Awards: Victor Mc-Laglen, Best Actor; John Ford, Best Director; Dudley Nichols, Adapted Screenplay; Max Steiner, Score.

Academy Award Nominations: Best Picture; George Hively, Editing.

John Ford and Victor Mc-Laglen, director and actor, worked together on *The Informer*. Actually, in this case, you couldn't say they were working *together*. When Ford was casting the film, he felt McLaglen was the only actor who looked brutal enough to portray Gypo Nolan. McLaglen had never given a truly emotional performance in any of his films, so Ford wasn't sure McLaglen was capable of portraying a man engulfed by his own lust and greed. He decided his only hope was to keep the actor in character at all times. How does a director help an actor play an unbalanced character? By keeping the actor off-balance.

Ford would tell McLaglen to prepare for a certain scene. When the actor showed up, they would be filming a different scene. That forced McLaglen to do scenes he wasn't familiar with, resulting in a tenta-tive, stumbling performance perfect for the character of Gypo Nolan. Some days Ford rushed him through his scenes so rapidly his head swam. On another occasion Ford called for a rehearsal of the scenes they were going to film the following day. Without McLaglen's knowledge, Ford rolled the cameras during this rehearsal and captured a fresh, impulsive performance.

The coup de grace came when Ford was ready to shoot the scene in the court of inquiry. The director told the actor to take a day off, knowing that McLaglen would go out and have a few drinks. Early the next morning Ford sent a car to McLaglen's house. The actor was brought to the studio suffering from a massive hangover. His performance in the court scene is a portrait of a man who's genuinely confused, a man whose thought processes are cloudy, a man who can't quite grasp what's going on. In other

words, he was perfect.

By the time they finished filming, Victor McLaglen, who had lost weight and was suffering from insomnia, swore he'd give up acting right after he killed John Ford. However, there's something about winning an Academy Award as Best Actor that tends to smooth things over. Victor McLaglen not only forgave John Ford, but also worked with Ford on four other films: *The Lost Patrol, Fort Apache, The Quiet Man,* and *She Wore a Yellow Ribbon.*

Although RKO spent only $218,000 to make the picture, *The Informer* lost money on its initial run. After it received an Academy Award nomination as Best Picture, RKO released it again and the movie made a profit. *The New York Times* said that the only reason *The Informer* lost the Best Picture Award to MGM's *Mutiny*

on the Bounty was that the winning picture was from "the more influential Metro lot."

While *The Informer* won four Academy Awards, that's only part of the story. 1935 was a crazy year for the Oscars. Actors, writers, and directors were unhappy with the Academy of Motion Picture Arts and Sciences, and each group formed a separate guild to represent its interests in labor negotiations. The newly formed guilds all boycotted the Academy Awards. John Ford, who was treasurer of the Screen Director's Guild, wasn't present at the ceremony, but when he accepted his Academy Award a week later, the members of the Guild kicked him out of office.

When Academy President Frank Capra sent Dudley Nichols his award for Best Adapted Screenplay, Nichols returned it, saying he couldn't turn his back

on the thousands of members who had risked everything to create a writers' organization. Capra sent the award back to Nichols with a note stating, "The balloting does not in any way take into account the personal or economic views of the nominees, nor the graciousness with which they may be expected to receive the nomination." Nichols again refused to accept, and the statuette was returned to the Academy.

There are two Fords in the credits in addition to John Ford. Wallace Ford, who plays Frankie, was no relation. Francis Ford, who appears in a bit part as a bearded judge, was the director's older brother.

Intermezzo

1939 Selznick International/United Artists
Produced by David O. Selznick
Directed by Gregory Ratoff

S·Y·N·O·P·S·I·S

A Swedish violinist (Leslie Howard) deserts his wife and children when he falls in love with his daughter's piano teacher (Ingrid Bergman).

Academy Award Nomination: Lou Forbes, Best Musical Score.

Kay Brown was excited: she had found something her boss wanted. Brown was producer David Selznick's representative in New York, and one of her jobs was to screen foreign films, looking for properties Selznick could remake for American audiences. What she found was a Swedish film called *Intermezzo* and a twenty-three-year old actress named Ingrid Bergman. Brown obtained a print of the film and sent it to her boss, who liked the story but wasn't overly impressed with its star. He instructed Brown to sail to Europe and buy the rights. In those days there were no transatlantic flights, so it took Brown two weeks to travel across the ocean, make the deal, and sail back. When she returned to New York, she found her boss had changed his mind. He wanted to bring Ingrid Bergman to Hollywood. Kay Brown turned right around and sailed back to Europe.

Ingrid Bergman was wary of American film offers, but she liked Kay Brown instantly and the two became friends. However, Bergman was a wife and mother, and she wasn't willing to leave her home for an extended period. The actress refused Selznick's offer of a seven-year contract, but she did agree to go to Hollywood to make one film.

When David Selznick met his newest discovery, he was horrified. Bergman was five feet, seven inches tall, in the days when most leading men were well under six feet. When Selznick threw a party to introduce Bergman to the Hollywood community, many of the established performers laughed at her behind her back, calling her "the Swedish cow." Bergman just didn't look like a traditional movie star. She had thick eyebrows, crooked teeth, and she spoke very little English.

The day after the party, Selznick met

with Ingrid at the studio, laying out plans to change her name, straighten her teeth, dye her hair, and pluck her eyebrows. Bergman flatly refused. When Selznick realized she was serious, he called in the publicity department. "I've had a brilliant idea," he told them. "Let's publicize Ingrid Bergman as the first natural Hollywood beauty. No capped teeth! Her own hair! Her own name!" David Selznick turned the actress's rebellion into a plus for his film.

He used a similar technique on his leading man, Leslie Howard. To understand Howard's connection with *Intermezzo*, we have to go back a year. David Selznick was casting *Gone With the Wind*, and he wanted Leslie Howard for the role of Ashley Wilkes. Howard flatly refused, saying he didn't want to play any more weak, ineffective men. Selznick knew that money wouldn't change Howard's mind, but he knew what would. The actor wanted to make a bigger contribution to the creative side of his films, so Selznick promised him that he could function as an associate producer on *Intermezzo* if he took the role in *Gone With the Wind*. Howard agreed, and the rest, as they say, is Hollywood history.

That's why Howard's name appears in the *Intermezzo* credits twice, once for his acting role and again as the film's associate producer.

Intermezzo would be Leslie Howard's last American film. When World War II broke out, he returned to his native England, where he produced, directed, and acted in films that would help the war effort. He died in 1943 as he was returning to London from a secret mission in Lisbon, Portugal. It was a tragic case of mistaken identity. German gunners shot the plane down be-

cause they thought Winston Churchill was on board. Churchill was safe in England, but the world lost a great acting talent.

An "intermezzo" is a short, dramatic musical or other entertainment between the acts of a drama or opera.

It Happened One Night

1934, Columbia
Produced by Harry Cohn
Directed by Frank Capra

S·Y·N·O·P·S·I·S

Screwball comedy about a bored heiress (Claudette Colbert) and a reporter (Clark Gable) who fall in love on a cross-country bus trip.

Academy Awards: Best Picture; Frank Capra, Best Director; Clark Gable, Best Actor; Claudette Colbert, Best Actress; Robert Riskin, Adaptation.

It Happened One Night was the picture nobody wanted, until it swept the Academy Awards.

When Frank Capra first told Columbia head Harry Cohn he wanted to make a picture from a story called "Night Bus," Cohn refused, saying bus pictures always bombed. Capra and screenwriter Robert Riskin went to the Desert Inn in Palm Springs, planted themselves and their typewriters under the palm tress, and wrote the script they called *It Happened One Night*. Cohn reluctantly gave the go-ahead. He still hated it, but at least they had gotten the word "bus" out of the title.

From a previous deal with Louis B. Mayer, Cohn was owed the services of an MGM star. Capra wanted Robert Montgomery, and Mayer agreed, but when the actor read the script, he thought it was one of the worst things he had ever read. Mayer, who was trying to punish Clark Gable for his disruptive attitude, suggested to Cohn that they use Gable. Capra was against it. When Gable came over to talk with the director, he showed up drunk and told Capra working at Columbia was "tantamount to exile in Siberia". Gable didn't have enough clout to refuse, and

he and Capra were stuck with one another.

Finding a leading lady was much harder. Myrna Loy, Margaret Sullavan, Miriam Hopkins, and Constance Bennett all turned the role of Ellie Andrews down in quick succession. When Capra went to Claudette Colbert's house to ask her to consider the role, she refused, saying she was on her way to Sun Valley that very day. He offered her twice her normal salary, which she accepted with the impossible provision that they would complete filming exactly four weeks from that day. Capra accepted the challenge, and the picture was underway.

Because he had so little time, Capra took a cavalier attitude toward filming. They breezed through the picture, often inventing business on the spot or ad libbing around the written dialogue. His objective, and that of leading man and lady, wasn't to make a great picture. They just wanted to get it over with.

Colbert complained throughout. When Capra wanted all of the people on the bus to start singing spontaneously, she said it was ridiculous to expect a group of strangers to know the words to the same song. In another scene Colbert and Gable are forced to share a room, so they hang a clothesline draped with a sheet between the twin beds. When Colbert refused to undress, Capra created one of the most seductive scenes on film. He had her undress behind the sheet, placing each garment over the clothesline as she removed it. Colbert also refused to do the famous hitchhking scene, in which Gable's thumb is ignored but she succeeds by hiking up her skirt. When Capra called for a stand-in to do the closeup of the leg,

Colbert relented, saying she wouldn't allow someone else's leg to be mistaken for hers. When filming was finished, she was off to Sun Valley, where she told her friends, "I have just finished the worst picture in the world."

New York critics were lukewarm, but someone forgot to tell the American public that they weren't supposed to like the film. As weeks passed, the box office receipts gained momentum, until the picture was the biggest money maker in the studio's history.

Despite its popular success,

no one, especially Frank Capra, expected what happened one night at the Biltmore Hotel. His low-budget, slam-it-out-in-four-weeks movie that nobody wanted swept the Academy Awards. Claudette Colbert was boarding a train for New York when Academy officials rushed up to tell her she had won. A police escort whisked her to the Biltmore, where she accepted the award, still dressed in her traveling suit. She began to walk off stage, then returned and admitted, "I owe Frank Capra for this." Louis B. Mayer, who tried to punish Clark Gable by sending him to Poverty Row, was forced to triple Gable's salary.

When Clark Gable removed his shirt and revealed that he wasn't wearing anything underneath, T-shirt sales plummeted nationwide.

It's A Wonderful Life

1946, RKO/Liberty Films
Produced and Directed by Frank Capra

S·Y·N·O·P·S·I·S

An angel (Henry Travers) shows a man who's about to commit suicide (James Stewart) how he's changed the lives of people he knows and loves.

Academy Award Nominations:
Best Picture; James Stewart, Best Actor; Frank Capra, Best Director; William Hornbeck, Film Editing; John Aalberg, Sound Recording.

In December of 1945, RKO studio head Charles Koerner received a Christmas card from Philip Van Doren Stern. Instead of the standard, "Peace on Earth, Good Will Towards Men," Stern sent out a holiday story called "The Greatest Gift". Koerner gave the story to Frank Capra, who was in the market for a script. After Capra read the four typewritten pages, he said it was the story he'd been looking for all his life.

Frank Capra was one of Hollywood's premier directors in the late 1930s. When the United States entered World War II, he enlisted and spent the war years making propaganda films for the Army. When the war was over, he returned to Hollywood, but he didn't go back to work for the studios. He was going to work for himself. With several friends, he founded Liberty Films, and began looking for just the right property. He found it in "The Greatest Gift," which became *It's a Wonderful Life* , one of the most beloved films of all time.

For Capra, making *It's a Wonderful Life* was a once-in-a-lifetime experience, and also one of the loneliest. He was returning to Hollywood after several years' absence. Most of his old colleagues were scattered among the various studios. Some of the faces he dealt with were familiar, many were not. He had to start almost from scratch, building his teams of writers, desig-

ners, costumers and technicians. For Capra, the biggest change was that making a great movie was no longer his only responsibility. He now had the added burden of making an entire company profitable.

For the lead in *It's a Wonderful Life*, he could imagine only one man: Jimmy Stewart. Capra went to the actor's home to pitch the story. After two hours of non-stop talking, Capra suddenly felt that the entire concept was wrong, the story line was terrible, and that it wasn't going to work. He left Stewart's house without even waiting for the actor's decision. Of course, Jimmy Stewart had already decided the project sounded wonderful, and he wanted to make the film. Capra was depressed, but after reading the final draft of the Francis Goodrich/Albert Hackett script, his confidence returned.

Capra saw the project as a way to tell the weary, the disillusioned, and the disheartened that no one is a failure, that each man's life touches many other lives, and that if he weren't around, it would leave an awful hole. He wanted to make a film that expressed its love for the homeless and the loveless. In his autobiography, *The Name Above the Title*, he wrote that he wanted it "to shout to the abandoned grandfathers staring vacantly in nursing homes, to the always-interviewed but seldom adopted half-breed orphans, to the paupers who refuse to die while medical vultures wait to snatch their hearts and livers... I wanted to shout, 'You are the salt of the earth, and *It's a Wonderful Life* is my memorial to you.'"

Frank Capra thought *It's A Wonderful Life* was not only the best movie he had ever made, he also felt it was one of the best movies anyone had ever made. Many people agree with him, and believe it should not be tampered with. When I attended the colorization hearings in Washington D.C., Jimmy Stewart told me that imposing artificial color on a classic picture like *It's A Wonderful Life* was nothing short of mutilation, and should be a crime. I couldn't agree more.

It's a Wonderful Life, which cost $2 million to make, lost $525,000 in its initial run.

Jane Eyre

1944, 20th Century-Fox
Produced by William Goetz
Directed by Robert Stevenson

S·Y·N·O·P·S·I·S

After a governess (Joan Fontaine) marries the lord of the manor (Orson Welles), she discovers his insane first wife imprisoned in the mansion.

Successful projects in Hollywood never die, they just keep getting remade. *Jane Eyre* has been brought to the screen no fewer than seven times, and that doesn't include numerous television and radio adaptations. While the 20th Century-Fox version with Orson Welles and Joan Fontaine is without a doubt the best, the project faced a long and torturous road from idea to completion.

In the late thirties, David Selznick acquired the film rights to the Charlotte Bronte novel. He asked Orson Welles to play Edward Rochester, but Welles was busy doing *Citizen Kane* and regretfully declined. When Selznick decided the story was too

similar to his own classic, *Rebecca*, he sold the entire project to Twentieth Century Fox. Fox didn't just buy the rights, they bought the whole package, which included the services of Joan Fontaine.

Robert Stevenson, Aldous Huxley, and John Houseman spent the next two years writing

the script. By the time production was ready to begin, Welles was finished with *Citizen Kane*. Since he and John Houseman were old friends, it was natural that Welles would again be offered the lead.

While Orson Welles was excited about playing Edward Rochester, he wasn't always excited about what he was called on to do. When he was asked to fall off a horse, Welles remarked sarcastically, "I'm supposed to have tried about anything else, so I'd like to try falling off a horse." He was obviously less than enthusiastic about the stunt. After a few feeble attempts, director Robert Stevenson decided to let the fall take place off-camera.

In a later scene Joan Fontaine was called on to bathe Welles' injured foot in hot water. She accidentally spilled some boiling water, scalding him. "While you might be willing to suffer for your art," said Welles dryly, "I most certainly am not." For the next take they used cold water and a carefully hidden steam generator.

According to studio publicists, the set of *Jane Eyre* was the first time Joan Fontaine ever saw any kind of snow, even the mixture of powdered gypsum and finely ground ice that Hollywood called snow. Fontaine was born in Tokyo and raised in Stockton, California, and had never played in snow as a child. While she was delighted with the artificial snow, Welles hated it. As the ice melted, the gypsum formed a plastic that stuck to the performer's shoes, making them extremely heavy. Welles was not a happy man when they filmed a scene that required him to trudge through the slush. His shoes were so heavy, he could hardly pick them up.

Few critics noticed the young actress making her third film appearance, as Helen Burns. Check the credits and you'll find her name . . . Elizabeth Taylor. Most of the publicity went to six-year old Margaret O'Brien, who learned to sing, dance, play the piano, and speak French for her role in *Jane Eyre*. O'Brien won a Special Oscar as Outstanding Child Star of 1944. Peggy Ann Garner, who played Jane as a child, won the award the following year.

For the garden scene, director Robert Stevenson told cinematographer George Barnes he wanted the moon to look "mellow with a suggestion of being aged." If there's one black and white scene you can point to as

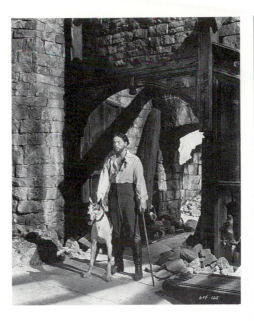

an argument against colorization, it's this work of art. The subtle gray tones and textures Barnes achieved would be ruined by the computer process that adds color to a black and white movie.

Orson Welles considered Charlotte Bronte's *Jane Eyre* the greatest novel ever written in the English language. He first played Edward Rochester on his radio show, *Mercury Theater of the Air*.

Jezebel

1938, Warner Bros.
Produced by Hal Wallis and Henry Blanke
Directed by William Wyler

S·Y·N·O·P·S·I·S

A spoiled Southern woman (Bette Davis), who shocks New Orleans society with her outrageous behavior, repents when the man she loves (Henry Fonda) is stricken with yellow fever.

Academy Awards: Bette Davis, Best Actress; Fay Bainter, Supporting Actress.

Academy Award Nominations: Best Picture; Ernest Haller, Cinematography; Max Steiner, Score.

In 1926, twenty-one-year-old Henry Fonda was on a double date with his best friend, Hunter Scott. Hunter was dating a girl named Bobbi Davis, and Henry had been fixed up with her sister Bette. Sitting in the back seat of a car parked at the Princeton Stadium, Henry Fonda experienced his very first kiss. Eleven years later, Henry Fonda and his one-time date were both movie stars, making

Jezebel under the watchful eye of director William Wyler.

On November 4, 1937, *Jezebel* producer Hal Wallis sent the following memo to his co-producer, Henry Blanke: "Do you think Wyler is mad at Henry Fonda or something because of their past? It seems that he is not content to okay anything with Fonda until it had been done ten or eleven takes. After all, they have been divorced from the same girl (Margaret Sullavan) and bygones should be bygones . . . I think if we will try printing up an occasional third or fourth take, after Wyler has okayed a tenth or eleventh take, you will find that the third or fourth is just as good. Possibly Wyler likes to see these big numbers on the slate, and

maybe we could arrange to have them start with the number six on each take, then it wouldn't take so long to get up to nine or ten." There is no record of whether they actually did begin numbering the takes by starting with six, but, despite admonitions from Wallis and Blanke, Wyler went twenty-eight days over his forty-two day shooting

schedule. This made things especially difficult for Bette Davis. Henry Fonda had signed to appear in *Jezebel* with the stipulation that he would be finished filming by early December so he could be in New York for the birth of his first child. Wyler was so far behind in the schedule that Fonda's closeup work had to be completed out of context. After he left, they filmed Bette Davis' closeups, with Davis playing many emotional scenes to an assistant reading Fonda's lines.

Warner Bros. made *Jezebel* to cash in on interest in Southern stories generated by the upcoming *Gone With the Wind*. Bette Davis, who had wanted to play Scarlett O'Hara, may have been given Jezebel as compensation. In fact, Selznick had seriously considered Davis for the role, but the studio refused to loan her to Selznick unless Warner's male star, Errol Flynn, played Rhett Butler. If Selznick didn't take Flynn, he couldn't have Davis.

Since the subject matter was so similar to *Gone With The Wind*, David Selznick followed the progress of *Jezebel* and attended one of its preview performances. In one of his famous memos he told Jack Warner it was a great pity that "so distinguished and costly a picture as *Jezebel* should be damned as an imitation... of *Gone With the Wind*." He referred to several scenes that he claimed were stolen directly from *G.W.T.W.*, specifically one in which a group of men seated around a dinner table discuss the differences between North and South. Warner replied with a memo of his own, saying he had investigated Selznick's concerns and that the scene in question was taken directly from the original Owen Davis play, not from *G.W.T.W.* He thanked Selznick for his "splendid interest," but didn't cut the scene.

What Jack Warner did change was the ending. When Miriam Hopkins played Jezebel on Broadway, the self-centered character never reformed. Hal Wallis' executive assistant, Walter MacEwen, contended that filmgoing audiences prefer to sympathize with their leading characters and suggested *Jezebel* "leave one feeling that a touch of the good old regeneration through suffering is going to make her a wiser and more palatable person after the final fade out."

While *Jezebel* suffers from the inevitable comparisons with *Gone With the Wind*, it remains one of the finest performances ever turned in by the inimitable Bette Davis.

Miriam Hopkins, who played *Jezebel* on Broadway, was furious when the film role went to her biggest rival, Bette Davis.

King Kong

1933, RKO Radio
Produced by Merian C. Cooper
Directed by Ernest B. Schoedsack

S·Y·N·O·P·S·I·S

A giant ape, brought to the United States as a money-making attraction, escapes and terrorizes New York City.

In the late 1920s Merian C. Cooper spent a lot of time dreaming about a movie in which a giant ape terrorizes a city. One day as he left his midtown Manhattan office, he looked up in time to see an airplane passing very close to the top of the New York Life Building. That's what his eyes saw. His mind saw his giant ape, perched on the top of the building as airplanes circled and attacked. But Cooper didn't know how to bring his vision to the screen.

A few months later David Selznick needed an assistant at RKO and offered Cooper the job. On the studio lot Cooper met the one man who could bring his vision to fruition: Willis O'Brien,

a special effects expert who had refined stop motion animation, the technique of taking a model, moving it in tiny increments, and filming each movement a few frames at a time. Cooper and O'Brien combined their visions and began creating the legend we know as *King Kong*.

Despite rumors that surface periodically, Kong was never played by an actor in a gorilla suit. An eighteen-inch model was animated for most of the action, while some of the closeups featured various life-sized body parts, including a foot, part of a leg, and the hand that clutched Fay Wray. The full-sized head required one operator to work the eyes,

one to work the ears, and a third to work the face.

During filming of the animation sequences, technicians looked to Cooper for advice on the movements. For the fight between Kong and the dinosaur, Cooper and any willing volunteer reenacted the holds he learned as a high school wrestler. Those movements were translated directly to the battle sequences.

For Kong's climb up the Empire State Building, Cooper also acted out the action for the animators. The first time they filmed it, Cooper so exaggerated his actions that when they were translated onto film, the ape looked like a bad ham actor milking a death scene. Cooper did the movements again, and once again the technicians copied them, creating a more realistic death scene.

It wasn't just the idea of *King Kong* that made the movie a hit, it was the unequaled creativity at all production levels, from the genius of O'Brien and his animators to the unprecedented scope of the musical score by Max Steiner. Even the sound effects were innovative. Sound effects expert Murray Spivak sent a crew to the San Diego Zoo to record gorilla roars, but the content, well-fed gorillas wouldn't cooperate, so they recorded the lions and tigers at feeding time. Kong's roar was created by playing the sounds backwards and dropping them an octave. Kong's footsteps were made by common toilet plungers, covered in sponge

rubber and "walked" over gravel. When he couldn't get definitive answers from the Museum of Natural History as to what prehistoric dinosaurs sounded like, Spivak picked up a microphone and made the noises himself, later processing the sounds to make them less human. Spivak, a former symphony percussionist, was afraid that his sound effects might clash with Steiner's powerful score, so he pitched all of his noises in the same key as the music.

When they shot the closeups of the planes that eventually bring Kong down, Cooper and director Ernest Schoedsack could not resist. Determined to be the ones who finally killed Kong, they cast themselves as the vic-

torious aviators.

The first rough cut, which did not contain music or sound effects, was seen by an RKO executive, who thought the whole thing was a terrible waste of money and told Cooper to cancel the project and not spend a single cent more. Cooper went to Selznick, who borrowed money from other productions to finish *King Kong*. It was a wise decision. *King Kong* not only rescued RKO from the clutches of bankruptcy, but also pioneered many visual and audio special effects techniques still in use today.

When Merian Cooper lived in New York City, the Third Avenue Elevated kept him awake at night. He got his revenge by having Kong destroy it.

Kitty Foyle

1940, RKO Radio
Produced by David Hempstead
Directed by Sam Wood

S·Y·N·O·P·S·I·S

After a working girl (Ginger Rogers) marries a Philadelphia socialite (Dennis Morgan), she exposes his family's hypocrisy and finds happiness with a middle class man (James Craig).

Academy Award: Ginger Rogers, Best Actress.

Academy Award Nominations: Best Picture; Sam Wood, Best Director; Dalton Trumbo, Screenplay; John Aalberg, Sound.

On the night of the Oscar ceremonies in 1940, the Biltmore Hotel was buzzing with excitement. For the first time the Academy of Motion Picture Arts and Sciences was using sealed envelopes and keeping the winners secret until formally announced. It was the Academy's reaction to *The Los Angeles Times's* refusal, the year before, to hold the results until after the official announcements.

When it came time for the Best Actress award, Alfred Lunt and Lynn Fontanne stepped forward and went through the now-familiar ritual of naming the nominees. The competition was stiff: Bette Davis for *The Letter*, Joan Fontaine for *Rebecca*, Katharine Hepburn for *The Philadelphia Story*, Martha Scott for *Our Town*, and Ginger Rogers for *Kitty Foyle*. "And the winner is . . . Ginger Rogers for *Kitty Foyle*!" Caught completely by surprise, Ginger ran up and grabbed the statuette out of their hands,

saying, "This is the happiest moment of my life." Not very original, but sincere. Because she was up against such legendary competition, she hadn't even rehearsed an acceptance speech. She thanked her mother for standing faithfully by her, which her mother certainly had; in fact Lela Rogers had rushed up to the podium in her daughter's wake and was literally standing by her.

When mother and daughter returned to their seats, fellow nominee Joan Fontaine approached their table and offered her congratulations. The year after Ginger Rogers won her Oscar for *Kitty Foyle*, Joan Fontaine won for *Suspicion*. Fred Astaire, who had costarred with Fontaine in *Damsel in Distress* commented, "They dance with me and then win Academy Awards for acting!"

Ironically, Ginger Rogers won her only Oscar nomination for a role she didn't want. In late 1939 Ginger had just finished a string of pictures for RKO and she was completely exhausted. Producer David Hempstead sent her the Christopher Morley novel about a woman named Kitty Foyle. She turned it down. Though she was looking for roles that would change her image as the girl who danced her way to success, she wasn't sure she could handle the emotional depth of Kitty Foyle. Hempstead did his best to convince Rogers she'd be great. His only demand was that she dye her blonde hair brown to look less glamorous.

In recognition of her contribution to the image of the working girl, Ginger Rogers received an award from a group of real-life Manhattan secretaries at the annual Stenographers' Ball. *Time Magazine* covered the event, commenting that "Ginger, with her shoulder-length tresses, her trim figure, her full lips, her prancing feet and honest to goodness manner, is the flesh and blood symbol of the United States working girl." I don't know what prancing feet and full lips have to do with being a stenographer, but *Time* seemed to think it was important.

After winning the Oscar for *Kitty Foyle*, Ginger Rogers turned down an offer to play a stripper in *Ball of Fire*, saying that henceforth she would play only ladies.

Laura

1944, 20th Century-Fox
Produced and Directed by Otto Preminger

S·Y·N·O·P·S·I·S

A detective (Dana Andrews) investigates the murder of a beautiful woman (Gene Tierney) and falls in love with the victim.

Academy Award: Joseph La Shelle, Cinematography.

Academy Award Nominations: Otto Preminger, Best Director; Clifton Webb, Supporting Actor; Jay Dratler, Samuel Hoffenstein, Betty Reinhardt, Ring Lardner, Jr., and Jerome Cady, Screenplay; Lyle Wheeler and Leland Fuller, Black and White Interior Decoration.

Making movies is not like writing a book. Writing is a solo act, with the writer singlehandedly making all the decisions that create a work of art. Making a film is always a group effort, and the group doesn't always agree. When two Hollywood egos clash, it can mean big changes in the creative vision.

When Otto Preminger was first slated to produce and direct *Laura* for 20th Century-Fox, William Goetz was the head of the studio. By the time the project got off the ground, Darryl Zanuck was in power, and Zanuck didn't like Preminger's directoral style. While he allowed Preminger to continue to function as the film's producer, he brought in Rouben Mamoulian to direct. It

wasn't long before Zanuck became angry with Mamoulian and fired him. When Walter Lang and Lewis Milestone both turned down the chance to finish the picture, Zanuck gave it back to Preminger. However, that didn't mark an end to the battles between the two men. Preminger was willing to cast several newcomers; Zanuck wanted to stick with established names. Preminger wanted Dana Andrews for the role of the detective; Zanuck wanted John Hodiak. Preminger wanted Clifton Webb; Zanuck was completely against casting Webb as the character based on the egotistical literary critic Alexander Woolcott. Webb, who had appeared in a few silent movies in the twenties, had spent the rest of his career on the stage and had never made a Hollywood movie. Although Waldo Lydecker had been written with Webb in mind, Zanuck thought casting him was too big a risk. Preminger prevailed and signed both Andrews and Webb.

The next fight was over who should photograph the picture. Preminger wanted Joe LaShelle as cameraman; Zanuck opposed it because LaShelle had never been a first-unit photographer. Once again Preminger prevailed, and LaShelle justified the director's faith in him by winning an Academy Award for cinematography.

The final confrontation between studio head and producer came over the choice of music. Zanuck assigned composer David Raksin to compose a theme, but Preminger wanted to use Duke Ellington's "Sophisticated Lady." Preminger called Raksin on a Friday and told him he had until Monday morning to come

up with a great theme, or they'd use the Ellington song. Raksin worked all weekend, and on Monday morning, he presented Zanuck and Preminger with the haunting theme from *Laura*, which has become a Hollywood classic.

One casting decision they did agree on was Gene Tierney as Laura, but she wasn't sure she wanted the part. After reading the script, she thought she was just playing a portrait, and in the end that proved to be prophetic. Rouben Mamoulian's wife, Azadia, was commissioned to do the portrait that was such an integral part of the story. When Preminger saw the portrait, however, he thought it lacked a certain mystical quality essential to the plot. There wasn't time to paint another one, so he sent Tierney to pose for studio photographer Frank Polony. They took the photograph, enlarged it, and had an artist brush paint over the photo to make it look like a painting.

Gene Tierney later

recalled that Otto Preminger worked the cast for long, grueling days, molding all the elements to fit his vision. In retrospect, she admitted, it was worth it. Of all the pictures she made over the years, people most associated her with *Laura*. She always felt that people related more to the portrait than to anything she brought to the role. I think she was much too modest.

Darryl Zanuck considered Jennifer Jones and Hedy Lamarr for the lead in *Laura* before casting Gene Tierney.

A Letter To Three Wives

1949, 20th Century-Fox
Produced by Sol Siegel
Directed by Joseph L. Mankiewicz

S·Y·N·O·P·S·I·S

Three women (Jeanne Crain, Linda Darnell, Ann Sothern) receive a letter from a fourth woman (Celeste Holm) who claims to have run off with one of their husbands.

Academy Awards: Joseph Mankiewicz, Best Director; Joseph Mankiewicz, Screenplay.

Academy Award Nomination: Best Picture.

Directors often use unusual techniques to get what they want from their actors. Joseph Mankiewicz needed Linda Darnell's face to register just the right amount of genuine distaste when she looked at a photograph in *A Letter to Three Wives*, so he played a trick on her. When it came time to shoot her close up, he substituted the picture called for in the script with a photo of Otto Preminger in a Nazi uniform. Mankiewicz knew that Darnell despised Preminger for the way he treated her when they were making *Fallen Angel* and *Forever Amber*. It worked. The expression on her face was one of genuine dislike.

Mankiewicz used a similar technique with Ann Sothern, who was supposed to be delighted as she entered a room and saw her husband, played by Kirk Douglas. When it came time for her close up, Mankiewicz had Douglas strip down to his shorts and pop out from behind the couch. Needless to say, Sothern's expression of surprise was also genuine.

Joseph Mankiewicz adapted the script from the John Klempner novel, *A Letter to Five Wives*, with two wives lost in the translation. In addition to drawing incidents and characters from the book, Mankiewicz borrowed liberally from his own life. In the movie version Linda Darnell lives next to a railroad, and conversations are punctuated with the roar of the trains rushing past. When Mankiewicz was growing up in New York City, his family lived next to the Third Avenue El. He remembered his father stopping in the middle of a tirade, waiting until a train passed, and then picking up the monologue without missing a beat. He used the incident in the script.

Other details for the film were inadvertently supplied by his friends. Once, when Mankiewicz was dating Judy Garland, she used the cigarette lighter in his car, shook it like a match, and threw it out the window. Years later he remembered her absent-minded action and incorporated the business into the film.

If you've seen *A Letter to Three Wives* on commercial television, chances are you didn't see all of it. Before running the film,

television stations usually cut one of Kirk Douglas's speeches. The subject: radio, but the speech could apply equally to television. Douglas's character says that radio writing is merely "precisely timed driblets of distraction between advertisements," and he blasts radio as a medium whose entire reason for being is to sell deodorant and mouthwash. That hits a little too close to home for many commercial television stations, and the speech is often edited out before the movie is shown.

While Joseph Mankiewicz won an Oscar for the screenplay, there was one little problem with the plot. Many viewers couldn't figure out which husband Addie ran away with. If you were confused, you're in good company. When the movie was shown to American troops in Tokyo, General Douglas MacArthur, chief of the Far East Occupation forces, was so confused by the film's ending that he had an aide write to Mankiewicz, asking, "With whom did Addie run off?" Let me try to clear it up once and

for all.

Mankiewicz threw in a red herring by having the butler give Deborah (Jeanne Crain) the message that her husband (Jeffrey Lynn) would not be home. He wanted you to think that Porter Hollingsway (Paul Douglas) had considered running off with Addie (Celeste Holm, who is never seen in the film, only heard) but changed his mind, just as he said he had. By his admission in front of witnesses, he gave his wife, Lora May (Linda Darnell) grounds for a divorce and a hefty alimony settlement. Now that we've cleared up that mystery, let's explore something that's easier to understand, like $E=MC^2$.

This movie was originally entitled, *A Letter to Five Wives*, but when Darryl Zanuck read the script, he said, "You've got two wives too many."

Lifeboat

1944, 20th Century-Fox
Produced by Kenneth Macgowan
Directed by Alfred Hitchcock

S·Y·N·O·P·S·I·S

Survivors of a clash between a ship and a German U-boat find themselves together in one lifeboat.

Academy Award nominations:
Alfred Hitchcock, Best Director; John Steinbeck, Original story; Glen MacWilliams, Black and White Photography.

The mood was tense on the 20th Century-Fox sound stage. Alfred Hitchcock was directing a picture that took place entirely in one lifeboat in the middle of an ocean, and nobody was happy. They shot everything in giant tanks, with three different vessels as various sections of the boat. Images for the sky and sea were projected on a screen behind the tanks.

The movie was physically demanding for all the actors, but for Hume Cronyn one moment was particularly harrowing.

Stormy seas were whipped up by enormous wind machines, and hydraulic lifts rocked the tank to create waves. During one storm scene Cronyn fell out of the boat and was dragged into a large metal agitator. He could have been killed if a professional lifeguard, Joe Peterson, hadn't been standing by just for that kind of emergency. Peterson took a deep breath, dove in, and was able to stay under long enough to free the actor from the machine.

Lifeboat was not an easy picture to make. Because the actors spent hour after hour, day after day, in a rocking boat, many of them became seasick. Every day thousands of gallons of water were hurled into their faces, and they were often covered with oily residue from a machine, which made fog by shooting oil over dry ice. Over the thirty-five days of filming their clothing had to remain dirty, and one by one they all came down with colds or pneumonia. William Bendix summed it up for his fellow cast members. When Hitchcock asked him why he was shaking his head, Bendix replied, "I'm thinking of all the people who want to be in the movies and here I am instead."

Lifeboat was an unusual picture with unusual challenges for the writer, director, and actor. It's a picture in which no scenes are hidden from the other characters, a picture in which a love story must unfold in front of witnesses who are always present. Before work began on the script, Hitchcock cabled Ernest Hemingway in Cuba and asked him to write the screenplay, but Hemingway was too busy with other projects. Hitchcock then hired John Steinbeck to write a prose version of the story. Steinbeck thought the idea of having one set throughout the entire movie was impractical, but Hitchcock was a master of making the impractical practical and, against the judgments of others, he made it work.

Since all the action took place in a boat, working in one of Hitchcock's cameo appearances seemed impossible. He solved the problem by using his picture on a newspaper ad for a weight loss program. He had recently lost a hundred pounds on a rigorously supervised diet, and used his own photo for both the "before" and "after" shots.

Another kind of weight loss was a challenge for makeup and costume designers. The cast had to look as if they were slowly starving, so when filming began, they were padded to look ten to fifteen pounds heavier than they actually were. Over the course of the picture, they slimmed down to their normal weights. Makeup made them look even more gaunt, and it didn't take much. Because they were often seasick, most of the cast actually lost weight over the course of filming.

One incident on the *Lifeboat* set has become part of the Hollywood legend. After a particularly rigorous scene, Tallulah Bankhead climbed out of the boat and was greeted by a standing ovation from the technical crew. Hitchcock turned to the publicity people who were present and explained that the crew was over-

whelmed by Bankhead's fine performance. That's the story that went out in the press releases, but Hitchcock knew the real reason for the applause. Tallulah Bankhead wasn't wearing anything under her skirt, and the crew applauded the show she gave every time she climbed in or out of the boat!

Aspiring actress Mary Andersen asked Alfred Hitchcock which was her best side. "My dear," he replied, "you're sitting on it!"

The Little Foxes

1941, RKO Radio
Produced by Samuel Goldwyn
Directed by William Wyler

S·Y·N·O·P·S·I·S

Lillian Hellman's intense drama about the greed and corruption that destroys a wealthy Southern family.

Academy Award nominations:
Best Picture; Bette Davis, Best Actress; William Wyler, Best Director; Teresa Wright, Patricia Collinge, Supporting Actress; Lillian Hellman, Screenplay; Stephen Goosson and Howard Bristol, Interior Decoration; Meredith Willson, Score; Daniel Mandell, Editing.

It's a shame the cameras filming *The Little Foxes* focused only on the action that took place on the set. If there had been a camera covering what happened between takes, the footage would have rivaled the film for drama and emotion.

When Sam Goldwyn hired William Wyler to direct the picture, Wyler could see only one actress starring in *The Little Foxes*: Bette Davis. Wyler accepted the assignment with the stipulation that Davis play the lead. If Goldwyn wanted another actress, he'd have to find another director. Never mind the fact that at one time Wyler and Davis had been lovers. They were now "good friends" and shouldn't have any problems working together. As it turned out, they

weren't good enough friends.

Their working relationship quickly deteriorated, and it wasn't long before they were at each other's throats. Wyler wanted Davis to play Regina as a congenial, hospitable woman who saw her way of life disappearing but kept up a civilized front. That's how Tallulah Bankhead had played the woman on Broadway. Davis saw Regina in an entirely different light, as a cold, emotionless shell of a woman who had lost all of her human warmth as a result of the effects of the Civil War on her family.

Davis and Wyler fought constantly. They fought about her hair; they fought about her costumes; they fought about her makeup. They stopped filming to argue; they didn't start filming because they were arguing. The tension that comes across on film isn't just a great acting job by Bette Davis. It's a very real manifestation of her emotional state.

While she knew the cast and crew witnessed the battles on the set, Davis was unaware she had an audience for private complaints in her dressing room. She would call Sam Goldwyn to her dressing room to let him know how she felt about the situation. Davis didn't know that there was a microphone stored in the next booth. If she had, she might not have yelled quite so loudly. While she complained about Wyler, the director was some distance away, listening to every word she said.

Unable to cope with the tension and unwilling to compromise her portrayal of Regina Giddens, Bette Davis was on the verge of collapse. One evening she called her doctor and requested a sedative, which somehow became mixed with a small bottle of household ammonia. After Davis drank it, she was wracked with convulsions. Quick action by her maid saved her life, and she was rushed to a hospital.

Davis took a few days off to recover from the effects of the poison and then returned to the battlefield. The war escalated, culminating with the filming of the dinner scene. Every time Wyler yelled "cut," Davis yelled back with vicious personal attacks. When the scene was completed, Wyler told Davis her work was terrible and he should have given the role to Tallulah Bankhead. That was all she could take. Davis broke down completely and left the set for a week.

During her absence, Sam Goldwyn suggested they scrap the footage and re-shoot the entire film with Davis' hated rival, Miriam Hopkins. Surprisingly, Wyler insisted he complete the picture with Bette Davis. Davis returned to the set when she was reminded about a clause in her contract that stipulated that if she did not complete the picture for any reason, she was responsible for the entire cost of the production.

Was the creative tension between leading lady and director worth it? *The Little Foxes* was nominated for nine Academy Awards, including Best Picture, Wyler as Best Director, and Davis as Best Actress. Despite their triumphs, Bette Davis and William Wyler were not anxious to repeat the experience, and they never

worked together again.

Sam Goldwyn borrowed Bette Davis from Jack Warner for *The Little Foxes* in exchange for Gary Cooper's services for *Sergeant York*.

Little Miss Marker

1934, Paramount
Produced by B.P. Schulberg
Directed by Alexander Hall

S · Y · N · O · P · S · I · S

A child (Shirley Temple) is left with a bookmaker (Adolphe Menjou) as security ("a marker") for a bet.

In 1933 Paramount declared bankruptcy, and the studio needed a miracle. What they got was a child named Shirley Temple, just after she filmed *Stand Up and Cheer* but before the movie was released. In other words, they got Shirley Temple before anyone knew who Shirley Temple was. They got their miracle.

After her mother had spent several years trying to interest every studio in Hollywood in her daughter, Shirley had scored a Fox contract as a result of her work in Baby Burlesk shorts—and one of Southern California's infrequent rain storms. On January 29, 1934, Shirley's parents, George and Gertrude Temple, took Shirley to the theater to see herself on screen. They didn't stay to see *42nd Street* but left after Shirley's short. It was raining, so George left his wife and daughter in front of the theater while he went for the car. With true Hollywood timing, songwriter Jay Gorney, who had auditioned 150 little girls to sing "Baby take a Bow" for *Stand Up and Cheer*, was entering the theater at that moment. He saw Shirley studying pictures of Ruby Keeler in the movie posters. When Shirley, who was looking at Keeler's feet, hummed and tried out a few tap steps of her own, Gorney was enchanted by the picture she presented. He asked Gertrude Temple to bring Shirley by for an audition, an audition that would change the course of Hollywood history. Shirley got the part and a Fox contract.

After Shirley had filmed her one number in *Stand Up and Cheer,* Mrs. Temple was afraid her child could spend years playing bit parts at Fox. She heard Paramount was looking for a child to star in *Little Miss Marker,* so she arranged a screen test with director Al Hall. He had Shirley say just three words, "Aw nuts" and "Scram," and he knew he had found his Miss Marker.

Filming *Little Miss Marker* was a thrill for Shirley. She rode her very first horse, and, in a scene where she was thrown, she was attached by wire to an overhead crane, which lowered her gently to the ground.

Everyone at Paramount was impressed with her performance, including her costar, Adolphe Menjou, who told friends that after one day on the set, he wanted to quit. He called her "an Ethel Barrymore at age four," (she was almost six, but that was a closely guarded secret) and said she "knows all the tricks. She backs me out of the camera, blankets me, crabs my laughs . . .

She's making a stooge of me."

No one taught Shirley her astounding sense of theatricality. She was a truly remarkable child and amazed adults with her talent and professionalism. John Ford, who directed her in *Wee Willie Winkie,* called her "One-Take Temple" because she never blew a line or an action. Bill "Bojangles" Robinson was impressed because no matter how complicated the dance routine, she could pick it up after seeing it just once. John Barrymore, the greatest actor of his day, said, "She has an extraordinary instinct for acting, a real naturalness . . . She's one of those miracles that sometimes occur in the theater." Opera star Rosa Ponselle was astonished by the clarity of her voice.

Shirley Temple was lucky, not only to have been born talented and just a few miles from Hollywood. She was lucky that her parents were more interested in her welfare than in her amazing salary. Shirley had a clause in her contract stating that if her parents ever decided the work was affecting their child adversely, they had the option of canceling the contract and letting Shirley retire. Her father, who was a banker, invested her money wisely, providing income for her at various stages of adulthood. And, not wanting public adulation go to their daughter's head, they severely restricted her personal appearances.

Years later, Shirley Temple Black remembered those years fondly, saying that while other children read fairy tales, she was allowed to play in them. It's a tribute to George and Gertrude Temple that their daughter remained a happy, secure child who, as an adult, was able to walk away from Hollywood and live happily ever after.

HER DADDY HOCKED HER FOR 20 BUCKS TO THE TOUGHEST MUGS ON BROADWAY

DAMON RUNYON
author of "Lady for a Day" writes another great human heart story.

"Little MISS MARKER"

A Paramount Picture with

ADOLPHE MENJOU   DOROTHY DELL   CHARLES BICKFORD   SHIRLEY TEMPLE

a B. P. Schulberg Production

Copyright 1934 by Paramount Productions, Inc. All Rights Reserved.   Country of Origin U.S.A.—Copyright waived to magazines & newspapers.

Lloyds of London insured Shirley Temple with the condition that she could not fight in a war.

The Lodger

1944, 20th Century-Fox
Produced by Robert Bassler
Directed by John Brahm

S·Y·N·O·P·S·I·S

A mysterious gentleman (Laird Cregar) roams the streets of London, killing women at random.

Take some beautiful young women, put them in period costumes in a foggy London setting, add a dash of terror and an honest-to-goodness legend, and you have a story Hollywood just couldn't resist. If Jack the Ripper had lived a hundred years later, he would have become a genuine media celebrity. It's no wonder that three film versions of *The Lodger* have been made.

This one's the best. It combines a great director and a classic cast and gives us one of our few opportunities to enjoy the work of actor Laird Cregar.

On the night the critics previewed *The Lodger* at the Roxy in New York City, Laird Cregar was in the audience. He had already seen the entire movie three times, but never with a real audience. He sat, unrecognized, in the first row of the balcony to observe how the audience reacted to his character. He wasn't prepared for what he saw. That preview audience laughed throughout the film, particularly at his character, a man who stalked and killed young women. *The New York Times* critic reported that Cregar mumbled "interesting reaction" as he left the theater. Cregar left the Roxy

depressed and upset; the film was obviously a failure. However, audiences in the rest of the country did not react the way the New Yorkers had. Moviegoers in the Midwest, in the South, in the Rocky Mountains, and in the Pacific Northwest were all properly frightened out of their wits. It's possible that, even in 1944, New Yorkers were already a bit blasé about the idea of a mass murderer living in a nearby rooming house.

20th Century-Fox wanted a director who was intimately familiar with London. They needed someone with a sharp eye for detail because they intended to achieve a genuine London look, even though they were film-

ing entirely on Hollywood sound stages. John Brahm was born in Germany but fled to England to escape Nazi persecution. His London background made him a natural to direct *The Lodger*.

The crew's theme song for this picture could have been "Smoke Gets in Your Eyes." To achieve those foggy London street scenes, director John Brahm used smoke pots, which were great for visuals but hard on the eyes. Frequent breaks were a necessity as the cast and crew sought the fresh air of a nearby parking lot.

Laird Cregar is *The Lodger*, a character who is supposed to look pale and gaunt. Like many of us, Cregar had a tendency to put on a few extra pounds, which caused him to go on intensive crash diets before each picture. His haggard, unhealthy look in this movie was created by make-up and the real effects of a starvation diet. His weight problem haunted

him as relentlessly as Jack the Ripper stalked his victims. A year after filming *The Lodger*, his life-style caught up with him. At the age of twenty-eight, Cregar died of a heart attack brought on by his excessive swings in weight.

Working on *The Lodger* changed the life of another of its stars. When filming began, Merle Oberon was married to British producer Alexander Korda. When filming ended, so did her marriage. She had fallen in love with Lucien Ballard, *The Lodger*'s cinematographer. After her divorce, she and Ballard embarked on a four-year marriage. Gossip columnist Hedda Hopper loved to criticize Oberon in print, especially during her affair and subsequent marriage to her cameraman. When Oberon confronted Hopper, asking what she had done to deserve such treatment, Hopper gave one of the most honest answers in Hollywood history. What had Oberon done? "Why nothing, dear. It's bitchery, sheer bitchery."

P·L·A·Y·E·R·S

Merle Oberon .... Kitty
George Sanders .... John Garrick
Laird Cregar .... The Lodger
Sir Cedric Hardwicke ... Robert Burton
Featuring
    Sara Allgood
    Aubrey Mather
    Queenie Leonard
    David Clyde
    Helena Pickard
    Lumsden Hare
    Frederick Worlock
    Olaf Hytten
    Colin Campbell
    Anita Bolster
    Billy Bevan
    Forrester Harvey
    Skelton Knaggs
    Charles Hall
    Edmond Breon
    Harry Allen
    Raymond Severn
    Heather Wilde

I must admit, I've included *The Lodger* as one of my favorites for purely sentimental reasons. When American Movie Classics(SM) went on the air in October of 1984, *The Lodger* was the very first movie we aired. It will always hold a special place in my heart.

The silent version of *The Lodger*, made in London in 1926, was the first suspense thriller directed by Alfred Hitchcock.

Lost Horizon

1937, Columbia
Produced and Directed by Frank Capra

S·Y·N·O·P·S·I·S

Five travelers find a hidden land where people live forever.

Academy Awards: Stephen Goosson, Interior Decoration; Gene Havlick and Gene Milford, Editing.

Academy Award nominations: Best Picture; H.B. Warner, Supporting Actor; John Livadary, Sound Recording; C.C. Coleman, Assistant Director; Dimitri Tiomkin, Columbia Music Department, Score.

A funny thing happened to Frank Capra on the way to a football game. He discovered Shangri-La.

He was in a train station on his way to the game when he picked up a paperback version of James Hilton's *Lost Horizon*. As he read, the film unfolded in his mind. The next morning he approached Columbia studio head Harry Cohn with the project,

saying it would cost a mere two million dollars to produce. In 1934 that was a ridiculous amount of money for a small studio like Columbia to consider spending on one film. In fact, two million dollars was more than Columbia's entire budget for all the films it produced that year.

Cohn was persuaded to take a six-month option on the story. Since Capra was working on *Mr. Deeds Goes to Town*, Cohn waited for the *Mr. Deeds* returns before making a decision. Mr. Deeds was a box office success, Capra won the Academy Award for Best Director, and Cohn approved the *Lost*

Horizon project.

For a film about the Sahara, in those days, they brought tons of sand on to a sound stage. For Venice they brought in lots of water. For *Lost Horizon*, they brought in Tibet.

How do you make a yak? Take a yearling steer and give him a hairy, hoof-length overcoat. Tibetan horses? Shetland ponies with toupees on their legs and chests. Tibetan blizzards? That was a bit of a challenge.

Capra found a cold storage facility in the Los Angeles commercial district that was kept at a constant zero degrees Fahrenheit, the perfect place to take a cast and crew. The weather inside was truly frightful, as wind and snow machines combined to create genuine blizzard conditions.

The cast and crew experienced all the problems of filming in sub-freezing temperatures. The cold fogged the film, so the magazines were covered with electrically heated covers. New cold-resisting lubricants were invented for cameras and motors. Cables cracked and short-circuited; human hands stuck to the equipment. The cast and crew suffered every day just by coming to work, walking in from the ninety degree California sun to the freezing conditions on the set.

When *Lost Horizon* was finished, Columbia tried it out in a preview in Santa Barbara. Producer/Director Frank Capra and studio head Harry Cohn knew their careers were on the line. This was the biggest monetary gamble of their lives, and Cohn had approved the production against the wishes of the Columbia board of directors. The three-hour preview bombed, and Capra went back to the editing room. He cut the entire first two reels, beginning the film with the burning of Baskul. Some scenes were re-shot, some were shortened, some were dropped entirely. Two years after Capra first proposed the idea to Harry Cohn, the picture was ready for release, and it's been in constant circulation ever since.

What happened to those original two reels? Capra said he burned them, but some good detective work by the American

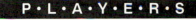

Ronald Colman ...... Robert Conway
Jane Wyatt........................... Sondra
John Howard.......... George Conway
Margo .... Maria
Featuring:
    Thomas Mitchell
    Edward Everett Horton
    Isabel Jewell
    H.B.Warner
    Sam Jaffe
    Hugh Buckler
    David Torrence
    Willie Fung
    Victor Wong
    Noble Johnson

Film Institute uncovered copies of most of the material. They have a print of the film, almost as it appeared the night of that fateful Santa Barbara preview. Six minutes of the film were never found, a fitting end to the story of a film about the unobtainable Shangri-La.

Despite the fact that his *Lost Horizon* was a nominee, Academy President Frank Capra presented Jack Warner with the Best Picture Oscar. It was one of the few instances where a loser presented an award to the winner.

The Lost Patrol

1934, RKO Radio
Produced by Merian C. Cooper
Directed by John Ford

S·Y·N·O·P·S·I·S

Members of a British Army patrol, lost in the desert during World War I, are killed, one by one, by Arab snipers.

Academy Award nomination: Max Steiner, Best Score.

John Ford was unhappy. He was preparing to direct *The Lost Patrol* for RKO, the script was absolutely terrible, and they were only ten days away from the start of filming. He called in his favorite writer, Dudley Nichols, and they threw out everything that had been done, went back to the original Philip MacDonald story, and started from scratch. Eight days later they had the script for *The Lost Patrol*. Ford then took the cast and crew to the Yuma location and shot the film in 110-degree heat in just ten days. Total elapsed time from the day Ford and Nichols began to write the script to completion of

filming: twenty-four days.

"It was a character study," Ford said: "You got to know the life story of each of the men." The movie, now considered one of Ford's classics, marked the first time the director worked with producer Merian C. Cooper, a partnership that would create some of the finest films of the next three decades.

The star of *The Lost Patrol* was one of John Ford's regulars, Victor McLaglen. Ironically, this role is remarkably similar to one he played in real life. As a member of the British Army in World War I, McLaglen had been posted to the Mesopotamian desert, the setting for *The Lost Patrol*. His desert duty was only a part of his colorful background. Victor McLaglen was born in 1885 in South Africa, the son of an Anglican Bishop. At the age of sixteen he ran away to America and became a prize fighter, boxing his way across

the United States and Canada. When he was twenty, he went to England, where he became the heavyweight champion of the British empire. When World War I broke out, he joined the Irish Fusiliers, serving in the desert and eventually becoming deputy provost marshal for the city of Baghdad. After the war he went back to England and became an actor, a vaudevillian, and a circus performer.

The Lost Patrol is one of those pictures in which the main characters are killed off, one by one. Ford and Nichols' script focuses not on the violence but on the way men behave in the face of certain death. If you pay attention to the credits, you can tell in what order they'll be killed. The longer they lived in the movie, the bigger the part and the better the billing.

John Ford was known for his stock company, meaning he had a tendency to use the same actors over and over again. Victor McLaglen was one of his regulars, along with John Wayne, Henry Fonda, Wallace Ford, Ward Bond, Harry Carey, Sr. (and later Harry Carey, Jr.), Maureen O'Hara, Barry Fitzgerald, Ben Johnson, Jim Kerrigan, and Mildred Natwick, among others. True to form, Ford used McLaglen, Ford, and Kerrigan in his next RKO film, *The Informer*.

With his performance as the religious fanatic, Boris Karloff, in his only Ford feature, proved he was capable of more than creating monsters. Another unusual bit of casting was Billy Bevan, star of silent films and scores of comedy shorts.

Lost Patrol was remade in 1939 by RKO as *Bad Lands*, with Robert Barrett and Noah Beery, Jr., but instead of a British patrol, it centered on a posse pinned down by an Apache war party. Douglas Walton, who was killed in Ford's version of *The Lost Patrol*, met the same fate in the remake, which also featured John Ford's brother Francis. The plot line was also used in *Sahara*, and *The Lost Patrol's* closing sequence was duplicated for the Robert Taylor World War II film, *Bataan*.

While Ford's version of *The Lost Patrol* was only a modest financial success, it has grown in stature over the years. When it was reissued on a double bill with *Gunga Din*, another RKO adventure featuring Victor McLaglen, critics and audiences took a second look at *The Lost Patrol*, now considered one of the finest John Ford films.

P·L·A·Y·E·R·S

Victor McLaglen .... The Sergeant
Boris Karloff .... Sanders
Wallace Ford .... Morelli
Reginald Denny .... George Brown
Featuring:
　　J. M. Kerrigan
　　Billy Bevan
　　Sammy Stein
　　Alan Hale Sr.
　　Douglas Walton
　　Brandon Hurst
　　Paul Hanson
　　Neville Clark
　　Howard Wilson
　　Francis Ford
　　Abdullah Abbas

The Lost Patrol was a remake of a 1929 film by the same name starring Victor McLaglen's brother, Cyril McLaglen. Four other McLaglen brothers were also professional actors.

The Lost Weekend

1945, Paramount
Produced by Charles Brackett
Directed by Billy Wilder

S·Y·N·O·P·S·I·S

Portrait of an alcoholic (Ray Milland) who struggles to get through a weekend.

Academy Awards: Best Picture; Ray Milland, Best Actor; Billy Wilder, Director; Charles Brackett and Billy Wilder, Screenplay.

Academy Award nominations: John F. Seitz, Cinematography, Miklos Rozsa, Score; Doane Harrison, Editing.

One Saturday morning in 1945, two women, friends of Ray Milland's wife, got the shock of their lives. They were walking along Third Avenue in New York City when they saw Ray Milland staggering down the street. He was unshaven and looked as if he had spent days in the same clothes, and he was very obviously drunk. They lost no time in telling friends in Hollywood what had happened, and before long the gossip columns were full of the alcoholic binge that had left Ray Milland in a New York gutter. What no one had told the women, or the columnists who printed the item, was that there had been a camera hidden in the ambulance that drove slowly along next to Milland as he staggered down the street. In the ambulance was director Billy Wilder, who hid his cameras to capture the real New York City. He and Milland were making *The Lost Weekend,* the story of one man's losing battle against alcoholism.

It was a picture no one wanted Wilder to make, most of all Ray Milland. Milland, who wasn't a drinker, was repulsed by the character and leery of appearing in a picture that was so overwhelmingly depressing. His wife convinced him to take the risk and stretch himself as an actor. It was an experience he would never forget.

When Milland arrived in New York City, he requested a one-night stay at Bellevue's infamous psychiatric ward to study the behavior of the drunks who were brought in. Around three a.m., he could no longer stand to hear the howling and screaming of the alcoholics and drug addicts. He walked out of the hospital,

kidding, but the technician bet him $5 that he'd not only be nominated, but he'd also win. Milland thought it was so improbable, he gave the man fifty to one odds.

determined to go back to his room at the Waldorf. Stopped by a policeman on 34th Street, Milland explained that he was a movie star and that he had been at Bellevue doing research. The cop took one look at his gown, stamped "Bellevue," and hustled Milland back into the psychiatric ward. Later Milland returned to that same ward to film a scene for the movie.

A few months later Milland was on the Paramount lot when a technician from the sound department told him he had seen a rough cut of *The Lost Weekend* and that Milland was sure to win an Oscar. Milland thought he was

As the weeks passed, Milland noticed that everyone at the studio was treating him with respect. The possibility of an Oscar nomination thrilled and terrified him. The morning the nominations were announced, he and his wife were up at 5:30, eagerly awaiting the first edition of the paper. When Ray Milland's picture appeared on page one with the other nominees, he sat down and wept.

On the night of the Awards Ingrid Bergman read the nominees and opened the envelope. When she smiled, he was sure he had lost. He and Bergman had never met, and he

assumed her smile could only mean she was looking at the name of a friend. When she called his name, he was literally speechless. After accepting the award, all he could do was grin and bow.

"If *To Have and Have Not* established Lauren Bacall as The Look, then *The Lost Weekend* should certainly bring Mr. Milland renown as The Kidney."

—Billy Wilder.

The Magnificent Ambersons

1942, A Mercury Production
Produced and Directed by Orson Welles

S·Y·N·O·P·S·I·S

Saga of the Amberson family and its fall from wealth.

Academy Award nominations: Best Picture; Agnes Moorehead, Supporting Actress; Stanley Cortez, B&W Cinematography; Albert S. D'Agostino and Mark-Lee Kirk, Art Direction; Al Fields and Darrell Silvera, Interior Decoration.

Orson Welles had the unique experience of making a film from a story about himself and his family. *The Magnificent Ambersons* was based on Booth Tarkington's Pulitzer Prize-winning novel of the same name. Tarkington had been good friends with Welles's parents and had used them as models for the novel's main characters, George and Isabel. Orson himself was most likely the model for Isabel's petulant son George, a suspicion corroborated by the fact that Welles's full name was George Orson Welles.

The film version wasn't Welles's only professional association with the Tarkington novel. Earlier in his career he had produced *The Magnificent Ambersons* as a radio play for his Mercury Theater of the Air. You can see the influence of Welles's radio background on the film version: the film opens and closes with extensive narration, and sound effects and off-camera voices are utilized throughout. By the way, this is the only film Welles directed in which he doesn't appear on camera. He does the opening and closing narration, but he's never seen.

The opening sequence of Welles's first film, *Citizen Kane,* was a series of newsreels briefing the audience on the life of Charles Foster Kane. Welles used a similar technique in his second film, opening it with a montage that takes the viewer all over town, introduces the leading characters, and establishes some of the story lines.

Two themes run throughout the film: times change and events repeat themselves. Although these may sound contradictory, Welles interwove them effectively.

Welles purposely used visual contradictions throughout the film. The screen actually lightens as Welles says "they saw their midland town spread and darken into a city." As Welles comments, "In those days, people had time for everything," the screen shows several generations passing so quickly the viewer can't distinguish individual events.

Another thing viewers cannot distinguish is the fact that the sleigh riding scenes were shot entirely indoors, at a Los Angeles ice house. Welles took twelve days just to film that one scene, making sure every detail was perfect right down to the clouds of condensation coming from the actors' breath.

Welles's ending of *The Magnificent Ambersons* included one of the most spectacular shots in the history of cinema. In one continuous take the camera completed a tour of the house, up and down the stairs and

through the rooms. At times the camera did a complete 360-degree pan of a room, showing all four walls. That shot involved forty lighting and sound technicians placed at strategic points along the path of the one continuous shot. Unfortunately, the shot was chopped up by a well-meaning studio executive.

After a preview audience laughed in all the wrong places, RKO President George J. Schaefer ordered editor Robert Wise to cut forty minutes out of the film and change the ending. In the adjusted ending Eugene visits Fanny (Agnes Morehead) in an old age home, which is actually the Amberson home, converted into an institution. As Eugene leaves, the camera pulls back to reveal that the city has taken over the beautiful grounds around the house. As it continues to pull back, the traffic noise gets louder and louder, until it drowns out the music and natural sound.

Despite the fact that the ending is obviously not the work of

the man who created the rest of the film, *The Magnificent Ambersons* is still an extraordinary piece of work. Although it received lukewarm reviews when it was released, it is regarded today as one of the masterpieces of the cinema and a tribute to the genius of a twenty-six-year old filmmaker named George Orson Welles.

Many of the people Orson Welles cast in his movies, including Joseph Cotten and Agnes Moorehead, were former members of his radio company, Mercury Theater of the Air.

Meet John Doe

1941, Warner Bros.
Produced and Directed by Frank Capra

S·Y·N·O·P·S·I·S

When a columnist (Barbara Stanwyck) is fired after writing a fictitious letter from a man who's planning to commit suicide, she's offered her job back if she can produce the man (Gary Cooper).

Academy Award nomination: Richard Connell and Robert Presnell, Original Story.

For years Frank Capra had the Rodney Dangerfield syndrome.

Although he directed some of America's best loved films, the critics never gave him any respect. The intellectual critics called him the "Pollyanna" filmmaker and dismissed his optimistic subjects and characters as mere "Capra-corn."

In 1940, when Capra's contract with Columbia ran out, he and screenwriter Bob Riskin formed their own company. Capra had one objective in making his first independent film: he wanted it to be a critical success. He and Riskin bought a treatment called *The Life and Death of John Doe* and headed for the desert. Sitting in shorts outside their red-tiled adobe bungalow, they hammered out the script for *Meet John Doe*. As they wrote page after page, their excitement mounted. Riskin proclaimed it would be the greatest film they had ever made. Capra went even further and said it would be the greatest film anybody had ever made. Then Capra and Riskin ran into trouble. They couldn't come up with an ending.

They broke Hollywood tradition by refusing to release advance publicity about the story line. They didn't do it to generate speculation; they did it to hide the fact that they didn't know where the script was going.

Capra began filming without a completed script, shooting during the day and working with Riskin on the script each night. They tried countless endings, but nothing seemed right.

When the rest of the film was in the can, Capra shot four endings to *Meet John Doe* and released four versions of the film, each with a different ending. In one Gary Cooper committed suicide. In another he returned to Skid Row. Audience reaction was unanimous: they loved the picture and hated the end, no matter which one they had seen.

Six weeks after the film was released, Capra got a letter from a man who had seen all four versions of the picture. He said the endings were all bad. Cooper should decide to commit suicide, he said, but be stopped at the last minute by Stanwyck's love and by support from a group of followers. The letter was signed, "John Doe." Capra knew immediately that Mr. Doe had hit upon the right ending. He called the cast back, shot the fifth ending, and pulled the other versions out of circulation.

Meet John Doe was met with the critical acclaim Frank Capra had dreamed of. Unfortunately, it didn't make him a rich man. The movie was a tremendous hit at the box office, and the money came pouring in. However, Frank Capra Productions was a new company, and at that time the IRS used that first success as a yardstick to tax future profits. After a year-and-a-half of working

without any salary, after borrowing money to pay corporation taxes in advance and paying personal income tax on their divided assets, Capra and Riskin were forced to pay Uncle Sam 90¢ out of every dollar of profit they made on their first picture. Capra learned a painful and expensive lesson: A start-up company can't be too successful or it will go bankrupt. He dissolved Frank Capra Productions and gave the United States government the only thing it hadn't taken: himself. He joined the Army and spent the next several years in support of the war effort, making the famous "Why We Fight" films.

"Once in a blue moon a picture comes along that makes one proud to be in the picture business..." Telegram to Frank Capra from David O. Selznick after he saw *Meet John Doe.*

P·L·A·Y·E·R·S

Gary Cooper Long John Willoughby
Barbara Stanwyck........Ann Mitchell
Edward Arnold............... D.B. North
Walter Brennan ....Colonel

Featuring:

James Gleason	Stanley Andrews
Spring Byington	Andrew Tombes
Gene Lockhart	Pierre Watkin
Rod LaRocque	Charles C. Wilson
Irving Bacon	Edward Earle
Regis Toomey	Mike Frankovich
Ann Doran	Harry Holman
Warren Hymer	Bess Flowers
Aldrich Bowker	Billy Curtis
Sterling Holloway	Johnny Fern
Mrs. Gardner	Suzanne
Crane	Carnahan
J. Farrell	Maris Wrixon
MacDonald	Vaughn Glaser
Pat Flaherty	Selmer Jackson
Carlotta Jelm	Knox Manning
Tina Thayer	John B. Hughes
Bennie Bartlett	The Hall Johnson
Sarah Edwards	Choir

Meet Me in St. Louis

1944, MGM
Produced by Arthur Freed
Directed by Vincente Minnelli

S·Y·N·O·P·S·I·S

The trials and tribulations of the Smith family of St. Louis shortly before the 1904 World's Fair.

Academy Award: Margaret O'Brien, Outstanding Child Actress (miniature statuette).

Academy Award nominations: Irving Brecher and Fred F. Finklehoffe, Screenplay; George Folsey, Color Cinematography; Ralph Blane and Hugh Martin, "The Trolley Song," Song; George Stoll, Scoring of a Musical Picture.

Margaret O'Brien knew how to wow an audience, even an audience of two. When Vincente Minnelli and Arthur Freed were looking for a child to play the important role of "Tootie" Smith in *Meet Me In St. Louis*, an agent brought in Margaret, dressed in a Scottish plaid kilt. The child walked right up to Freed, grabbed his arm and exclaimed, "Don't send my father to the chair. Don't let him fry!" Freed and Minnelli not only cast the little girl, they used the kilt and the line as well, both of which appeared in *Meet Me in St. Louis*.

While Minnelli couldn't have been more pleased with seven-year-old Margaret's performance, he didn't always like what he had to do to get it. For one emotional scene, in which Margaret hysterically broke up the snowmen in the yard, Margaret couldn't seem to bring tears to her eyes. Gladys O'Brien, Margaret's mother, said that if Minnelli would just tell her someone was going to kidnap her pet dog and kill it, Margaret would cry. Minnelli felt like the worst kind of child abuser, but he told Margaret her pet wasn't long for this world, and Margaret went on to the set and did the hysterical scene in one take. Afterwards Margaret went happily home, and Minnelli remained wracked with guilt, saying, "I never want to go through that again."

While Minnelli had minor problems with Margaret O'Brien,

he had major problems with Judy Garland, who hadn't wanted to make the film at all. During filming Garland was extremely impatient with her director and became annoyed at the excessive number of takes and retakes. One day Mary Astor, who was playing her mother, told her that Minnelli knew what he was doing and that if Judy would pay attention, she would learn something. When Judy saw the results of his painstaking technique, she realized he had brought out of her a depth of emotion and a truly adult performance that no other director had been able to achieve. She began to trust him, and eventually that trust blossomed into love.

Songwriters Ralph Blane and Hugh Martin knew their assignment to write the songs for *Meet Me in St. Louis* constituted their "Big Break," but when Arthur Freed told them to write a song about a trolley, they couldn't get a handle on it. Four times they presented Freed with a song they thought would be great to sing on a trolley, and four

times Freed told them "It's a great song, but I want a song *about* a trolley." For inspiration Blane went to Beverly Hills Public Library and looked up books about old St. Louis, where he found a picture of a trolley captioned "Clang clang clang went the trolley." Starting with that line, he and Martin wrote the song in just ten minutes.

One of Blane and Martin's biggest challenges was coming up with a Christmas song that would bring something new to the legion of existing carols. The first time they wrote it, it went,

"Have yourself a merry little Christmas
It may be your last
Next year we will all be living in the past..."

When Judy heard it, she said it was so sad the audiences would leave the theater. Their second attempt was better:

"Have yourself a merry little Christmas
Let your heart be light
Next year all our troubles will be out of sight..."

©1944 EMI Feist Catalog, Inc.

Like *Meet Me in St. Louis*, the song has become a Christmas classic.

Vincente Minnelli wanted a voice that did not sound professional, so producer Arthur Freed (who had no performing experience) dubbed the singing of Leon Ames.

Miracle on 34th Street

1947, 20th Century-Fox
Produced by William Perlberg
Directed by George Seaton

S·Y·N·O·P·S·I·S

A child (Natalie Wood) who doesn't believe in Santa Claus learns the meaning of faith when she meets Kris Kringle.

Academy Awards: Edmund Gwenn, Supporting Actor; Valentine Davis, Original Story; George Seaton, Screenplay;

Academy Award nomination: Best Picture.

Sometimes filmmakers owe a debt of gratitude to those who came before them; other times they curse their predecessors. Director George Seaton wanted to shoot a segment of *Miracle on 34th Street* at New York's famous Bellevue Hospital. Unfortunately Billy Wilder and *Lost Weekend* got there first.

To obtain permission to film in a ward, Billy Wilder had shown hospital officials a fake script. When hospital executives saw the scenes in *The Lost Weekend*, in which hospital attendants brutalize alcoholic Ray Milland, they vowed that Hollywood would never again be allowed to film within their walls. When Seaton approached them with his script, they refused to allow even a single frame to be shot at Bellevue. They had been tricked once with a phony script, so why should they believe Perlberg was filming an innocent story about Santa Claus? Seaton's only comment was, "Wilder's a tough man to follow."

With Santa Claus, all things are possible. Seaton wanted to make a film about the spirit of giving at Christmas so often overlooked by commercialism. He found a story by Valentine Davis, who got the idea for the plot while waiting in line at a department store.

Officials at Macy's were more obliging than the people at Bellevue and allowed Seaton to take his cameras into their main store in Manhattan during the Christmas rush. When the movie was released as a popular and critical success, Gimbels took out

a full-page advertisement in *The New York Times* commending the film and and their biggest competitor, Macy's Department Store.

Miracle on 34th Street is such a staple of December television schedules that it's hard to think of movie audiences seeing it for the first time at the height of summer. While the film was in production, Fox head Darryl Zanuck didn't think it had any chance of becoming a Christmas classic, so he released it in July.

The stars were Maureen O'Hara and John Payne, but the picture belonged to Edmund Gwenn and ten-year old Natalie Wood. As a result of her work in *Miracle on 34th Street*, Natalie's salary was raised to $1,500 a week, the level of a top Hollywood star. While the majority of her salary was put in trust for her, it also raised her Russian immigrant family out of desperate poverty. Her father was an alcoholic, and her mother often took Natalie and her sisters out of the house until he recovered from one of his drunken rages. The safety of a

movie set, where she was invariably cast as a much-loved member of a typical American family, may have been good therapy for her.

When Edmund Gwenn was on his deathbed in 1959, *Miracle* director George Seaton visited him and asked how he was doing. Paraphrasing another Edmund (Edmund Kean), Gwenn said: "It's tough, but not as tough as playing comedy."

Miracle on 34th Street has itself become part of the Christmas tradition. Each year, as the holiday season unfolds, millions of television viewers are treated to an idealistic vision of a world where life is simple, honest, uncomplicated, and free of commercialism. Ironically, this

picture, like Frank Capra's *It's A Wonderful Life*, is usually presented as seasonal filler amidst a plethora of commercials, and subjected to the idiocy of colorization.

If you believe in the spirit of these films, join me in demanding that they be seen in their original form, the way they were designed by the artists who made them. Take a stand against commercialism; insist on glorious black and white!

When he won his Oscar for *Miracle on 34th Street*, Edmund Gwenn said, "Now I know there is a Santa Claus."

Mr. and Mrs. Smith

1941, RKO Radio
Produced by Harry E. Edington
Directed by Alfred Hitchcock

S·Y·N·O·P·S·I·S

A married couple (Carole Lombard and Robert Montgomery) discover they're not legally married.

An unhappy actor once remarked that Alfred Hitchcock "herded his actors like cattle," and most of Hollywood had heard the comment when the director began working on *Mr. and Mrs. Smith.* Since it was Hitchcock's first and only screwball comedy, Carole Lombard was determined to begin in the proper mood. When Hitchcock appeared on the set for the first day of filming, he was confronted with a tiny corral containing three live heifers. One of the cows was labeled "Carole Lombard," one "Robert Montgomery," and the third "Gene Raymond."

Part of the success of *Mr. and Mrs. Smith* lies in the talents of Carole Lombard, who not only starred in the picture but also was the unofficial operative producer. She oversaw the budget and chose the director, the cast, and the entire technical crew, which included Pat Drew, an electrician who had lost his leg in an airplane accident. Lombard had a clause in her contract that stipulated Drew would be employed on all her films.

Lombard and Hitchcock met through their mutual friend, David O. Selznick, shortly after the producer brought Hitchcock to Hollywood to direct *Rebecca.* When Carole moved in with Clark Gable, Hitchcock rented her house in Bel Air. After his success with *Rebecca* and *Foreign Correspondent,* she asked him if he'd like to do a comedy. He said, "No, not particularly." But when she asked him to direct her in *Mr. and Mrs. Smith,* he replied that he was a gentleman and would acquiesce to the lady's request.

Both Hitchcock and Lombard wanted Cary Grant for the lead, but he was firmly booked for the next two years. They both agreed that Robert Montgomery was the only other actor who could carry the light and witty script. Montgomery liked the part and agreed to play it for $110,000, which was $40,000 more than Hitchcock was paid.

Working with Carole Lombard was a joy; she insisted on having fun with everything and everyone. When they filmed Hitchcock's cameo appearance, she appointed herself director of the scene. She sat in Hitchcock's chair, criticizing the director's posture and walk. After calling for several takes and yelling, "Give! Give!" to the amusement of the crew, she was finally satisfied with his performance and called for a print. She followed through on her directorial responsibilities by personally supervising the editing of the short scene.

Alfred Hitchcock wasn't the only butt of Lombard's practical jokes. She also picked on Robert Montgomery. 1940 was a Presidential election year, with Carole a Roosevelt supporter and Montgomery favoring Wendell Wilkie. Every morning Carole hid in the bushes on the studio lot, and after her co-star

parked his Rolls Royce, she'd cover it with FDR bumper stickers. Every night he'd carefully remove them. While he knew she was doing it, and she knew he knew she was doing it, they never once spoke about the prank. It just kept happening.

Mr. and Mrs. Smith is one of the last times the comic genius of Carole Lombard was captured on film. After completing her next picture, *To Be or Not To Be*, she embarked on a cross-country war bond drive. She was bumped from her returning flight but talked her way on to it, saying she was on official government business and should receive priority. She and her mother were allowed to board the doomed flight, which crashed into Table Rock Mountain, thirty miles southwest of Las Vegas. All twenty-two passengers on board were killed instantly, and an entire nation joined her husband Clark Gable in mourning the loss of Carole Lombard.

"She brought great joy to all who knew her and to millions who knew her only as a great artist. She gave unselfishly of time and talent to serve her government in peace and war. She loved her country. She is and always will be a star, one we shall never forget, nor cease to be grateful for."

—Franklin D. Roosevelt, on Carole Lombard.

Mister 880

1950, 20th Century-Fox
Produced by Julian Blaustein
Directed by Edmund Goulding

S·Y·N·O·P·S·I·S

True story of a Treasury Department investigator (Burt Lancaster) who tracks down a counterfeiter (Edmund Gwenn), and finds that the man manufactures only enough money to support himself and his neighbors.

Academy Award nomination:
Edmund Gwenn, Supporting Actor.

Depending on their responsibilities, everyone involved with making a motion picture has a different perspective. An actor looks at a script for his or her lines and actions, a cinematographer looks for possible camera angles, and the prop person makes a list of what must be found or made. When the prop man received his copy of the script for *Mister 880*, he found that most of it was pretty straightforward—all but for one item, an old printing press.

Studio carpenters couldn't build a working press, so assistants were sent to print shops and antique stores throughout Los Angeles. They went to hundreds of places without finding a working press. Then they stumbled on to a little print shop in southern California, where an 1872 model card press had been stashed away in storage. With a few minor modifications the seventy-eight-year old printing press was ready for its film debut as "Cousin Henry."

Finding a working press wasn't the only technical problem 20th Century-Fox faced in making

Mister 880. Because the story revolves around an endearing old counterfeiter, large amounts of currency were included in the prop list. However, at that time it was illegal to photograph U.S. currency in any manner, and that included using a movie camera. The Treasury Department cooperated by issuing a special permit to film real currency, and it even supplied actual footage of

the workings of the Department in Washington, D.C.

The stars of *Mister 880* are Burt Lancaster and Dorothy McGuire, but the performance that captured my heart was turned in by Edmund Gwenn. You know who he is . . . everyone recognizes him as the prototypical Santa Claus from his Oscar-winning performance in *Miracle on 34th St.* He was nominated again for *Mister 880*, but he lost to George Sanders for *All About Eve.* Gwenn began his professional career on the British stage in 1896. He became friends with George Bernard Shaw and was often cast in the first runs of Shaw's plays.

Mister 880 provided chances for the director and his assistant to step out of their customary roles. In 1946 Edmund Goulding wrote the song "Mam'selle" with Mack Gordon for *The Razor's Edge.* When he used his own song in *Mister 880*, he received a second listing in the credits. Far down in the cast list was the name Mike Lally, who was Goulding's assistant. Lally had always wanted to be an actor, so the director gave him one of his first speaking parts. At least he got billing. In an unbilled

bit part was a man named Scott Seaton, a San Francisco millionaire who had lost all of his money in a mining venture. He never made it big as an actor, but he appeared in several films, including *Father of the Bride* and *Donovan's Reef.*

The press material released with the film included a lot of trivia about the art of counterfeiting. For example, did you know that the Roman emperor Nero was supposed to be the first counterfeiter? One wonders, though, if he was emperor, why he would turn to counterfeiting. Studio publicity also dispelled the myth that if you can rub the ink off a bill, it's counterfeit. That's not true. The ink should rub off real money, too. However, if a bill seems unusually dull, smudgy, or unnaturally white, chances are it's illegal tender.

Like Skipper Miller in *Mister 880*, most counterfeiters are eventually caught. One master engraver tried to get away with his crime by changing one

phrase on the bill to read, "This bill is legal tender for all those stupid enough to take it." The judge was not amused. Like Skipper Miller, the man found out that counterfeiting doesn't pay.

"Mister 880" refers to the case number the Secret Service assigned to the counterfeiting operation.

Mr. Smith Goes to Washington

1939, Columbia
Produced and Directed by Frank Capra

S·Y·N·O·P·S·I·S

When a naive, honest man (James Stewart) is chosen to fill a vacated Senate seat, he exposes political corruption and speaks out for the common man.

Academy Awards: Lewis R. Foster, Original Story.

Academy Award nominations: Best Picture; Frank Capra, Director; James Stewart, Best Actor; Harry Carey, Claude Rains, Supporting Actor; Sidney Buchman, Screenplay; Lionel Banks, Interior Decoration; John Livadary, Sound Recording; Dimitri Tiomkin, Score; Gene Havlick and Al Clark, Film Editing.

There are times when you see a scene on film that has such a ring of truth, you know it wasn't something a screenwriter made up sitting next to a Hollywood swimming pool. That's true of several scenes in *Mr. Smith Goes to Washington*. Before writing the script, producer/director Frank Capra and screenwriter Sidney Buchman took a trip to Washington. They did what any new visitor does in Washington; they took a tour. By mixing in with the regular tourists, they were able to appreciate the awe felt by Americans from around the country when seeing the Senate, the Capitol, and the monuments for the first time.

Of course, Capra was also given views of Washington no tourist would ever see. The director was allowed to attend a presidential news conference, and the experience almost made him cancel the picture. As an immigrant, Capra had a reverence for America that comes through in his pictures. As he sat in the news conference, listening to reporters ask President Roosevelt about issues that would shape the world, he began to think making this picture was a mistake. Capra wondered if he was doing our government a disservice by making a film about a common man who exposes corruption at the highest levels. He left the press conference and went to the Lincoln Memorial, where he overheard a young boy reading Lincoln's words to his blind grandfather. Capra was overwhelmed by the experience and decided it was indeed appropriate to assert that a democratic government belongs to the people. He vowed to make the film, if only for the opportunity to include a scene in which a young boy reads Lincoln's words to his grandfather.

The picture premiered in Washington under the auspices of the National Press Club, and for Frank Capra the night was one of the great disasters of his life. The Washington elite walked out on the film, which portrayed politicians as corrupt influence peddlers. The next day the Senate voted ninety-six to zero against the movie and began considering legislation that would limit the power of the studios. The other studios, afraid Washington was out for revenge, offered Columbia two million dollars to shelve the picture and never release it. A telegram from Ambassador Joseph P. Kennedy in London asked Columbia not to release the film in Europe, saying it would be seen as Nazi propaganda and proof that democracies were run by corrupt individuals out for their own gain. Capra responded by sending Kennedy hundreds of clippings extolling Mr. Smith as the highest American ideal: the little guy fighting for what he

believes in and winning.

Columbia bravely released the picture, and, while American power brokers hated it, the American people loved it. So did the Europeans, proving Kennedy wrong. The film didn't tarnish the American image abroad, it polished it.

When the Nazis overran France, they gave French theater owners thirty days to comply with an order to run only German pictures. During that month many of them presented *Mr. Smith Goes to Washington,* and the French packed the theaters, cheering the speech about liberty. On November 4, 1942, *The Hollywood Reporter* quoted a European correspondent who had attended the final showing. It was "as though the joys, suffering, love and hatred, the hopes and wishes

of an entire people who value freedom above everything, found expression for the last time."

For the filibuster scene in which James Stewart's voice becomes hoarse, a doctor painted his throat with a mercury solution, causing his vocal cords to swell.

Morning Glory

1933, RKO Radio
Produced by Pandro S. Berman
Directed by Lowell Sherman

S·Y·N·O·P·S·I·S

A talkative young woman from New England (Katharine Hepburn) achieves success on the New York stage.

Academy Award: Katharine Hepburn, Best Actress.

Why is it that so many talented people in Hollywood are also self-destructive? Lowell Sherman was assigned to direct Katharine Hepburn's third film, *Morning Glory*. As well as being a creative director, Sherman was a skilled actor. His specialty was playing wealthy cads, the kind who wear velvet smoking jackets and populate elegant drawing rooms. Before directing *Morning Glory*, he had just starred in the triumphant *What Price Hollywood?* Sherman could have made a tremendous impact on Hollywood, but his alcoholism made him an unreliable talent. He was able to stay sober during the production of *Morning Glory*, partly because the film was made at breathtaking speed.

Sherman told producer Pandro Berman that if he could have a week with the cast, just sitting around a table reading the lines, he'd make the fastest picture in Hollywood history. He was as good as his word. After a week spent just reading the script, Sherman was ready to shoot. He finished the film in eighteen days, and he did it in an unusual way. When making a feature film, standard operating procedure calls for all the scenes that take place on one set to be shot together. Often, shooting out of sequence means that the actors play scenes from the end of a movie before they do the beginning. That wasn't the case with *Morning Glory*. It's one of the few Hollywood films shot entirely in sequence, from beginning to end.

Katharine Hepburn wasn't originally slated to play the lead, but Pandro Berman was no match for her. She was in Berman's office when she saw the *Morning Glory* script on his desk. She began reading it and instantly fell in love with the character of Eva Lovelace. She took the script home with her and finished it; the next day she told Berman she wanted the part. He said absolutely not; the part, which had been modeled after Tallulah Bankhead, was meant for Constance Bennett. Hepburn was persistent and finally wore Berman down. Constance Bennett didn't have a chance.

The leading man was Douglas Fairbanks, Jr., who met Katharine Hepburn for the first time at *Morning Glory* rehearsals. As he got to know her, he became more and more attracted to her. He asked her repeatedly for dates, but she refused. When she finally did agree to go out to dinner with him, she asked to be taken home early, pleading that she had a headache. Fairbanks was so enamored of Hepburn that, after escorting her home, he sat in his car outside her house, savoring the enchanted evening. A few minutes later the back door flew open and Hepburn dashed out and jumped into a waiting car. Unknown to Fairbanks, Hepburn was seriously involved with her agent, Leland Hayward, a relationship that would last for four years. (Hayward was never faithful to Hepburn and eventually married Margaret Sullivan.) Fairbanks was too much of a gentleman to tell Hepburn he knew about her second assignation. Years later he admitted to her he had seen her run out the back door that evening, and they both got a good

laugh out of it.

The original script for *Morning Glory* called for a wonderful sequence in which Hepburn and Fairbanks played scenes from *Romeo and Juliet*. Fairbanks thoroughly enjoyed the experience but said his green tights made him look like a decadent string bean. Lowell Sherman decided that the actors couldn't do Shakespeare without a real audience, so on the day they shot those scenes, chairs were set up on the sound stage and they performed to a real audience. Unfortunately, most of the Romeo and Juliet scenes were left on the cutting room floor when the picture proved to be too long.

Katharine Hepburn and Adolphe Menjou virtually repeated their *Morning Glory* roles in the 1937 *Stage Door*. The latter film was not an official remake, but it did have similar

characters, story lines, and themes.

Katharine Hepburn has received twelve Academy Award nominations for acting. Her four awards as Best Actress set a Hollywood record.

My Darling Clementine

1946, 20th Century-Fox
Produced by Samuel G. Engel
Directed by John Ford

S·Y·N·O·P·S·I·S

John Ford's classic retelling of the gunfight between the Earps and the Clantons at the O.K.Corral.

There are many cliches associated with Westerns. In a badly made film, cliches come off as unreal at best and downright comic at worst. But in the hands of a master filmmaker like John Ford, even a cliche can be moving and emotional. There are a lot of cliches in *My Darling Clementine*, but they seem so natural that other filmmakers have copied Ford's style and technique.

It was Darryl Zanuck who assigned Ford to make *My Darling Clementine*. Ford didn't want to do it; he was trying to raise money for his own production company at the time. But he had a contract with 20th Century-Fox that obligated him to make one more picture, so he had no choice: he had to make the story of Wyatt Earp and the gunfight at the O.K. Corral.

Ford had been

acquainted with the real Wyatt Earp, who had spent time in Hollywood before his death in 1929. Earp had told Ford the true story behind the most famous gunfight in the Old West. While Ford incorporated many of those authentic details into the picture, he also took a few liberties with the facts. Earp told Ford that the Mc-Lowery Brothers were present at the fight, but Ford cut them from his version. Old Man Clanton, played by Walter Brennan, wasn't at the real fight, but in the film he showed up right on time. The

real gunfight at the O.K. Corral involved two Earps and three Clantons, all of whom had shotguns, not pistols. Pistols were so inaccurate in those days that, even at a short distance, the vast majority of bullets fired would miss their mark by a wide margin.

Ford also made the ultimate decision as to who lived and who died, without concerning himself with historical accuracy. While Virgil Earp was wounded in the battle, he didn't die, nor did Doc Holliday. They did in *My Darling Clementine.*

Because filmmakers don't operate in a vacuum, it's important to know what was happening in Ford's life to understand how it affected the picture. He had just come back from active duty in World War II and, like other returning veterans, he had a sense of being an outsider, of coming from the wilderness of war to a community full of rules and order. That feeling, and other concerns of the combat veteran, are reflected in the story. When Henry Fonda stands at his

brother's grave and promises "to make a country where kids can grow up safe," it's a statement of what most Americans were fighting for.

While this picture is considered one of his classic Westerns, John Ford did not shoot the ending to *My Darling Clementine.*

His picture ended with Wyatt Earp remaining in Tombstone as permanent marshal. When Darryl Zanuck saw the completed film, he didn't like it. Zanuck cut a full thirty minutes out of the film, changed the ending, and had it reshot.

Here's an interesting side note to *My Darling Clementine.* In 1943 Charles Bidwell, an unemployed steel worker from Houston, Texas, went to Hollywood to see the sights before he enlisted in the service. Like most tourists, he took a tour of the studios. Everywhere Bidwell went people thought he was

Henry Fonda. Studio executives were so impressed with his resemblance to Fonda that they took his name and told him to contact them after he got out of the service. In 1946 he did so, and the studio hired him as Henry Fonda's stand-in for *My Darling Clementine.* Charles Bidwell held his position as Henry Fonda's stand-in for the next thirty-five years.

The "O.K." in the O.K. Corral stands for "Old Kinderhook."

My Favorite Wife

1940, RKO Radio
Produced by Leo McCarey
Directed by Garson Kanin

S·Y·N·O·P·S·I·S

A wife (Irene Dunne) who has been lost at sea for seven years returns on the day her husband (Cary Grant) has her declared legally dead so that he can marry another woman (Gail Patrick).

The credits often tell only part of the story of who contributed to the success of a movie. Leo

McCarey came up with the original concept for *My Favorite Wife* and was going to produce and direct it for RKO. When he was seriously injured in an auto accident, the picture was turned over to a relative newcomer named Garson Kanin. McCarey still received credit as producer, and you could say he "ghost directed" from his hospital bed. Kanin later said that McCarey remained in charge of the day-to-day course of the direction. Kanin, who may have benefitted from the master's instruction, went on to direct many classic comedies, including *Pat and Mike*, *Adam's Rib*, and *Born Yesterday*.

Jean Arthur was originally slated to play the lead, but that same year Columbia cast her in *Too Many Husbands*, in which she played a woman whose missing husband turned up on the eve of her wedding to another man. Columbia wouldn't loan her out for a picture that had virtually the same plot, so Leo McCarey signed Irene Dunne for the lead. She received $100,000, a percent-

age of the profits, and top billing over Cary Grant.

Irene Dunne was so pleased with *My Favorite Wife* that she agreed to attend a special premiere in her home town of Louisville, Kentucky, before the film's official debut at Radio City Music Hall. Dunne had a reputation of being a real lady, off-screen as well as on. A devout Catholic, her life was so free of scandal that publishers weren't interested in her autobiography. Although she was one of Hollywood's most successful leading ladies, the publishers felt her life was too boring!

Randolph Scott plays the man who's been shipwrecked on an island with Irene Dunne for the past seven years. Cary Grant, of course, becomes terribly jealous when he learns Randolph Scott was his wife's "roommate." Ironically, when they were still unknown, struggling actors, Randolph Scott and Cary Grant had been roommates. They shared an apartment to cut expenses while waiting for their big breaks.

Gail Patrick, who plays Bianca, was a Paramount starlet when she co-starred with Randolph Scott in *Murders in the Zoo* in 1933. After years of playing "the other woman," she gave up acting to enter TV production. She and Erle Stanley Gardner collaborated to create the television series *Perry Mason,* which Patrick produced for many years.

Scotty Beckett, who played the son, started his career at the age of three as a member of the *Our Gang/Little Rascals* comedies. After leaving *Our Gang,* he was often cast in

as *Something's Got to Give,* with Marilyn Monroe and Dean Martin. Marilyn rarely showed up on the set, and when she did, she refused to accept changes in the script. The few scenes that director George Cukor got in the can proved to be Marilyn's last work in front of a camera. Fox announced that Lee Remick was signed to replace Marilyn, but Dean Martin objected. He said he had signed to do a picture with Marilyn, not Lee Remick. The entire project was scrapped and

Favorite Wife unavailable for television.

pictures where he played the star as a boy, most notably as the young Jolson in *The Jolson Story.* Like many of the *Our Gang* kids, he died young. His death at the age of thirty-nine was ruled a probable suicide.

In 1962 20th Century-Fox tried to remake *My Favorite Wife*

brought back a year later as *Move Over, Darling* with Doris Day and James Garner. Like many remakes it wasn't nearly as good as the original. However, more people are familiar with the Doris Day version. For many years legal problems between Fox and RKO over the remake kept *My*

In addition to *My Favorite Wife*, Irene Dunne and Cary Grant costarred in *The Awful Truth* in 1937 and in *Penny Serenade* in 1941. In all three pictures Irene Dunne received top billing.

Nightmare Alley

1947, 20th Century-Fox
Produced by George Jessel
Directed by Edmund Goulding

S·Y·N·O·P·S·I·S

A sideshow barker (Tyrone Power) teams up with an unscrupulous psychiatrist (Helen Walker) to pass himself off as a psychic. He ends up back at the circus as a sideshow freak, where his wife (Joan Blondell) rescues him.

Tyrone Power was the biggest name at the box office in the early forties, but he was dissatisfied. He played essentially the same character in picture after picture: the dashing man of action, often nattily dressed in the costume of a bygone era. Critics liked him but rarely raved about his acting ability. While he enjoyed his fame, he wanted more than mere celebrity status; he wanted the respect that comes from being recognized as a great actor.

After Power returned from serving in World War II, he found himself stuck in the same old costume pictures, beginning with his swashbuckler role in *Captain from Castile.* Fox did take a small gamble and cast him as a sensitive, introspective hero who seeks the goodness in life in *The Razor's Edge.* Power's notices were adequate, but the studio wasn't ready to let him do more than fight the bad guys and romance a leading lady.

Power went to studio head Darryl Zanuck and asked him to buy the rights to a novel called *Nightmare Alley.* The character fascinated him, and he wanted the chance to play an unmitigated heel. At first Zanuck categorically refused. The American public did not want to associate Tyrone Power with an unsympathetic character. Power argued that his character in *The Razor's Edge* had also been unusual and that the picture had made a lot of money. Zanuck relented, bought the rights, and assigned *The Razor's Edge* director Edmund Goulding to the picture. Zanuck assigned veteran producer and all-around performer George Jessel to produce, which was also out of the ordinary because Jessel normally handled lighthearted musicals.

This unusual team combined to make a picture that has come to be regarded as a cult classic. When you call a film a cult classic, it usually means one thing: during its original run it totally flopped at the box office. That's what happened to *Nightmare Alley.* While the movie-going public couldn't stand to see their favorite hero playing such an unsavory character, the critics were overwhelmed, and many called it Power's greatest performance. Edmund Goulding was so impressed, he called Power "the greatest actor of his generation."

While filming *Nightmare Alley,* Tyrone Power was enjoying a much-publicized romance with Lana Turner. They visited carnivals and sideshows together, where he soaked up the ambiance and witnessed firsthand the lives of the people known as "Carnies." After his work on the picture was over, he took an extended vacation. Lana gave him an elaborate going away party and planned to join him as soon as her latest picture was completed.

Power, who was in Africa when he heard he had received rave reviews for *Nightmare Alley,* was looking forward to celebrating his triumph with Lana when they met in Casablanca. But the Hollywood gossip mill never rested, and its reach extended overseas. Tyrone Power was in Rome when he found out that Lana had been seeing Frank Sinatra. From that moment on he refused to accept her calls and did not respond to her wires.

He wasn't left heartbroken for long. There was an incredibly beautiful twenty-three year old actress named Linda Christian staying at the same hotel. She fol-

lowed him to Hollywood, and they were married on January 27, 1949.

Tyrone Power once told Elia Kazan that, for anyone who wants to be a great actor, it is a tragedy to be born handsome. Kazan replied that it is a greater tragedy to be born homely.

Nothing Sacred

1937, Selznick International/United Artists
Produced by David O. Selznick
Directed by William Wellman

S·Y·N·O·P·S·I·S

A newspaperman (Fredric March) brings a dying girl (Carole Lombard) to New York to tell the story of her final days, then finds out she's not really sick.

Director William Wellman heard strange sounds coming from the set of *Nothing Sacred*, but that was nothing unusual. With Carole Lom-

bard on the set, almost anything could happen. She was famous for her practical jokes and crazy stunts; in fact, the phrase "Nothing Sacred" could sum up her philosophy of life. Wellman couldn't figure out what those noises could be. There was a sort of "ca-ching! ca-ching!", followed by the sound of breaking glass and applause. Wellman was right. Carole Lombard was responsible for those odd sounds. The previous day she had made a bet with one of the crew members, and the entire cast and crew got in on the action. Carole Lombard

brought in her air pistol and proceeded to prove her contention that she could shoot out all the lightbulbs on the set. Electricians, set dressers, prop men, assistants . . . everybody wagered money on the outcome. All those who backed Carole won their bets.

There was one bet producer David Selznick covered when he decided to make *Nothing Sacred*. He had all the elements necessary for a hit movie. Selznick had just finished *A Star is Born*, directed by William Wellman and starring Fredric March. It's no coincidence that he started with the same team, added Carole Lombard, and made *Nothing Sacred*. By the way, Carole Lombard's character was named Hazel Flagg, a variation on Harriet Flagg, Selznick's faithful executive secretary.

Selznick shot the film in the newly improved but still very expensive process known as Technicolor. Since much of the filming was done on location in New York City, film audiences around the country were treated to their very first color views of the Empire State Building, Radio City, Park Avenue, the Polo Grounds, and the Statue of Liberty. That was pretty exciting stuff back in 1937! Shooting in Technicolor also created problems. Because there weren't many color cameras available, Selznick was forced to commit to a shooting schedule and reserve the cameras well in advance. This was a small problem compared to the ending of the film, which Selznick hated. The original Ben Hecht script called for the reporter and the girl to publicly expose the lie, revealing the gullibility of the American press and people. When Hecht refused to rewrite it, Selznick was left with a picture that had no ending and a schedule he couldn't postpone. Screenwriters Ring Lardner, Jr., and Budd Schulberg quickly wrote the new ending, in which Lombard agrees to fake her suicide and save the reporter's reputation. Selznick didn't love it but he approved it, because there wasn't time to write

anything else.

The scene in *Nothing Sacred* in which Carole Lombard put a strait jacket on Fredric March took a great deal of rehearsal. Wellman spent time with Carole teaching her how to work with the jacket, which led to obvious jokes concerning how Wellman had acquired this peculiar knowledge. After they finished shooting, the studio threw the traditional cast party, and Carole and her costar bought Wellman his very own personalized strait-jacket. They made a formal presentation, and then Carole attacked him with the jacket. Wellman had done such a good job of teaching her how to use it on a struggling opponent that he was no match for her. Of course, once she had him in it, she wasn't about to let him out. Wellman spent the entire

evening in the strait jacket, eating and drinking whatever his friends would hand feed him. Publicity chief Russell Birdwell knew a good thing when he saw it and sent photos of Wellman in a strait jacket to newspapers all over the country.

Of the $465,000 Carole Lombard made in 1937, eighty-five percent   went to government income taxes.

Notorious

1946, RKO Radio
Produced and Directed by Alfred Hitchcock

S·Y·N·O·P·S·I·S

An American agent (Cary Grant) falls in love with the woman he recruits for a dangerous mission (Ingrid Bergman).

Academy Award nominations: Claude Rains, Supporting Actor; Ben Hecht, Original Screenplay.

Directors in the 1940s worked under restrictions that contemporary filmmakers don't have to deal with. In the case of a love scene between Cary Grant and Ingrid Bergman in *Notorious*, those restrictions caused the director to be more creative.

The censors who enforced the Production Code were adamant that love scenes could not contain what they called "protracted kissing." By having Cary Grant and Ingrid Bergman nibble at each other's lips and ears while discussing their dinner, Alfred Hitchcock became the first director to slip a three-minute kissing scene past the censors. He wanted the viewer to feel like an active participant in the scene, making it a ménage à trois between Grant, Bergman, and the audience. Cary Grant and Ingrid Bergman told the director that they were uncomfortable with the scene, but Hitchcock told them to trust him, that it would work beautifully on film. He was right.

Cary Grant complained that Hitchcock was favoring Bergman, not just in the dinner scene but in all the scenes the two shared. There could be some truth to the accusation, since Hitchcock often did favor his leading ladies. The photography and the lighting in the final bedroom scene, which all but cuts Cary Grant out of the picture, seems to support this theory.

Notorious was the first film Alfred Hitchcock made that was conceived entirely as a love story. All of his earlier films had been suspense thrillers with a love interest added. He and scriptwriter Ben Hecht co-wrote the dialogue, much of which was later rewritten by Hitchcock. Analysts of the director's life claim that the two main male characters, played by Cary Grant and Claude Rains, represent the two sides of Hitchcock's own personality. Much of the dialogue between Rains and the actress who plays his mother could easily have been an exchange between the director and his own domineering mother, who had recently died. Hitchcock visually expressed the link between mother and son when their shadows merged into one image.

When Alfred Hitchcock was working on the story line for *Notorious*, he wanted the plot to revolve around something the Germans were doing in Rio, but he and Ben Hecht couldn't come up with the proper illegal activity. Hitchcock suggested the bad guys could be collecting samples of Uranium 235. The story was sent around to several Hollywood studios, but they all turned it down. The idea that uranium could be used to make an A-bomb was too farfetched. Hitchcock became so frustrated that he was willing to let the plot revolve around anything: industrial diamonds, military secrets, anything. As he explained to one producer, he was making a love story, and it didn't matter what the MacGuffin was.

According to Hitchcock, a MacGuffin is anything spies are after in an espionage story. The audience doesn't really care what the MacGuffin is: it could be microfilm hidden in the heel of a shoe or secret formulas found only in the mind of a scientist. In a later film, *North by Northwest*, Hitchcock disposes of the Mac-Guffin in one line. When Cary Grant asks James Mason what the enemy agents are after, Mason merely answers, "Government secrets."

Notorious grossed more than $1,000,000 and met with critical acclaim, including making *The New York Times* list of the ten best pictures of 1946. It stands the test of time and remains one of Alfred Hitchcock's best romantic thrillers.

The F.B.I. put Alfred Hitchcock under investigation when he began trying to sell the idea for *Notorious*, months before the general public learned that Uranium 235 could be used to create atomic bombs.

The Philadelphia Story

1940, MGM
Produced by Joseph Mankiewicz
Directed by George Cukor

S·Y·N·O·P·S·I·S

On the eve of her marriage, a wealthy woman (Katharine Hepburn) discovers she still loves her ex-husband (Cary Grant).

Academy Awards: James Stewart, Best Actor; Donald Ogden Stewart, Screenplay.

Academy Award nominations: Best Picture; George Cukor, Director; Katharine Hepburn, Best Actress; Ruth Hussey, Best Supporting Actress.

Katharine Hepburn, Marlene Dietrich, and Greta Garbo. . .box office poison? That's what movie distributors labeled all three legends in the late 1930s. Hepburn, smarting from the negative publicity as well as six unprofitable films in a row, went East to try to recoup her stage career. She became excited by a play Philip Barry had written expressly for her. She asked the Theater Guild to produce the play, but the Guild, which had also had a string of non-money-makers, could not come up with the necessary funds. The Guild put up half, Katharine Hepburn put up 25 percent, and Howard Hughes, who was dating Kate at the time, put up the rest. Hepburn also paid Barry $25,000 for the film rights. While she didn't know it at the time, that action would significantly affect the rest of her film career.

When *The Philadelphia Story* was a smash hit and ran for 415 performances on Broadway, a movie was the obvious next step. Since Hepburn personally owned the rights, the studios negotiated directly with her. She turned down an offer from Warner Bros. for $225,000 for the rights, because they wanted Bette Davis to star. MGM made the offer she couldn't refuse: If she could get a top box office name as a co-star, the studio would pay $175,000 for the rights and an additional $75,000 for her services.

Director George Cukor suggested Cary Grant, a logical choice because he and Hepburn had proven their on-screen compatibility in *Bringing Up Baby* and *Holiday*. Negotiations almost broke down when Grant demanded top billing, but Hepburn relented and settled for second. Grant was also given his choice of which of the two male leads he would play.

When two characters were combined to form one stronger role, he chose the part of Dexter Haven. Van Heflin, who had played the other male lead on Broadway, was crushed when the film role went to James Stewart. Once casting was settled, screenwriter Donald Ogden Stewart began adapting the script. Producer Joseph Mankiewicz had an audio recording made of the Broadway version, which he turned over to the writer with firm instructions that every laugh from the stage version should be included in the film script. Films and plays are different media, however, and stage laughs couldn't necessarily be adapted for a fast-paced picture. Needless to say, Stewart found the restriction irritating. Mankiewicz eventually relented and let him do the adaptation his way.

Filming went smoothly and was completed on time in eight weeks, with no call-backs for retakes. The only real problem with the production was that the first cut ran thirty minutes too long. Many sparkling moments had to be left on the cutting room floor.

The Philadelphia Story broke all previous attendance records at Radio City Music Hall, taking in $600,000 in just six weeks. Hepburn's triumphant return to Hollywood proved that people would indeed pay to watch a Katharine Hepburn film. The success of *The Philadelphia Story* convinced MGM executives to allow her, on her next film, to work with a man she had not yet met—a man named Spencer Tracy.

P·L·A·Y·E·R·S	
Cary Grant	C.K. Dexter Haven
Katharine Hepburn	Tracy Lord
James Stewart	Macauley Connor
Ruth Hussey	Elizabeth Imbrie

Featuring:
- John Howard
- Roland Young
- John Halliday
- Mary Nash
- Virginia Weidler
- Henry Daniell
- Lionel Pape
- Rex Evans
- Russ Clark
- Hilda Plowright
- Lita Chevret
- Lee Phelps
- David Clyde
- Claude King
- Robert De Bruce
- Veda Buckland

"There's magnificence in you, Tracy. You're lit from within. You're the golden girl, full of life and warmth and delight."
—James Stewart to Katharine Hepburn in *The Philadelphia Story*.

The Pride of the Yankees

1942, Samuel Goldwyn Studios/RKO Radio
Produced by Sam Goldwyn
Directed by Sam Wood

S·Y·N·O·P·S·I·S

The true story of baseball player Lou Gehrig (Gary Cooper) and his courageous fight against a terminal illness.

Academy Award: Daniel Mandell, Film Editing.

Academy Award nominations: Best Picture; Gary Cooper, Best Actor; Teresa Wright, Best Actress; Paul Gallico, Original story; Herman J. Mankiewicz and Jo Swerling, Screenplay; Rudolph Mate, Black and White Cinematography; Perry Ferguson, Howard Bristol, Interior Decoration; Thomas Moulton, Sound Recording; Leigh Harline, Score; Jack Cosgrove, Ray Binger, Thomas T. Moulton, Special Effects.

In 1942, studio executives had strong reasons not to make a baseball picture. With so many men away fighting World War II, they reasoned, Hollywood had to make pictures that interested women. Since they as-sumed women couldn't possibly understand baseball, a baseball picture was a sure-fire box office flop. It wouldn't be helped by the foreign markets, because foreigners would never be interested in baseball, would they?

Screenwriter Niven Busch didn't agree with the conventional wisdom. He wanted to tell the story of Lou Gehrig, the Yankees' gallant first baseman who died in 1941. This wasn't a baseball story; it was a moving battle against a terminal illness fought by a man who happened to be a baseball player. Busch tried to talk Sam Goldwyn into letting him write the script, but Goldwyn wasn't convinced. Niven then acquired the newsreels of Lou Gehrig Day at Yankee Stadium, when fellow players and fans paid tribute to their hero. Goldwyn was so moved by the emotion that came through on the screen that he agreed to produce the picture.

Sam Goldwyn was an immigrant and didn't have the advantage of playing sandlot baseball as a youth. Consequently, his understanding of the game was sketchy at best. He agreed when Irving Fine, his publicity chief, suggested they use some of Gehrig's teammates to play themselves. The players were all offered $500 for one week's work, along with transportation and lodging in Hollywood for themselves and their wives. The only man who didn't agree was Red Rolfe, the third baseman, who said that at his present salary he couldn't do it for less than $1,500. Goldwyn was furious and told Fine to forget Rolfe. After all, if he got a first baseman for $500, how dare a mere third baseman ask for more?

The producer's ignorance of baseball contributed to another vintage Goldwynism. Seated next to Yankee catcher Bill Dickey at a luncheon, Sam enthusiastically told Dickey that the first time the catcher was seen in the film was when they faded in on him in the dugout. Dickey, who didn't know what a "fade-in" was, said he didn't understand. Goldwyn proudly explained that a dugout was the place where the players sat and waited for their turn to play.

When Goldwyn Studios announced its intention to make the Lou Gehrig story, Eddie Albert, William Gargan, and Dennis Morgan were all mentioned as possible stars. Director Sam Wood only considered one actor: Gary Cooper. If you look at photos of Gehrig, the resemblance between the two men is amazing. While

Cooper physically resembled Gehrig, however, his baseball ability was nonexistent. Cooper admitted he had never picked up a baseball in his life, a claim that seemed to be confirmed when retired major-leaguer Lefty O'-Doul saw how the actor threw. He characterized Cooper's throwing style as reminiscent of an old woman tossing a hot biscuit. To make matters worse, Gehrig had been left-handed and Cooper was a righty. In the wide shots they used a double to throw left-handed, something Cooper couldn't get the hang of. But when it came to batting, they almost canceled the picture. Close-ups were essential, but Cooper just couldn't swing a bat left-handed. Art director William Cameron Menzies came up with an innovative solution. They made up a uniform with the number and the Yankee insignia printed backwards. When they

shot the scene, Cooper batted right-handed and ran to third base. They printed the film backward, and Cooper seemed to be batting left-handed and running to first.

As Lou Gehrig, baseball player, Cooper didn't fool the experts. But his portrayal of Lou Gehrig, the man, was so moving it earned him his third Academy Award nomination.

Amyotrophic lateral sclerosis, or ALS, is also commonly referred to as "Lou Gehrig's Disease."

Public Enemy

1931, Warner Bros.
Produced by Darryl Zanuck
Directed by William Wellman

S·Y·N·O·P·S·I·S

A Chicago slum kid (James Cagney) rises within the ranks of the underworld to become one of the city's crime bosses.

Let's play word association. What citrus fruit do you associate with the film *Public Enemy*? (A) lemon (B) orange (C) grapefruit. Give yourself ten points for answering C. While no one was aware of it the day they filmed it, James Cagney's overreaction to Mae Clarke's chatter would go down as the most famous moment in grapefruit history. Whose idea was it? Everyone's, it seems.

Darryl Zanuck liked to claim credit for it, saying he came up with it at a story conference. Most experts now discount his claim. William Wellman also wanted credit. He said that when his wife was angry with him, she'd walk around with a totally blank look on her face. One day,

when she was particularly expressionless during breakfast, he wondered how she'd react if he shoved a grapefruit in her face. He decided it would cost him a lot less money if he let James Cagney do it to Mae Clarke.

The truth of the matter was that the incident was in the original script, but it was an omelette, not a grapefruit, that Cagney shoved in Clarke's face. Writers Kubec Glasmon and John

Bright based the incident on a very real gangster, Hymie Weiss, who was so annoyed with his girlfriend, he did the honors with a steaming hot omelette. That's the way it appeared in the script, but an omelette was too messy, so a grapefruit was substituted.

The cruelty of the scene caused a national outcry, but no one was more surprised than Mae Clarke. She had been told that Cagney would fake the action, and that the grapefruit would never actually touch her face. Surprise! One person who got some malicious enjoyment from the scene was Clarke's ex-husband, Monte Brice. After their messy divorce, he got into the habit of stopping by the Strand Theater just in time for the scene and leaving just after.

If director William Wellman lied to Mae Clarke about the grapefruit, James Cagney suspected the same thing happened when Donald Cook was supposed to throw a punch at him. Instead of pulling the punch, Cook let Cagney have it full force. Cagney didn't move fast enough, and production was stopped while he dealt with a broken tooth.

He might not have moved fast enough to avoid the punch, but he didn't have that problem ducking bullets. In those days special effects did not include simulated gun fire, so when James Cagney ran past a brick wall with the bullets flying, those were real bullets he was dodging. The studio hired an ex-World War I gunner named Bailey to man the machine gun. Cagney said later that if he had hesitated for the briefest fraction of a second, he would have been pulverized just like the wall.

Public Enemy made James Cagney a household name, which is ironic, because

when they began filming, Eddie Woods was in the lead and James Cagney was playing the secondary role of his friend. After three days of filming, director William Wellman looked at the rushes and agreed with the judgment of the writers. Wellman went to Zanuck and said that the two men should switch roles. Zanuck wasn't crazy about the idea. Woods was dating the ever-powerful Louella Parsons, and the studio was afraid that if Eddie were upset, Louella would be too. Wellman was persuasive, and Zanuck agreed to the change,

which raised Cagney to the star status he retained for six decades.

Public Enemy, which was shot in just twenty-six days at a cost of $150,000, made more than a million dollars for the studio. When *Public Enemy* was made in 1931, the Production Code had not yet been adopted by the studios. When Warner Bros. tried to reissue the film in 1936, the Breen Office, which enforced the Code, refused to give its approval. The film wasn't seen again in public until 1953, when it was issued on a double bill with *Little Caesar*.

When *Public Enemy* first opened in 1931, the theaters in New York stayed open all night to accommodate the crowds.

The Quiet Man

1952, Argosy Pictures/Republic
Produced by John Ford and Merian C. Cooper
Directed by John Ford

S·Y·N·O·P·S·I·S

An Irishman (John Wayne) who has been living in America returns to his homeland and falls in love with a woman (Maureen O'Hara) in a Galway village.

Academy Awards: John Ford, Best Director; Winton C. Hoch and Archie Stout, Color Cinematography; Merian C. Cooper, honorary award for his many innovations and contributions.

Academy Award nominations: Best Picture; Victor McLaglen, Supporting Actor; Frank S. Nugent, Screenplay; Frank Hotaling, John McCarthy, Jr., and Charles Thompson, Art Direction; Daniel J. Blomberg, Sound Recording.

You would think a director of John Ford's stature would be able to make any picture he wanted. His films were already legendary, and no one doubted that he was one of the best directors ever to walk a sound stage. When he wanted to make *The*

Quiet Man, however, no one in Hollywood trusted his judgment.

He bought the rights to the Maurice Walsh short story in 1936, and for years he tried to interest any studio in making the story of an Irish-born man who returns to his homeland after living in Pittsburgh. No one wanted it. Most studio executives thought it would make an "artsy" picture, one that would not be commercially viable; besides, they suspected that Ford only wanted to make it because his

parents had been born in Ireland.

Finally Ford thought he had the backing he wanted. It was a three-picture deal between his company, Argosy, and RKO. If the first picture he directed made money, *The Quiet Man* would be his second. The movie he made was called *The Fugitive*; it was not a success at the box office, and RKO canceled plans for *The Quiet Man.*

Three years later Ford struck a similar three-picture deal with Herbert Yates of Republic, but their association didn't run smoothly. Like the other executives, Yates hated *The Quiet Man,* and he offered Ford a much smaller budget than the director wanted. Republic never made multi-million dollar pictures, and Yates grilled Ford on every penny that was spent. Ford's frustration mounted when he sent rushes back to Hollywood containing some of the most beautiful color photography ever captured on film and Yates complained that Ireland looked too green.

The production of *The Quiet*

Man was both a homecoming and a family affair for Ford and other cast members. Ford felt at home in Galway, not far from the birthplaces of his mother and father. His sense of family was reinforced by the fact that his daughter worked as an assistant editor on the film, her husband, Ken Curtis, and Ford's elder brother, Francis, were cast in the movie, and his son Patrick was a second unit director. The family connections didn't stop with the Ford clan. Three of John Wayne's children appeared in the film, as did Maureen O'Hara's brother Charles fitzSimons, while Victor McLaglen's son Andrew worked as Ford's assistant.

Ford, who would go to any lengths to put an actor in the proper mood, took advantage of the fact that McLaglen's son was present. He needed McLaglen to be angry for the scene in which he throws Maureen O'Hara's dowry on the floor. The night before they did the scene, Ford told McLaglen, in front of Andrew, that it was useless to continue filming: he had turned in such a poor performance that Ford was afraid he wasn't capable of doing the scene. Ford knew exactly what would happen. McLaglen was so upset he couldn't sleep, and by the next morning, his anger boiled over to the point where he had to be physically restrained from hitting the director. They filmed the scene, and McLaglen's rage came through loud and clear.

When the picture was finished, it was 129 minutes long, which Herbert Yates said was unacceptable. He ordered Ford to cut nine minutes from the film, but Ford said that any further cuts would ruin it. Yates then arranged for a screening for the Republic distributors, and insisted that the version they were shown be no longer than 120 minutes. During the screening the audience was enthralled, and both Ford and Yates knew they had a hit on their hands. Then, at the instant when John Wayne agrees to the famous fight, the screen went blank. Ford turned to Yates and told him that, since he couldn't find anything to cut, he had just ended the picture there. Yates knew the picture could be a box office hit even if it went 129 minutes, and he agreed to let Ford finish the picture his way.

John Wayne's character was named Sean Thornton, after John Ford and one of his relatives. "Sean" is the Gaelic equivalent of "John," and "Thornton" was one of Ford's Irish rebel cousins whose house was burned by the Black and Tans.

Rear Window

1954, Paramount
Produced and Directed by Alfred Hitchcock

S·Y·N·O·P·S·I·S

A professional photographer, confined to his apartment with a broken leg, spies on his neighbors and becomes convinced that a man living across the courtyard murdered his wife.

Academy Award nominations:
Alfred Hitchcock, Best Director; John Michael Hayes, Screenplay; Robert Burks, Color Cinematography; Loren L. Ryder, Sound Recording.

Who would have the gall to tell an eight-time Academy Award winning costume designer how to do her job? Alfred Hitchcock, that's who.

When Edith Head designed the costumes for Hitchcock's *Rear Window*, she received very specific instructions from the director, right down to the type of shoes he wanted to go with each outfit. He paid particular attention to Grace Kelly's costumes, insisting on white chiffon for one scene, a gold number for another, and a pale green suit which subtly linked the leading lady to Judith Evelyn's brilliant green outfit. Hitchcock controlled every detail—or so he thought. When the director told Edith Head to pad the bustline of one of Kelly's sheer nightgowns, both women balked: they thought the idea was ridiculous, and conspired to come up with their own solution. Head made a few tucks in the material around the bustline; Kelly took it from there. When the leading lady emerged from the dressing room, she stood extremely straight and tall, and changed her walk slightly to lead with her chest. When Hitchcock saw the results, he turned to Head and said, "See what a difference they make?"

Since all of the action in *Rear Window* takes place in James Stewart's Manhattan apartment, the challenge for Hitchcock and his crew was to make the relationship between Stewart and the people in the apartments across the courtyard look real. Hitchcock refused to use trick photography. Instead, he took an entire sound stage at Paramount and constructed one of the largest indoor movie sets of all time: a four-story building that featured a fully landscaped courtyard and

Stewart's character, L.B. Jeffries, is meant to represent Hitchcock himself: they note the similarities between the wheelchair and a director's chair, and the fact that Jeffries makes up histories for the people he spies on. But a better suggestion might be that *Rear Window* works well because the audience identifies so closely with the character. Like a member of the movie audience, Jeffries is seated in a chair, witnessing people and events that are removed from his own experience. In effect, he is an audience of one, identical to the audience in the theater—until reality invades his private world and very nearly kills him.

"We've become a race of Peeping Toms. People ought to get outside and look in at themselves."
—Thelma Ritter to James Stewart in *Rear Window.*

thirty-one apartments— twelve of which were completely furnished. The director later said that if he had tried to make the picture on location, it would have been impossible to light the various apartments properly.

Alfred Hitchcock always supervised every detail of his productions, and that extended to the film's promotional campaign. He personally wrote the advertising copy, which read, "If you do not experience delicious terror when you see *Rear Window,* then pinch yourself—you are most probably dead." Can't you just hear him saying that in his droll, deadpan voice?

Critics have speculated that

Rebecca

1940, Selznick International/United Artists
Produced by David O. Selznick
Directed by Alfred Hitchcock

S·Y·N·O·P·S·I·S

A new bride (Joan Fontaine) suspects that her husband (Laurence Olivier) still loves his first wife.

Academy Awards: Best Picture; George Barnes, Black and White Photography.

Academy Award nominations: Laurence Olivier, Best Actor; Joan Fontaine, Best Actress; Alfred Hitchcock, Best Director; Judith Anderson, Supporting Actress; Robert E. Sherwood, Screenplay; Lyle Wheeler, Art Direction; Hal C. Kern, Editing; Jack Cosgrove and Arthur Johns, Special Effects; Franz Waxman, Original Musical Score.

In June of 1939 Alfred Hitchcock came to America to direct *Rebecca* for David O. Selznick. Selznick was involved with making *Gone With the Wind* and didn't have time to supervise the first draft of the script. When he finally read it, he was absolutely horrified. He sent the director a lengthy memo which began, "It is my unfortunate and distressing task to tell you that I am shocked and disappointed beyond words by the treatment of *Rebecca* . . ." It got worse from there. Hitchcock had diverged from the original Daphne du Maurier novel, inventing a mad grandmother locked away in a tower and comic scenes depicting a woman's seasickness. Selznick demanded that Hitchcock scrap

the whole script and begin again, this time adhering to the book as closely as possible. Selznick also decided that Joan Fontaine's character should not have a first name. He thought it would add to Rebecca's presence if no one ever called the new Mrs. de Winter by her given name.

While Selznick was adamant that the book be followed as closely as possible, the censorship office forced him to change the ending. In the book Max de Winter murdered his first wife; in the movie she died accidentally, because the censorship office could not allow a murderer to go unpunished. Selznick sent a long apology to author Daphne du Maurier,

reminding her that he had been faithful to her creation in all other respects.

Once Selznick and Hitchcock had a working script, they needed a cast. Laurence Olivier, who was signed to play the male lead, wanted his fiancee, Vivien Leigh, as his leading lady. After several tests, Selznick decided she wasn't believable as the weak and shy young girl. Selznick considered many actresses, but it came down to Joan Fontaine and Anne Baxter. Most of Selznick's associates pushed for Anne Baxter, saying she was the better actress. Up to that time, Fontaine had only starred in mediocre "B" pictures and had a reputation for turning in wooden performances. Why did Selznick choose Fontaine? He said Baxter was "ten times more difficult to photograph than Fontaine, and I think it is a little harder to understand Max de Winter marrying her than Fontaine." In other words, Selznick didn't think

Anne Baxter was attractive enough for the part.

Joan Fontaine was on her honeymoon when she received word that Selznick had chosen her, and she was forced to return to Hollywood the next day. Cutting short her honeymoon with Brian Aherne wasn't much of a sacrifice. The night before the wedding he had told her he didn't want to marry her, and he only showed up at the church to keep from being humiliated by the press. Both parties were relieved when Joan returned to Hollywood.

One of the reasons Joan Fontaine was able to express tension and anxiety on the screen was that she was feeling those emotions on the set. Since Olivier had wanted Vivien Leigh to play the role, he kept Fontaine at a distance. When crew members arranged for an on-set birthday party for Fontaine's twenty-second birthday, Olivier and the other British cast members refused to attend. Hitchcock escalated this tension between them by telling Fontaine that Olivier hated her and that no one else in the cast thought she could handle the part.

Whatever Alfred Hitchcock's methods, he inspired a stellar cast to outstanding per-

formances, making *Rebecca* a masterpiece of romantic suspense.

Columnist Louella Parsons asked Joan Fontaine's mother to comment on her daughter's performance in *Rebecca*. "Joan has always seemed rather phony to me in real life," Fontaine's mother replied, "but she's quite believable on the screen." *Rebecca* was the only one of her daughter's movies she ever saw.

Scarface

1932, United Artists
Produced by Howard Hughes and Howard Hawks
Directed by Howard Hawks

S·Y·N·O·P·S·I·S

A Chicago gangster (Paul Muni) struggles for power in the 1920's.

Howard Hawks was teeing off at the Lakeside Country Club when the golf pro informed him that Howard Hughes wanted to join him for a round. Hawks's reply was concise: "Get lost." At the time, Hughes had filed suit against Hawks for a copyright infringement, and Hawks was in no mood to confront his courtroom enemy. The pro left but returned to say that Hughes would drop the suit if Hawks would agree to play one round of golf.

What Hawks didn't know was that Hughes had purchased the rights to *Scarface*, and felt that Howard Hawks was the only director in Hollywood who could do justice to the material. By the end of the eighteenth hole they had reached an agreement. Hughes would drop the suit and Hawks would direct *Scarface*.

Hawks went right to work, breaking down the script into film's visual imagery. He was a great storyteller and always looked for one image to further the story line. *Scarface* is a violent film in which many people are killed, so Hawks borrowed an image from the crime reporters of the day. Whenever the newspapers printed a photo from a murder or an accident, they put an "X" to mark the spot where the body was found. Hawks used X's throughout the film and even offered members of the crew a $100 bonus if he used one of their suggestions for placement of additional X's. In the opening credits Howard Hawks's name is printed over an X. When Boris Karloff is killed during the bowling match, the camera cuts to the scoresheet, where strikes were marked with X's. During the St. Valentine's Day massacre, the pattern on the grid above the bodies form X's, and one of the bodies has its arms crossed to form an X. Finally, George Raft lives in apartment ten, marked by the Roman numeral X.

Hawks's brilliance wasn't limited to visual imagery. He also knew how

PAUL MUNI

to get the most out of his actors, including an unknown actor named George Raft. Born and raised in Hell's Kitchen in New York, Raft became a prizefighter and a night club dancer. Ironically, he knew many of the top racketeers of the 1920s, men who bore a strong resemblance to the leading characters in *Scarface*. He arrived in Hollywood in the late twenties but didn't make much of a splash in his first few pictures. Howard Hawks hadn't seen Raft in a movie; nor did he find him at a casting call. The director noticed him in the audience at a boxing match and thought he looked exactly like the character of Guido Rinaldo. He approached Raft and asked him if he wanted the role. On the set, however, Raft was so nervous that he had trouble delivering his lines. He was particularly uncomfortable with his hands, so Hawks gave him a coin and told him to flip it throughout the

scene. Raft was so intent on the coin that his lines sounded casual and natural. The coin flip, which became a Hollywood symbol of the ultimate tough guy, was actually invented to soothe the nerves of a novice actor.

While *Scarface* is now considered a classic, many people weren't happy with it in 1932. Will Hays, who administered the then-voluntary Motion Picture Production Code, refused to give the film its seal of approval unless changes were made. Because the movie didn't state clearly enough that Crime Doesn't Pay, and since audiences couldn't be expected to figure it out on their own, Hays added an office scene in which a group of men deplore the violence of the mob.

Hays also objected to the ending. The way Hawks filmed it, Paul Muni was gunned down on the street, but the censor demanded that Muni's character be brought to justice and executed for his crimes. Filming had already been completed, however, and Paul Muni was not available for retakes, so Hawks filmed the new scenes with a stand-in. In the courtroom scene viewers saw the back of his head as he was pronounced guilty, and the execution scene showed only his feet. Because censorship is a local issue, different states chose to show different versions. In New Jersey audiences watched the original, while across the river in New York they saw the sanitized version. When Howard Hughes sued the New York Censor board and won the right to show the original unchanged film

in New York City, most states accepted the film the way Howard Hawks had ended it.

Director Howard Hawks made a cameo appearance in *Scarface* as "Man on Bed."

Shall We Dance

1937, RKO Radio
Produced by Pandro Berman
Directed by Mark Sandrich

S·Y·N·O·P·S·I·S

An American dancer (Fred Astaire), pretending to be a Russian ballet star, falls in love with an internationally known night club dancer (Ginger Rogers).

Academy Award nomination: George and Ira Gershwin, "They Can't Take That Away From Me," Best Song.

In the 1920s, if you had any hopes of being a performer or a musician, a composer or a writer, New York was the place to be. It was there that a young vaudeville hoofer became friends with a man who played the piano in shop windows to encourage customers to buy sheet music. When the dancer wasn't performing on stage with his sister, he and the piano player discussed their dreams. These dreams were compatible because the dancer wanted to star in musical comedies and the piano

player wanted to write them.

"Wouldn't it be great," the musician would say, "if we could someday work on the same musical together! I'll write it and you'll star in it." The piano player's name was George Gershwin, and the dancer was Fred Astaire. As you may have guessed, they both got their wishes.

While Fred Astaire and George Gershwin worked together on Broadway and later on films, *Shall We Dance* was the only Astaire/ Rogers musical for which George Gershwin and his brother Ira composed the entire score. It includes "Let's Call the Whole Thing Off," in which Fred and Ginger dance on roller skates, and "They Can't Take That Away From Me," which was nominated for an Oscar as the Best Song of 1937.

Shall We Dance was the seventh Fred Astaire/Ginger Rogers movie, and both performers thought it might be their last. They carefully monitored the box office receipts, wondering when the public would tire of the same formula in movie after movie. While 1937 found them still on the Top Ten Money Making list, they had slipped from third to seventh in just one year.

They had reason to be concerned. Reviewer Archer Winsten of *The New York Post* echoed many fans' thoughts when he wrote, "The only drawback, if anything of such proved popularity can be so considered, is the familiarity of the Astaire-Rogers act." To test audience reaction, Fred performed "They Can't Take That Away From Me" with Harriet Hoctor, while Ginger, clad in a daring costume that exposed her midriff, did a rumba with Pete Theodore.

Astaire, who was nervous about making films without Rogers, worried that reviews would accuse him of a "gingerless" performance. His fears proved groundless; Joan Fontaine was his dancing partner in his next movie.

While most performers relied on the counsel of a manager, an agent, or studio executives, Ginger Rogers consulted her mother, Lela Rogers, on important decisions. Lela wanted her to get away from all that singing and dancing and prove herself as a serious dramatic actress. Ginger broke away from her dancing partner by accepting a serious role in *Stage Door* with Katherine Hepburn. Rogers knew she had successfully overcome her image when she won an Oscar for her

work in *Kitty Foyle* in 1940.

Shall We Dance wasn't the last musical Fred Astaire and Ginger Rogers made together. The fact that it earned $413,000 proved to RKO that the old magic wasn't gone. While Fred and Ginger broadened their horizons over the next few years, they also made two more movies together: *Carefree* and *The Story of Vernon and Irene Castle*.

The hit song *They All Laughed* from *Shall We Dance* was inspired by a 1920's magazine ad headline for a correspondence school: "They all laughed when I sat down to play the piano."

She Wore a Yellow Ribbon

1949, Argosy Productions/RKO Radio
Produced by John Ford and Merian C. Cooper
Directed by John Ford

S·Y·N·O·P·S·I·S

A cavalry officer (John Wayne) who is about to retire thwarts an Indian massacre.

Academy Award: Winton Hoch, Color Cinematography.

he Wore a Yellow Ribbon has been called the most beautiful Western ever filmed, and that was ex- actly John Ford's intention. He used as his inspiration the paintings of Frederic Remington, those very realistic-looking portraits of a solitary cowboy or Indian mounted on a horse, often standing near a cliff. The horse has its head bowed against the wind, and a softly glowing sunset leaves the mountains awash in subtle reds and oranges. These are the images Ford painted into the film.

He made the picture at his favorite location: Monument Valley, which spans the border of Arizona and Utah. He was so intimately aware of every vista in the valley that he breezed through the picture, shooting at the incredible pace of eight to ten script pages per day and finishing nearly $500,000 under budget. Ford praised the work of cinematographer Winton C. Hoch for capturing the glow of the campfire and the aura of the sun and moon. The rest of the movie industry also recognized Hoch's contribution by awarding him one of his three Oscars for Cinematography. As a former chemist, however, Hoch was often more concerned with technical standards than with art. One of his battles with Ford almost kept one of the most memorable scenes in *She Wore a Yellow Ribbon* from being shot.

They were filming a line of cavalry when a nasty storm blew in. Ford wanted to take ad-

vantage of the thick black clouds, but Hoch argued that there wasn't enough light to make the proper exposure. Ford was furious, because, while they were arguing, the clouds could disappear at any moment. Hock finally rolled the camera, but he filed an official protest with the American Society of Cinematographers, claiming the scene wasn't acceptable to him. When they processed the film, the shot was beautiful, and Ford kept it.

Ford was master on the set and in the edit room, and no one forced him to include anything he didn't want. In *She Wore a Yellow Ribbon*, his screenwriters tried to talk him into using a shot of gunslingers riding through town. To end the argument, he shot it and used it in the movie, but not the way the writers envisioned. He used it in the credits, putting the names of the writers directly over the horses' rears.

One of the most memorable scenes in *She Wore a Yellow Ribbon* is the one in which John Wayne talks to his dead wife. Early in his career Ford had said to him, "Duke, you're going to get a lot of scenes during your life. They're going to seem corny to you . . . Play 'em. Play 'em to the hilt . . . You'll get by with it, but if you start trying to play it with your tongue in your cheek and getting cute, you'll lose sight of yourself and the scene will be lost." Wayne took that advice, and during the graveyard scene there wasn't a dry eye in the house.

She Wore a Yellow Ribbon was the first film in which John Wayne played an old man, a tough, efficient cavalry captain who can follow orders as well as give them. The scene in which he accepts a silver watch from his men is one of his very best. Wayne was nervous about making the scene too maudlin, so Ford suggested he take out a pair of glasses and struggle to read the inscription. The bit of business was exactly what the scene needed, and the break in Wayne's voice as he reads "Lest We Forget" was real and touching.

Wayne was disappointed when his performance wasn't nominated for an Oscar. He said, "I had played a man sixty years old, which was seventeen years older than I was at the time. I have always believed this was my best achievement in pictures."

"So here they are, the dog-faced soldiers, the regulars, the fifty-cents-a-day professionals, riding the outposts of a nation. From Fort Reno to Fort Apache, from Sheridan to Stark, they were all the same. Men in dirty shirt blue, and only a cold page in the history books to mark their passing. But wherever they rode, and whatever they fought for, that place became the United States."

—Close of *She Wore a Yellow Ribbon.*

Since You Went Away

1944, Selznick International/United Artists
Produced by David O. Selznick
Directed by John Cromwell

I n 1943 DavidO. Selznick wanted to get into World War II, but he was classified 4-F and the draft board didn't want him. He decided that he could make his contribution to the war effort by producing the definitive war movie, so he assigned his staff to submit stories for his consideration. For nine months the staff evaluated more than 1,800 stories, 270 of which were condensed and sent to Selznick. He rejected every one of them.

He finally found a magazine serial that consisted of letters from a wife to her husband, who was fighting in Europe. Selznick liked the idea of a story about the Home Front so much, he wrote the screenplay himself. In the credits he was billed as Jeffrey Daniel, the first names of his two sons.

Selznick needed all of his talents as a salesman and amateur psychologist to cast the picture. First he stunned Hollywood when he coaxed sixteen-year old Shirley Temple out of her two-year retirement. Then he went after Claudette Colbert, even though he knew she would never agree to play the mother of two teenaged girls. He resorted to psychology and told Hedda Hopper that he wanted Colbert for the role but didn't think she could do it. Hopper called Colbert and told the actress it was one of the best roles she would ever play. The $150,000 Selznick offered Colbert was also a powerful inducement.

He also talked Jennifer Jones into playing Jane, despite the fact that her estranged husband, Robert Walker, was cast as Jane's sweetheart. Add the fact that Jones and Selznick were just beginning their romantic involvement and you have an idea how strained relations were on the set.

This movie was extremely difficult to make: it contained hundreds of short scenes and involved 200 speaking parts and more than 5,000 extras. Wartime restrictions made it difficult to get the proper furniture and props to decorate the set, so much of the furniture in the Hilton house came from Selznick's own home.

When they filmed the big dance scene at the Chamberlain field hangar, Selznick refused to use the usual studio extras. He wanted people who looked like "decent high school kids in the middle west, not like a lot of peroxided extras." Since real kids look a lot like real kids, he brought in 700 college students from around the Los Angeles area.

Selznick also wanted a real sailor for the part of Harold Smith, so he sent his staff out to find one. U.S. Navy sailor Robert Mosley was sitting in the audience at a Lux radio presentation when one of Selznick's staff spotted him. Selznick liked Mosley, signed him to a contract, and changed his name to Guy Madison, which he came up with while looking out his window at a Dolly Madison cake wagon. After the war Guy Madison starred in many "B" movies, and eventually gained fame as television's Wild Bill Hickock.

Claudette Colbert's husband in *Since You Went Away* is seen only in a photograph. Neil Hamilton, who posed for the picture, later played Commissioner Gordon on television's *Batman*.

P·L·A·Y·E·R·S

Claudette Colbert .... Anne Hilton
Jennifer Jones .... Jane Hilton
Joseph Cotten .... Lt. Tony Willett
Shirley Temple
.... Bridget "Brig" Hilton

Featuring:
Monty Woolley
Lionel Barrymore
Robert Walker
Hattie McDaniel
Agnes Moorehead
Nazimova
Albert Basserman
Gordon Oliver
Keenan Wynn
Guy Madison
Craig Stevens
Lloyd Corrigan
Jackie Moran
Jane Devlin
George Chandler
Florence Bates
Irving Bacon
Addison Richards
Barbara Pepper
Adeline de Walt Reynolds
Ann Gillis
Dorothy Garner
Andrew McLaglen
Helen Koford
Robert Johnson
Dorothy Dandridge
Johnny Bond
Bryon Foulger
Edwin Maxwell
Doodles Weaver
Warren Hymer
Jonathan Hale
Ruth Roman
Grady Sutton
Rhonda Fleming
Neil Hamilton

Singin' in the Rain

1952, MGM
Produced by Arthur Freed
Directed by Stanley Donen & Gene Kelly

S·Y·N·O·P·S·I·S

In the transition from silent films to talkies, a young actress (Debbie Reynolds) dubs the voice of an established star (Jean Hagen).

Academy Award nominations: Jean Hagen, Supporting Actress; Lennie Hayton, Scoring of Musical.

It was five p.m. on a warm summer day on the MGM back lot, where an entire production crew was puzzled. They were set up to rehearse the title song for *Singin' in the Rain*, with black tarpaulin covering the entire exterior street, turning the day into night. When they turned on the valves controlling the rain, they got more of a drizzle than a downpour. With the help of the local water department, technicians finally tracked down the problem. As residents of Culver City came home from work, they turned on their sprinklers, causing a substantial drop in the water pressure. If the studio wanted a deluge, they would have to wait until morning.

While the movie was made in 1952, the story behind *Singin' in the Rain* actually began in the late 1920s when an ex-Tin Pan Alley composer named Arthur Freed produced *The Broadway Melody*, the first all-talking, all-singing film musical. The transition from silents to talkies were crazy days in Hollywood, with vocal coaches trying desperately to help silent stars overcome nasal voices or insidious regional accents and retain their movie careers.

Three decades later, Freed hired Betty Comden and Adolph Green to write a musical based on many of the songs he had written in that era, including "Singin' in the Rain." Comden and Green remembered the fate of John Gilbert, whose weak voice and inability to adjust to the understated acting of the talkies ended his career. Instead of adapting the songs for a contemporary plot, they decided to showcase that tumultuous period in Hollywood history.

Older studio employees were interviewed for their recollections about the transition between silent and sound. When technicians remembered the problems they faced finding places to hide microphones, Comden and Green wrote it into the script. Designers researched the equipment of the era, and lights and cameras were dragged out of storage and dusted off to be used in one more motion picture. Microphones were copied from museums, and a glass sound stage, which had been used for decades as a storeroom, was emptied and became a working sound stage once again. Instead of creating new set decorations, designers used the furniture, rugs, and chandeliers from the Greta Garbo/John Gilbert silent,

Flesh and the Devil. Andy Hardy's old jalopy was tuned up and given to Debbie Reynolds.

Before a single frame was shot, the Breen office became involved, reminding Freed that none of the showgirls who changed their clothes could be seen in their underwear. Part of the memo sent to Freed read, "Page 65: Don's line, 'What are you doing later?' approaches the element of sex perversion and we ask that it be eliminated." Don's speech was changed, once again saving the American public from a salacious thought.

Singin' in the Rain was a milestone for Debbie Reynolds, a Miss Burbank of 1948 who had played only a few bit parts and had no dancing experience. One of her key scenes was dubbing Jean Hagen's voice, which in the film was weak and squeaky. For Hagen's singing voice, Reynolds' voice was actually supplied by professional singer Betty Noyes. Hagen's *speaking* voice in this scene was supposed to sound cultured, and Reynold's Midwestern

twang wasn't up to it. Ironically, Jean Hagen dubbed the voice for Debbie Reynolds when Reynolds was on screen dubbing Hagen's.

After filming was completed, the studio held the traditional cast party, but with a twist. The party was held on stage 28, which was rigged for its own rain shower. As guests approached the party, they were given umbrellas and entered, appropriately, through the rain.

Careful choreography and photography in the ballet sequence hid the fact that Cyd Charisse was taller than Gene Kelly.

Sister Kenny

1946, RKO Radio
Produced and Directed by Dudley Nichols

Before anyone gets the wrong idea, Rosalind Russell does not play a nun in this picture! The word "sister" was an honorary title given to nurses in England or Australia. If Elizabeth Kenny had been an American, the movie probably would have been called *Nurse Kenny*.

There wouldn't have been a picture called *Sister Kenny* if it hadn't been for Rosalind Russell's father. He taught his children that no matter how busy they were, it was important to devote a certain amount of time to charity. Rosalind Russell believed he was right, and she joined the Los Angeles branch of The League for Crippled Children. While working for that organization, she heard a lot about Elizabeth Kenny, an Australian nurse who had some revolutionary theories about treatment for young polio victims. When Sister Kenny came to Los Angeles, Russell volunteered to let the Australian stay at her house, and Rosalind Russell and Elizabeth Kenny became friends. Whenever possible, the actress accompanied the nurse on her travels, and once she helped her fight a polio outbreak in Minneapolis.

Russell became almost obsessed with the idea of making a movie about this woman's life. She felt it was important that audiences see not only Kenny's dedication but also how much of a difference one woman can make. She approached all of the studios time and again, but all rejected the idea. For six years she was relentless. Then, in 1946, RKO approached her about doing three pictures for them. She made a deal . . . she would do the three pictures as long as one of them was *Sister Kenny*.

The script was based on Kenny's autobiography, *And They Shall Walk*, written in collaboration with Martha Ostenso. Dudley Nichols not only served as screenwriter, but he also produced and directed the film.

Because Russell knew her subject so well, this is probably the most accurate Hollywood biography ever made, although there was one major inaccuracy. Russell was the first to admit that she and the good sister bore absolutely no physical resemblance to one another. She laughingly repeated a journalist's contention that Sister Kenny most closely resembled an M4 tank, but went on to say, "Her eyes were the loneliest and loveliest I've ever looked into." Maybe she wasn't as far removed from the nurse as she thought. *New York Times* critic Bosley Crowther said that Rosalind Russell in her makeup at the end of *Sister Kenny* looked like a cross between George Washington and Ethel Barrymore.

Russell was not the kind of woman to blow her own horn, so most of Hollywood was unaware of her long-standing relationship with Elizabeth Kenny. Russell was very hurt when her good friend, Hedda Hopper, alleged that Russell accepted the role to benefit from the nurse's image and the publicity surrounding her good works. Later Hopper found out about the long friendship between the two women and sent a friend over to Russell's house to apologize. Russell was still upset and didn't know what to say. Hopper finally did what she should have done in the first place. She visited Russell's home and apologized in person.

Rosalind Russell received an Oscar nomination for her portrayal of Elizabeth Kenny. While she didn't win the top award, she won the Golden Globe from the Hollywood Foreign Press Association, the

Blue Ribbon Award from Box Office Magazine, a medal of merit from Parents Magazine, and the New York Foreign Press Circle Award. Although this film doesn't often appear on film critics' lists of top movies, Russell's extraordinary dedication to the story makes *Sister Kenny* an inspiring movie that can be viewed over and over again.

At five feet five inches, Rosalind Russell was considered exceptionally tall for a leading lady.

The Snake Pit

1948, 20th Century-Fox
Produced by Anatole Litvak and Robert Bassler
Directed by Anatole Litvak

S·Y·N·O·P·S·I·S

A young, mentally disturbed woman (Olivia de Havilland) works with a psychiatrist (Leo Genn) to come to terms with her past.

Academy Award: Twentieth Century Fox Sound Department, Sound Recording.

Academy Award nominations: Best Picture; Olivia de Havilland, Best Actress; Anatole Litvak, Best Director; Frank Partos and Millen Brand, Screenplay; Alfred Newman, Score.

In 1948, neighbors of Olivia de Havilland were concerned. They kept hearing the most blood-curdling screams emanating from her house. What was even more puzzling was that while all this screaming was going on, de Havilland's husband, Marcus Goodrich, was sitting calmly on the patio as if nothing were wrong.

Nothing *was* wrong. Olivia de Havilland was merely practicing for her latest role, that of a victim of mental illness in *The Snake Pit*.

The story behind the picture began in the latter days of World War II, when director Anatole Litvak was making films for the war department. He read some galley proofs for a new book by Mary Jane Ward and was so impressed with the story, written by a woman who had actually been a patient, that he contacted her and offered her $75,000 for the motion picture rights. The problem was that he didn't have $75,000. Although she accepted the fee in installments, he almost went bankrupt paying them, because he wasn't making much money working for the war department.

After the war he went to the various studio bosses, trying to sell them the story. None of them wanted it. Nobody had ever made a film about mental illness, so how could they know whether people would go and see it? Besides, at that time entertainment films were making it big, and no one wanted to touch a social issue. Finally, Litvak convinced his friend Darryl Zanuck to take a chance. Zanuck paid Litvak $175,000 for the rights to *The Snake Pit*, giving the director a $100,000 profit before a single frame was shot. Litvak then directed and co-produced the picture, which was critically acclaimed by psychiatrists as well as movie critics for dispelling some of the myths about mental illness.

Anatole Litvak and the entire cast worked hard to give an accurate portrayal of life in a mental institution. They visited many hospitals and even recorded the cries and muttering of the patients. When the superintendent of nurses at one of the institutions visited the set, she said, "Why, they look just like my own girls." Part of that realism was dictated by the director, who banned hairdressers from the set and eliminated bras and girdles from the costumes.

Anatole Litvak originally wanted Ingrid Bergman for the leading role, but she wasn't interested. Olivia de Havilland was. She even lost fourteen pounds before filming because she thought she looked too healthy to play Virginia Cunningham.

When Celeste Holm found out that Fox was making this picture, she asked to be in it. She wanted to be associated with pictures that didn't merely entertain but changed people's lives, or at least influenced their opinions. This picture was part of her lifelong interest in helping those who are mentally ill. Many years later she was named the honorary head of the National Association for Mental Health and for the Creative Arts Rehabilitation Center for people with emotional and mental problems.

P·L·A·Y·E·R·S

Olivia de Havilland .... Virginia Stuart Cunningham
Mark Stevens .. Robert Cunningham
Leo Genn .... Dr. Mark Kik
Celeste Holm .... Grace
Featuring:
    Glenn Langan
    Helen Craig
    Leif Erikson
    Beulah Bondi
    Lee Patrick
    Isabel Jewell
    Victoria Horne
    Tamara Shayne
    Howard Freeman
    Natalie Schafer
    Ruth Donnelly
    Katherine Locke
    Frank Conroy
    Minna Gombell
    June Storey
    Ann Doran
    Damian O'Flynn
    Lora Lee Michel
    Esther Somers
    Jacqueline de Wit
    Betsy Blair
    Lela Bliss
    Virginia Brissac
    Queenie Smith
    Mae Marsh
    Jan Clayton
    Helen Servis
    Celia Lovsky
    Lester Sharpe
    Mary Treen
    Victoria Albright
    Dorothy Neumann

As a result of the abuses brought to the public's attention by *The Snake Pit*, many states reformed laws covering psychiatric hospitals.

Spellbound

1945, Selznick International-Vanguard Films/United Artists
Produced by David O. Selznick
Directed by Alfred Hitchcock

S·Y·N·O·P·S·I·S

A psychiatrist (Ingrid Bergman) in a fashionable sanatorium falls in love with a colleague (Gregory Peck), then learns he has amnesia.

Academy Award: Miklos Rozsa, Scoring of a Dramatic or Comedy Picture.

Academy Award nominations: Best Picture; Alfred Hitchcock, Best Director; Michael Chekov, Supporting Actor; George Barnes, Black and White Cinematography; Jack Cosgrove, Special Effects.

W hen film people become interested in a subject, they'll find a way to make a movie about it. In the mid-forties there were so many producers, directors, and writers undergoing psychoanalysis, it was inevitable that, sooner or later, someone would incorporate therapy as an element in a suspense thriller.

Alfred Hitchcock was trying to interest David O. Selznick in

The House of Dr. Edwardes, a novel about a cult of devil worshipers. Selznick wasn't impressed, but he had a contract to make a picture with Hitchcock, so he hired Ben Hecht to write the screenplay. Hecht, who was undergo-

ing psychoanalysis at the time, wanted to turn it into a murder mystery that drew heavily upon new theories about the subconscious. Since Selznick was also undergoing therapy at the time, he loved the idea of a film rooted in psychological theory.

Any movie dealing with the subconscious must include a dream sequence. At that time, most filmmakers used the same techniques to convey the idea of a dream: soft focus, a little swirling smoke, and Vaseline around the edge of the camera lens to give the scene a floating feeling.

Hitchcock wanted to do something radically different.

To create Gregory Peck's nightmare, he hired surrealist artist Salvador Dali, who submitted black and white sketches, five of which were chosen for the picture. Dali was then paid $5,000 to make full-sized oil paintings from the sketches. That dream sequence almost became Selznick's private nightmare. Technicians told him that translating Dali's sketches into full-sized sets would cost more than $150,000, which would put the picture well over budget. Since Selznick's own company was making the film, he was personally responsible for cost overruns.

Hitchcock intervened, showing Selznick how Dali's images could be created using miniatures and models for a more reasonable $20,000. Selznick agreed, but reminded the director he had $1.2 million for *Spellbound* and not a penny more.

Hitchcock came up with some unusual methods of achieving special effects in this film. Near the end of the picture there's a dramatic shot in which the audience

sees a gun from the point of view of the man who's holding it. Hitchcock wanted a shot with the gun in the foreground and Ingrid Bergman in the background. Technically, this seemed impossible: the camera lens could focus either on the gun or on Ingrid Bergman, but not on both. Hitchcock could keep both in focus by bringing Bergman much closer to the gun, but the closer she came, the larger she would appear, and that wasn't the visual effect he was looking for. He wanted her to be dwarfed by the gun in the foreground.

His solution was brilliant. Prop people built a huge gun as well as the hand holding it, which two technicians moved on a special dolly. Although the gun almost fills the foreground, the viewer perceives the gun as normal-sized and Bergman as far off in the background.

While the shot of the gun impressed Hollywood insiders, it was the gunshot itself that awed the fans. While *Spellbound* was filmed entirely in black and white, the gunshot momentarily turned the screen blood red. To achieve the effect, film technicians hand-painted four frames of each release print. After two hours of watching black and white images in a darkened theater, the explosion of color had a spectacular subliminal effect on audiences.

Hitchcock not

only stayed within his budget, he also worked so efficiently that he finished a week ahead of schedule. Selznick was impressed and issued one of his famous memos, praising Hitchcock and the crew for their efficiency and professionalism.

Of the twenty nominations for the 1945 Oscar for Best Musical Scoring of a Dramatic or Comedy Picture, Miklos Rozsa received three. When he won for *Spellbound*, he became one of the few people in Hollywood history to beat himself out for an Academy Award.

Springtime in the Rockies

1942, Twentieth Century Fox
Produced by William LeBaron
Directed by Irving Cummings

S·Y·N·O·P·S·I·S

A broadway team (Betty Grable and John Payne) take on other partners (Cesar Romero and Carmen Miranda) to make each other jealous.

During World War II everyone had to cut back, even the people in Hollywood. The studios cut back on the materials they used for sets, the stars cut back on limo rides, and Carmen Miranda cut back on the amount of sugar she put in her coffee. Of the three, it was probably Carmen Miranda's sacrifice that contributed the most to the war effort. Before sugar rationing went into effect, the Brazilian entertainer was accustomed to drinking a beverage consisting of half a cup of coffee mixed with half a cup of sugar. While filming *Springtime in the Rockies*, her co-workers kidded her about the incredible sacrifice she was making. Throughout the war years Miss Miranda subsisted on coffee with just one lump of sugar. Her closely guarded secret, however, was that each cup of coffee consisted of half coffee and half honey!

A not-so-closely guarded secret was her unusual command of the English language. Her odd accent wasn't surprising, considering the fact that one of her teachers had spoken English with an Italian accent. When she stepped onto the set of *Springtime in the Rockies*, her English was more unusual than ever. She had spent three months with her mother,

speaking nothing but Portuguese. "It is very difficult to explain what happen to my English," she said. "All those nice English words, they leave me."

While English words left Carmen Miranda, it was extra calories that left Betty Grable. Grable was not only a talented actress, singer, and dancer, she also had the most enviable talent of all. For those of you who are trying to lose a few pounds (and who isn't?), let me tell you about Betty Grable's dieting habits. During her years as a number-one box office attraction, she rarely dieted and regularly ate ice cream and rich desserts. One day on the set of *Springtime in the Rockies*, she polished off not one, not two, not three, but four hot fudge sundaes. No matter what she ate, her weight stayed between 112 and 117. Now there's a talent we'd all love to have!

Betty Grable never forgot working on *Springtime in the Rockies*, because while she was falling in love with John Payne on screen, she was falling in love with Harry James off screen.

James and his band were at the height of their popularity. In a network radio poll, his group was named the number-one jive orchestra in the country. In those days popular musicians didn't have the advantages of appearing on MTV, so getting cast in a motion picture was important exposure. Before *Springtime in the Rockies* came out, he received four to six thousand pieces of fan mail every week. After its release, the number jumped to nine thousand. James had to employ three people full time just to answer his mail.

The song "I Had the Craziest Dream," which was written for the movie, became the theme song for Harry James and his Music Makers. In addition to gaining a song, he also gained a wife. A year after appearing in *Springtime in the Rockies*, he and Betty Grable began their twenty-one-year marriage.

Despite her charmed Hollywood life, Betty Grable died relatively young. She was just fifty-six years old when she succumbed to lung cancer in 1973. Throughout her long illness, her doctors and nurses said she never lost the sunny, optimistic disposition she was famous for.

P·L·A·Y·E·R·S

Betty Grable .... Vicky
John Payne .... Dan
Carmen Miranda .... Rosita
Cesar Romero .... Victor
Featuring:
    Bando da Lua
    Harry James and his
        Music Makers
    Charlotte Greenwood
    Edward Everett Horton
    Frank Orth
    Harry Hayden
    Jackie Gleason
    Trudy Marshall
    Roseanne Murray
    Billy Wayne
    Chick Chandler
    Patrick O'Moore
    Anthony Marsh
    Iron Eyes Cody
    J.W. Cody
    Bill Hazlitt
    Claire James
    Dick Elliott
    Bess Flowers

Jackie Gleason was given a small part in *Springtime in the Rockies*, but he didn't impress studio executives, and his contract was dropped. Gleason didn't become a household name until he went into television in the fifties.

Stagecoach

1939, Walter Wanger Production/United Artists
Produced by John Ford and Walter Wanger
Directed by John Ford

S·Y·N·O·P·S·I·S

Passengers on a cross-country stage face many adventures, including an Indian attack.

Academy Awards: Thomas Mitchell, Supporting Actor; Richard Hageman, Franke Harling, John Leipold, Leo Shuken, Score.

Academy Award nominations: Best Picture; John Ford, Best Director; Bert Glennon, Black and White Cinematography; Alexander Toluboff, Interior Decoration; Otho Lovering and Dorothy Spencer, Editing.

Nobody wanted to do the picture that John Ford wanted to make. One by one, every major studio turned down the chance to produce a film based on the Ernest Haycox story, "Stage to Lordsburg." Ford did interest Selznick International vice president Merian C. Cooper in the project, enough to get him to sign Ford to a two-picture deal. But Selznick read the story and balked. He wanted Ford and Cooper to make a classic, not just another Western, and he would only agree to make the picture if it starred Gary Cooper and Marlene Dietrich. Merian Cooper was so incensed at Selznick's decision that he quit, forfeiting $65,000 the company owed him.

Producer Walter Wanger of United Artists was coming off a series of pictures that had been financial failures. He agreed to fund the picture, but for a mere $392,000, much less than most

pictures of the heavy technical demands of *Stagecoach.*

To meet the reduced budget, Ford cut his own fee in half to $50,000. Under the restrictive budget he had only $65,000 for all actor's salaries, making it impossible to get a big-name star. Instead, he cast a man he'd known for ten years, a man who had worked on his earlier films, first as a prop man and later as a stunt man and bit player, a man who had been starring in Grade "B" Westerns made in eight days. He cast John Wayne.

They shot in Monument Valley, Ford's first film in the location he made a legend. There are four stories about Ford's discovery of the valley. Take your pick. One: Harry Carey was driving through the desert in the late twenties, found the valley, and told Ford about it. Two: John Wayne stumbled on it and told Ford about the magnificent location while working for him as a prop man. Three: John Ford found it himself. Four: Harry Goulding, who ran a nearby trading post, traveled to Hollywood with photographs of the valley, trying to interest production managers in filming there. While this last story may not be true, it is true that the money John Ford

pumped into the drought stricken area was welcomed by both the owner of the trading post and the impoverished valley residents. Local Navajo Indians made Ford an honorary chief, dubbing him Natani Nez, or Tall Soldier.

Stagecoach is also memorable for the incredible stunts performed and directed by Yakima Canutt. The script called for him to jump onto one of the horses pulling the coach, then to be shot by John Wayne. The script didn't say how he should fall, and John Ford left that up to him. The director just checked with the stuntman to make sure he was ready, then sent the three cameras to cover the action from various angles. Ford couldn't believe what happened next. Canutt made the jump from his horse to the team pulling the coach. John Wayne shot him and he fell between horses, holding on to the tongue, the piece of wood the harnesses are attached to. Then, traveling at forty-five miles an hour, he let go, allowing the galloping horses and the coach to pass over him. If the horses hadn't run perfectly straight in harness, he would have been trampled. When it was finished, Canutt

asked Ford if he wanted another take. Ford said he would never allow Canutt to do it again.

How did the public react to what Selznick called, "Just another Western?" John Wayne was present at the preview in Westwood, when the audience clapped and cheered wildly, giving *Stagecoach* a standing ovation. The picture nobody wanted was a hit.

When Thomas Mitchell received his Oscar as Best Supporting Actor for his performance in *Stagecoach*, he confessed that he didn't have a speech prepared because "I didn't think I was that good."

Stanley and Livingstone

1939, 20th Century-Fox
Produced by Darryl F. Zanuck
Directed by Henry King

S·Y·N·O·P·S·I·S

When a reporter (Spencer Tracy) finds a missing Scottish missionary (Sir Cedric Hardwicke), the Royal Geological Society brands him a liar.

In 1938, Louis B. Mayer was planning to make a picture called *Marie Antoinette*. He wanted Tyrone Power to star opposite Norma Shearer, but Darryl Zanuck owned Power's contract, so Mayer offered him a deal. In exchange for Tyrone Power's services, Mayer gave Zanuck Spencer Tracy to use in *Stanley and Livingstone*. Tracy was pleased with the deal for two reasons. First, he had read through Henry Stanley's journals and was eager to play the part. Second, the commitment would release him from a fiasco he was working on with newcomer Hedy Lamar. It was called *I Take This Woman*, but they had gone through so many directors and scripts that insiders had jokingly called it *I Re-Take This Woman*. The demands of the *Stanley and Livingstone* schedule meant he could leave that project, at least for a while.

Even before this picture was made, the phrase "Doctor Livingstone, I presume?" was legend, so one of the trickiest problems for the scriptwriters and for the star was how to deal with the meeting between Stanley and Livingstone. Every time Tracy said, "Dr. Livingstone, I presume?" he would crack up. They made take after take, but Tracy couldn't deliver the line. Finally, the writers gave him a 640-word speech, which he delivered in one continuous take. Tracy's performance was so strong that insiders were sure he was well on his way to winning his third consecutive Academy Award. When he wasn't even nominated, many Academy members said they hadn't voted for him because exceptional performances were *expected* of Spencer Tracy.

Tracy's outstanding performance in this film is supported by some of the best character actors in the business, including Walter Brennan, Henry Hull, Charles Coburn, Henry Travers, and Sir Cedric Hardwicke.

The life of the real Henry M. Stanley was filled with adventure. He was born in Wales but managed to spend the Civil War in the United States, where he served in the Confederate Army. After being captured at the battle of Shilo, he volunteered to fight for the Union, and served in the fledgling U.S. Navy. After the war, his job as a reporter for the New York Herald took him to Magdala with the British Army. In 1869 the paper asked him to find Dr. Livingstone, which resulted in his successful two-year search. According to the movie version, he returned to Africa after finding the doctor to carry out Livingstone's missionary work. That was fiction. Stanley continued to work as a reporter and made three more visits to Africa, where he explored many of the continent's uncharted regions.

Dr. David Livingstone was a Scottish physician and missionary who devoted his life to the exploration of Africa. He was the first European to see Victoria Falls, and personally charted the upper reaches of the Congo. He was in failing health when he crossed the Southwestern shore of Lake Tanganyika, and died in a small African village in May of 1873. His faithful followers carried his body to the coast and shipped him back to England. He was buried in Westminster Abbey

in April of the following year.

While the story of journalist Henry M. Stanley's search for Dr. David Livingstone was based on fact, Hollywood took a few liberties. The rivalry between Stanley and the character played by Richard Greene was entirely the product of a screenwriter's imagination. Although stock footage shot in Africa adds to the ambiance, Spencer Tracy and the rest of the cast never left the studio lot.

P·L·A·Y·E·R·S

Spencer Tracy ...... Henry M. Stanley
Nancy Kelly .... Eve Kingsley
Richard Greene .... Gareth Tyce
Walter Brennan .... Jeff Slocum
Featuring:
  Charles Coburn
  Sir Cedric Hardwicke
  Henry Hull
  Henry Travers
  Miles Mander
  David Torrence
  Holmes Herbert
  Montague Shaw
  Paul Stanton
  Brandon Hurst
  Hassan Said
  Paul Harvey
  Russell Hicks
  Clarence Derwent
  Joseph Crehan
  Robert Middlemass
  Ernest Baskett
  Everett Brown
  Frank Orth

"Just know your lines and don't bump into the furniture."
—Spencer Tracy on acting.

A Star Is Born

1937, Selznick International/United Artists
Produced by David O. Selznick
Directed by William Wellman

Ideally, making a movie should be a logical, controlled process, where decisions are made after intense thought and careful planning. In reality the process is often chaotic, and sometimes depends as much on external influences as on any unified vision. In 1937, David Selznick was immersed in making *A Star Is Born*. In those days there were only five Tech-nicolor cameras in Hollywood, so a producer had to arrange for their rental well in advance and commit himself to a specific filming schedule. When the cameras were available, you shot the picture, whether you were ready or not. When the cameras were ready to begin filming *A Star is Born*, Selznick and director William Wellman weren't. They began filming before the script was finished, without knowing how the picture would end.

Selznick was still writing additional scenes when Wellman gave his boss the bad news. Three-quarters of the way through the shooting schedule, the movie was already twenty minutes too long. And they still had a quarter of the picture plus the ending to shoot! Selznick immediately stopped writing and shifted his attention to finding scenes he could cut. He decided that Esther Blodgett's grandmother should be the first to go. But Wellman said the scenes with the grandmother showed the source of Esther's strength. Selznick agreed, and instead of eliminating the grandmother he trimmed several of the behind-the-scenes activities, a montage of Vicki Lester's successes, and a honeymoon sequence.

Even after the picture was edited, it still wasn't finished. Selznick tried the first version of *A Star Is Born* on a preview audience in Pomona, California. They liked it, but they didn't love it, and Selznick knew why. The ending just wasn't there. The original ending called for Janet Gaynor to notice Norman's footprints in the cement. Her eyes well up with tears, and as she stares off into space, the music comes to a romantic closing crescendo. They almost had it, but it needed something more. That something was added by John Lee Mahin, who was borrowed from MGM to do the rewrites. He added just one line, but it's one of the most important lines in the picture. In fact, it became one of the most famous lines in

the history of film. Janet Gaynor sees the footprints, walks up to the microphone and says, "Hello everybody, this is Mrs. Norman Maine." Its hard to imagine the picture without that wonderful closing line. Selznick and Wellman immediately knew it was the perfect ending, and so did everyone else.

A Star is Born was nominated for six Academy Awards, but won only for Best Original Story. Hollywood legend says that as William Wellman came down off the stage after accepting the award, he walked over to David Selznick's table and said, "Here. You deserve this. You wrote more of this than I did." Over the years, both men have claimed that *A Star is Born* was their own creation. In reality the story was a combination of three things: *What Price Hollywood?*, an earlier version of the story Selznick produced in 1932; the real-life

suicide of former silent star John Bowers; and several incidents from Wellman's life.

Future stars Carole Landis and Lana Turner were two of the extras in the scene at the bar at Santa Anita.

State Fair

1945, 20th Century-Fox
Produced by William Perlberg
Directed by Walter Lang

S·Y·N·O·P·S·I·S

The excitement builds in an Iowa farming community when its residents prepare for the state fair.

Academy Award: Richard Rodgers and Oscar Hammerstein, Best Song, "It Might As Well Be Spring."

Academy Award nomination: Charles Henderson and Alfred Newman, Score for a Musical.

Whenever there's a huge success on Broadway, you can be sure someone on the other coast wants to capitalize on it. In 1943 the Rodgers and Hammerstein musical *Oklahoma!* was breaking all records at the box office. 20th Century-Fox went to work to find a property with an *Oklahoma!* feel that would have a similar appeal. They had only to look as far as their own archives. In 1933 Fox had made a non-musical called *State Fair*, starring Will Rogers, Louise Dresser, Janet Gaynor, and Norman Foster based on a best-selling novel by Phil Stong. A musical remake of *State Fair* proved to be exactly what the studio was looking for.

For the starring role of Margy Frake, Fox chose its up-and-coming young starlet, Jeanne Crain. While Crain's biggest number in the picture also won an Oscar as Best Song, Crain had little to do with the song's success. The voice on the sound track was that of Louanne Hogan. Jeanne Crain's success in *State Fair* inspired the studio to raise her salary to $1,000 per week and to cast her in many more musicals, all of which were dubbed by professional singers.

Crain was twenty years old when she made *State Fair*; her costar Dana Andrews was thirty-six. While Crain didn't have a strong enough singing voice to carry her role, Andrews, who was a classically trained baritone, could have handled his own singing duties. The studio didn't seem to agree, however; it paid a professional singer $150 to do the job. Andrews wasn't upset. He said, "I could have saved the studio some money and sung the tune a lot better, but I kept my mouth shut. I don't like what happens to singers in Hollywood." He was allowed to join in for the chorus of "It's A Grand Night for Singing."

Third billing went to Dick

Haymes, who was better known for singing than for acting. Andrews' observation about singers may have been correct. Although Haymes was one of the top recording stars of the forties, his movie work never made an impression on studio executives. Immigration problems and financial difficulties brought on by five divorces may also have contributed to his lack of success.

Rounding out the cast in *State Fair* are a few of Hollywood's top character actors. Charles Winninger's portrayal of the father is considered the highlight of his career, which began before the turn of the century in his family's vaudeville act. Playing his wife was the always-motherly Fay Bainter, whose double Oscar nominations in 1938 as Best Actress and Best Supporting Actress

led to a rules change for the Academy. And what would a "country" picture be without Percy Kilbride, better known to thousands of movie fans as Pa Kettle. Donald Meek, Frank McHugh, and Henry Morgan (before he was known as "Harry") filled out this incredibly strong supporting cast.

You may have seen *State Fair* on television and thought you were watching a different picture. It was released for TV under the title *It Happened One Summer*. To add to the confusion, there was also a 1962 musical called *State Fair*, starring Pat Boone, Pamela Tiffin, Tom Ewell, and Alice Faye. Jose Ferrer directed and Richard Rodgers wrote new songs to supplement the old standards written for the earlier version. In the Pat Boone version the newspaper reporter became a television

P·L·A·Y·E·R·S

Jeanne Crain.............. Margy Frake
Dana Andrews................ Pat Gilbert
Dick Haymes.............. Wayne Frake
Vivian Blaine .... Emily

Featuring:
- Charles Winninger
- Fay Bainter
- Donald Meek
- Frank McHugh
- Percy Kilbride
- Henry Morgan
- Jane Nigh
- William Marshall
- Phil Brown
- Paul E. Burns
- Josephine Whittell
- Paul Harvey
- Emory Parnell
- Tom Fadden
- William Frambes
- Coleen Gray
- John Dehner
- Ralph Sanford
- Neal Hart
- Will Wright
- Francis Ford
- Ray Barons
- Cathy Downs
- Mae Marsh
- Ruth Clifford

reporter, the main event at the fair was a sports car race, and instead of Iowa, the whole thing took place in Texas. Frankly, the later version isn't nearly as good as the Jeanne Crain/Dana Andrews picture. There was also a stage version starring America's favorite homebodies, Ozzie and Harriet Nelson.

> "It's as happy as a hayride down the middle aisle of *Oklahoma!*"
> —Review of *State Fair*.

Sun Valley Serenade

1941, 20th Century-Fox
Produced by Milton Sperling
Directed by H. Bruce Humberstone

S·Y·N·O·P·S·I·S

When the band is booked at Sun Valley, an orchestra manager (John Payne) falls in love with a war refugee (Sonja Henie).

Academy Award nominations: Edward Cronjager, Black and White Cinematography; Emil Newman, Score for a Musical Picture; Mack Gordon and Harry Warren, "The Chattanooga Choo Choo," Best Song.

In the mid-thirties, Sonja Henie was the only female Olympic athlete who used her celebrity status as an entré into Hollywood. (What about Esther Williams? While Esther was a national swimming champion, she never competed in the Olympics.)

Sonja Henie started ice skating at the age of eight. Four years later she skated in the 1924 Olympics, and four years after that she had her first Gold Medal, followed by Gold Medals in the games of 1932 and 1936. When she decided to give up her amateur status, 20th Century-Fox made her a movie star. Over the years Sonja proved that she wasn't just a superb skater and a beautiful woman: she was also an astute business woman. Her contract stipulated that she would have the time to perform in the ice shows she also produced.

Between her income from the studios and the big profits from her ice shows, Henie was a self-made millionaire well before the age of thirty. At the ripe old age of twenty-eight she had done enough in her life to justify writing her autobiography.

In 1940 she married fellow millionaire Dan Topping and temporarily retired from the screen. Darryl Zanuck, who was vacationing in Sun Valley, Idaho, when he came up with the idea for *Sun Valley Serenade*, coaxed Henie back to the screen for what the musical critics called one of the best of the decade. Zanuck made one stipulation: Henie had to go on a diet before the cameras would roll! While critics were pleased both by her appearance and her performance, Sonja Henie wasn't pleased with Darryl Zanuck. She wanted to include a third ice number in the film, but Zanuck told her that if she wanted it, she'd have to pay for the production costs. She declined, and *Sun Valley Serenade* was finished with only two ice ballets.

After filming was completed, Darryl Zanuck decided he no longer wanted to put up with Sonja Henie's demands. Moveover, he thought that Henie's power as a box office draw was waning. He sent one of his top executives to tell her that Fox was no longer in need of her services, later admitting that he didn't go himself because he was afraid of getting hit in the head with an ice skate.

Sonja Henie had the last laugh. *Sun Valley Serenade* was a popular success, Henie was back at the top of the popularity polls, and Zanuck was forced to persuade her to return to Fox. She knew when to negotiate from a position of strength, and she agreed to come back for considerably more money than she made on *Sun Valley Serenade*. She made one movie for Fox in 1942 and one in 1943 before she ended her association with the studio.

Although *Sun Valley Serenade* is usually thought of as a Sonja Henie movie, it's historical-ly important because it gives us the opportunity to see the Glenn Miller Orchestra at the height of its popularity. The Miller arrangement of "Chattanooga Choo-Choo," which includes the Nicholas Brothers' high energy dance routine, is possibly the greatest big band production number ever filmed. Unfortunately, the Miller Band was seen in only one other movie, *Orchestra Wives* in 1942, before Miller's untimely death in World War II.

Natural ice looked dull in black and white, so hundreds of gallons of milk were added to the water before it was frozen for Sonja Henie's skating numbers.

Suspicion

1941, RKO Radio
Produced and Directed by Alfred Hitchcock

S·Y·N·O·P·S·I·S

A young bride (Joan Fontaine) suspects that her husband (Cary Grant) is planning to kill her.

Academy Award: Joan Fontaine, Best Actress.

Academy Award nomination: Best Picture.

What's in a name? RKO believed that the name of a movie was an important factor in its success. When Alfred Hitchcock adapted Francis Iles' novel *Before the Fact* for the screen, the studio commissioned the George Gallup organization to poll the movie-going public. The results showed that the title *Before the Fact* just didn't make it with movie fans. Hitchcock wanted *Fright*, but that sounded too much like a story about a haunted house. Gallup tested fifty titles for RKO, including *Love in Irons*, *Last Lover*, *Sable Wings* (don't ask me what that

means) *Girl in the Vise*, *Romantic Scapegrace*, *Search For Tomorrow* (before the soap opera), and, if you can believe it, *Men Make Poor Husbands*. Not surprisingly, all of the titles were found to be unacceptable. In desperation, Hitchcock picked up the original novel and found what he wanted in the second paragraph: "Suspicion is a tenuous thing, so impalpable that the exact moment of its birth is not easy to determine..."

Considering the struggle that went into choosing the title, it's not suprising that it took even more effort to settle on an ending. Some alternate endings for *Suspicion* existed only on paper, including the one that had Cary Grant joining the

Royal Air Force, where he died expressing regret for his checkered past. Other endings made it all the way through the production process.

Hitchcock filmed scenes in which Joan Fontaine was unfaithful to her husband and eventually committed suicide, but when

that option was shown to a preview audience, they laughed. Hitchcock also shot his choice, in which Fontaine's suspicions were correct, and she chose to drink the poisoned milk rather than live with her disillusionment. Another preview audience hated that one. They didn't want to think of Cary Grant as a murderer. That was ironic: Grant had accepted the role because he wanted to play a bad guy.

Several previews and alternate endings later, the studio decreed that Joan Fontaine's suspicions were all in her imagination and that her husband wasn't trying to poison her at all. Hitchcock was annoyed, because he wanted the film to end the way the book had, with the husband guilty of plotting his wife's death. Hitchcock didn't realize the worst was yet to come.

After he finished *Suspicion* Hitchcock went out of town. When he returned to Hollywood, he found to his dismay that the studio had not only changed the ending, but had

also cut every scene or line of dialogue that suggested Grant might be a murderer. The result was a picture that lasted only fifty-five minutes and had nothing whatsoever to do with *Suspicion*. Hitchcock was understandably upset. The studio recognized the absurdity of releasing the fifty-five minute version and allowed him to restore the scenes the executive had cut.

Suspicion was finally released to the theaters and was nominated for two Academy Awards: Best Picture, and Joan Fontaine as Best Actress.

Although Joan Fontaine appreciated the honor of receiving the nomination, she had originally decided not to attend the award ceremony. She was up against Bette Davis, Barbara Stanwyck, Greer Garson, and her own sister, Olivia de Havilland, and she felt she had no chance of winning.

The morning of the awards, Olivia was appalled to learn that her sister wasn't planning to attend. Joan said she didn't have any-

thing to wear and didn't have time to shop because she was filming that day. An hour later, Olivia and a saleslady from I. Magnin appeared at the studio with a stack of size six dresses, and between takes, Joan chose a black, ballet-length lace dress with matching mantilla.

That night, when Ginger Rogers read, "And the winner is . . . Joan Fontaine," the audience let out a collective gasp before breaking into applause. Many Academy members later admitted they had voted for Joan Fontaine because they thought she should have won the preceding year for her work on *Rebecca*.

Alfred Hitchcock put a light bulb in the glass of milk Joan Fontaine suspected was poisoned, giving the milk an unearthly glow.

Swing Time

1936, RKO Radio
Produced by Pandro Berman
Directed by George Stevens

S·Y·N·O·P·S·I·S

A professional dancer (Fred Astaire) pretends he can't dance and enrolls in a dance academy to get close to a pretty instructor (Ginger Rogers).

Academy Award: Jerome Kern and Dorothy Fields, "The Way You Look Tonight," Best Song.

Academy Award nomination: Hermes Pan, Dance Director, "Bojangles."

Fred Astaire and Ginger Rogers went into production on *Swing Time* just as *Follow the Fleet* opened to packed houses around the country. Since the plots of their musicals were essentially the same, Astaire was aware that he had to give the audience new and fresh dance numbers. In *Swing Time* his big number was a Jerome Kern melody called "Bojangles of Harlem." Astaire pushed the special effects technology of 1936 to the absolute limit. That one number took several weeks to film, with Astaire working alone with the crew and cameras after the rest of the cast had been released.

Because of the additional shooting time, *Swing Time* took longer to film than any of the other Astaire/Rogers musicals. Most critics now agree it was their best. While Fred Astaire's dancing was always picture perfect, Ginger's dancing had improved immeasurably. In the earlier films she appeared to be struggling to keep up; in *Swing Time* she established herself as Astaire's equal.

Astaire/Rogers fans were also pleased with *Swing Time* because it marked the return of comedians Helen Broderick and Eric Blore, who had impressed everyone with their performances in *Top Hat* but had been passed over in *Follow the Fleet* in favor of a second romantic inter-est. Producer Pandro Berman realized that the comedic element was much more important, and Broderick and Blore were brought back.

While Fred Astaire was working on *Swing Time*, he agreed to host and perform on a radio show called "The Packard Hour," named for the car company that sponsored it. When he danced for the radio show, he worked on a small, four-foot-by-four-foot dance mat, which meant he couldn't move very far. Microphones on the floor pick-

ed up the sounds of his shoes, and surprisingly, people enjoyed listening to Fred Astaire dance almost as much as they enjoyed watching him. Astaire found that for the radio, tap dancing worked best, so he confined himself to that style.

If the show had been done for a modern audience, it would probably have included a play-by-play announcer to let the audience know what was happening. Can you imagine it? "Astaire goes for the corners; he turns, he taps, he waves his arms over his head as his feet wow the studio audience!" Fortunately, radio audiences of the thirties preferred to use their own imagination.

After thirty-nine weeks, the producers were interested in continuing the show, but Astaire found he was too tired after a full day of rehearsing or filming to be up for the radio show. When the

contract was up, he decided not to renew, and the phrase, "Let's go hear Fred Astaire dance" slipped out of the English language forever.

Years before she became a spokesperson for Westinghouse, Betty Furness had a supporting role in *Swing Time*.

These Three

1936, Goldwyn/United Artists
Produced by Samuel Goldwyn
Directed by William Wyler

S·Y·N·O·P·S·I·S

A spiteful child accuses her teacher of adultery.

Academy Award nomination: Bonita Granville, Supporting Actress.

Lillian Hellman was still in her twenties when her first play became a smash hit on Broadway. It was called *The Children's Hour,* and dealt with the consequences when a young girl at a boarding school, who is angry with two of her female teachers, tells her parents that the women are lovers. The play made its author an overnight success, and Sam Goldwyn hired her as a full-time writer. Part of the deal was that she could choose her own projects. It was Hellman who convinced the studio to pay her $50,000 for the rights to redo *The Children's Hour* for the screen.

Any script that suggested homosexuality might exist was totally out of bounds for Hollywood. That didn't bother Sam Goldwyn. When he was told not to buy the rights to *The Children's Hour* because it was about lesbians, he replied, "That's OK. We'll make them Americans."

The Hays office demanded that the entire script be rewritten and the name changed, and even prevented the studio from publicizing the fact that Goldwyn had bought the rights to the Broadway hit. Goldwyn expressed his doubts that the play could be modified enough to suit the censor board, but Hellman was persuasive. She told him the play wasn't about homosexuality as much as it was about how a lie can destroy people's lives. She went to work and rewrote it as a story of alleged marital infidelity. Critics in 1936 said that the rewrite was even better than the original stage play.

The stars of the film were Merle Oberon and Miriam Hopkins, but the real honors went to Bonita Granville as the brat who decided to get back at her teachers. Her performance was so convincing that, at age twelve, she became one of the youngest actresses ever nominated for an Academy Award.

This was the first film William Wyler directed for Sam Goldwyn, and it was very nearly the last. Wyler had been hired at $2,500 a week after Goldwyn saw

The Gay Deception, a fluffy comedy with Francis Lederer and Frances Dee. Wyler, who considered comedy his forte, was dismayed to learn that his first assignment would be the Hellman play.

Wyler and editor Danny Mandell were present when Goldwyn saw the first cut of *These Three*. For an hour and a half Goldwyn didn't say a word. Then, when the lights went up, he stared straight ahead and said, "I'm very disappointed." Then he turned to the editor and pointed a finger at him, shouting "I'm very disappointed! I'm very disappointed! You loused up this picture!" Wyler jumped in, and the three men argued well into the night. The bottom line was that Wyler and Mandell had shortened the graduation sequence and cut the scene at the railroad station. Goldwyn demanded that they put the footage back in. Mandell complied, and the picture was previewed the following week. Afterward, Goldwyn walked up to Danny Mandell and said, "I think it went very well. But tell me, why did you have to put back that dull graduation scene and that stinking scene at the railroad station?"

These Three won critical acclaim and inspired Goldwyn to trust Wyler with seven more films, including the classics *Come and Get it*, *The Little Foxes*, *Dodsworth*, *Wuthering Heights*, and *The Best Years of Our Lives*.

Twenty-five years after making *These Three*, William Wyler directed the first accurate film version of the original Hellman play. By this time standards had relaxed enough for it to be called *The Children's Hour*. Audrey Hepburn and Shirley MacLaine were in the leading roles. Wyler again cast Miriam Hopkins, but instead of playing one of the teachers, this time she played the unreliable Aunt Lily.

After Bonita Granville grew up and married producer Jack Wrather, she became partner in his corporation and part owner of *The Lone Ranger* and *Lassie* television programs.

The Toast of New York

1937, RKO Radio
Produced by Edward Small
Directed by Rowland V. Lee

S·Y·N·O·P·S·I·S

The semi-biographical story of Jubilee Jim Fisk, a ruthless Wall Street tycoon.

Frances Farmer represented one of the most tragic stories in the history of Hollywood. She was a young actress who quickly rose to the top of her profession and just as quickly fell. She spent years in mental institutions, and in later life wrote about her fight with drugs and alcohol. But her road to Hollywood and a successful career was a fascinating one.

In 1931 she joined the theater department at the University of Washington and became the school's leading actress. One of her teachers became her mentor and gave Frances a piece of advice she never forgot: "Climb. Knock down anyone who stands in your way. But climb."

Frances's overwhelming ambition was to go to New York, but her schooling had taken all her money and her parents had none to spare. Then fate and her drama coach stepped in. The teacher had heard about a contest sponsored by a Communist newspaper. First prize was a trip to Moscow with stopovers in New York. Although Frances was definitely *not* a Communist, she managed to win the contest. When her mother found out about it, Frances was disowned and accused of being a spy and contributing to the Red Menace. The newspapers loved anti-communist stories, and journalists had a field day with banner headlines that read, "Coed to Act for Reds" and "Mother Uncovers Red Vice Ring." Mrs. Farmer threatened via the newspapers to commit suicide if her daughter left town. (Frances left anyway, but her mother didn't carry out the threat.) When the young actress returned to New York City, she cashed in her bus ticket back to Seattle for twenty-five dollars and began life as a struggling actress.

Within six months she landed a screen test for Paramount and was offered a six-month contract in Hollywood. When Frances wrote to her mother about her new opportunity, Mrs. Farmer wrote back, full of praise for "her daughter, the movie star." It was the first time Frances had heard from her since leaving Seattle.

She went to Hollywood in 1936, where Paramount starred her in a series of A and B pictures. For the next six years she received good notices, but her personal problems were overwhelming, and she was committed to a mental institution for many years. Her autobiography, published two years after her death in 1972, recounts the harrowing details of her stay there.

Looking back on her career, she admitted that she had been difficult on the set of *Toast of New York*. While she thought her character a cheap vixen, they wanted her to play an innocent ingenue. She argued with everyone, from the producer and director to the writers and costumers. When that wasn't effective, she gave interviews to the press in which she aired her grievances

against the entire Hollywood system.

Part of her problem was simple exhaustion. She had contracts with both RKO and Paramount, and the studios thought nothing of working her for incredibly long hours. She spent her days at Paramount, making a picture called *Ebb Tide*. Every night she was at RKO, filming *Toast of New York*. And the producers of the two films could not understand why she seemed out-of-sorts.

While producer Edward Small had his hands full dealing with Frances Farmer, director Rowland Lee was having problems with Edward Arnold. His fellow actors complained that he had a habit of pretending to blow his lines, take after take, just to wear the others down. When he was ready to give a real performance, the others were tired and didn't give their best effort. It was supposedly his way of making sure he looked better than the others so his performance would stand out.

Though Jack Oakie had only fourth billing on *Toast of New York*, he went on to become one of Hollywood's top comedy stars. It's hard to believe, but when he first went to Hollywood in 1929, he was very thin. Within a few years he had grown into the role of

the pleasantly plump comedian. Just before his death in 1978, Hollywood established an award for comic excellence. They call it the Jokie, a play on "Jack Oakie."

Frances Farmer found her co-star aloof and remote, solely intent on remaining Cary Grant, the personality.

Top Hat

1935, RKO Radio
Produced by Pandro S. Berman
Directed by Mark Sandrich

Brushin' off my tails."

©1935 Irving Berlin Music Corp.

For Fred Astaire, a good idea was never lost. Sometimes it just took a while for it to find its place. In 1931 Astaire was the star and choreographer of a Broadway musical called *Smiles*. One morning he awoke at four a.m. with images flashing through his head. He saw himself dancing with a cane, accompanied by a chorus line of men wearing top hats. He leaped out of bed, grabbed an umbrella, and danced around the apartment. He incorporated the number into the show, but *Smiles* was a total flop.

Four years later Astaire was working with Irving Berlin on an as-yet-untitled picture. As Fred described that number from the ill-fated Broadway musical, Berlin became excited. He sat down at the piano and played,

"I'm puttin' on my Top Hat
Tyin' up my white tie

"Top Hat" not only became the title song of the picture, it's probably the one song most closely associated with Fred Astaire.

Fred loved the new song, but he couldn't say the same for another composition Irving Berlin tried out on him. Berlin played it on his famous key-shifting piano, singing it in what was charitably described as his "weak" voice—meaning he couldn't hit any of the high notes and just sort of strained his voice in the right direction. Despite Astaire's initial, negative reaction, he recognized that the song would be good to dance to and went ahead and worked on the choreography. What was the song that disappointed Fred Astaire? It was one of the most graceful, most memorable of the Astaire/Rogers numbers, Irving Berlin's classic "Cheek to Cheek."

Classic or not, the number was a disaster the day they tried to film it. Fred and Ginger always did at least one rehearsal with Ginger in costume, because, as Fred once said, "Her dress becomes our dress." If the skirt was too full, it could wrap itself around Fred's legs, making it necessary to modify the dress or the choreography. Unfortunately, the wardrobe department was late with Ginger's dress for the "Cheek to

floated around the set like millions of white moths, Fred and Ginger pulled feathers out of their eyes, their mouths, and their ears.

The wardrobe people said the dress just needed to be shaken out and the fallout would stop. They were wrong. Fred and Ginger tried the number again, and once again the floor was covered with white fluff. Costume designer Bernard Newman finally solved the problem by

their own. To the tune of "Cheek to Cheek," they sang,

"Feathers, I hate feathers
And I hate them so that I can hardly speak
And I never find the happiness I seek
With those chicken feathers dancing cheek to cheek."

Cheek" number, and on the day of filming Ginger was wearing the feather-covered dress for the first time. They took their positions and began to dance. As Astaire wrote in his autobiography, the feathers started flying "as if a chicken were being attacked by a coyote." While the feathers

having each feather individually knotted to the dress. The next time you see *Top Hat*, look carefully and you'll see a few feathers fly.

The day after the feather episode, Astaire and choreographer Hermes Pan entertained the crew with a little number of

The florist's assistant was played by an aspiring actress named Lucille Ball.

Twelve O'Clock High

1949, 20th Century-Fox
Produced by Darryl F. Zanuck
Directed by Henry King

S·Y·N·O·P·S·I·S

After an 8th Air Corps officer (Gary Merrill) is replaced for getting too close to his men, his successor (Gregory Peck) has the same problem.

Academy Awards: Dean Jagger, Supporting Actor; W.D. Flick, Thomas Moulton, and Roger Heman, Sound.

Academy Award nominations: Best Picture; Gregory Peck, Best Actor.

When Gregory Peck first read the script for *Twelve O'Clock High*, he turned down the part, explaining to producer Darryl Zanuck that it was too much like MGM's flop, *Command Decision*. A year later Zanuck contacted Peck again, saying he had run *Command Decision* over and over until he saw why it was unsuccessful and had changed the concept for *Twelve O'Clock High*. Peck read the revised script and agreed to play General Frank Savage.

While signing the right leading man is vital to the success of a production, finding the right location is also important. When director Henry King made a nationwide scouting trip for *Twelve O'Clock High*, he had some very specific requirements. Since King had been a pilot since 1918, he used his own plane to fly around the country, looking for places that could double as British airfields. After logging 11,000 miles, he finally found Eglin Field, near Fort Walton, Florida, which had been the proving grounds for U.S. Army and Navy

arms during World War II. It was perfect for many of the scenes of wartime British airfields. Twentieth Century-Fox shipped in men and materials and built authentic Nissen and Quonset huts.

However, there were three problems with filming at Eglin. During the war the British painted their runways black so they couldn't be seen when enemy bombers flew over. The

Eglin runways were the usual light concrete color. Second, one of the scenes called for the field to appear overgrown and abandoned, but the Eglin airfield was well kept and the Army wasn't willing to let the weeds grow out. Third, the vegetation around the field looked more tropical than English.

King needed a second location, and he found it at the Third Army's Ozark Field near Dothan, Alabama. A chartered DC6 shuttled people and equipment between airfields, completing the trip in just twenty-two minutes. Using Ozark solved all three problems: the Ozark runways could be painted black, they were able to bring in vegetation native to less temperate climates, and they were allowed to let the weeds and grass grow until the runway looked abandoned.

First Henry King shot the opening scenes at the overgrown field. When they were finished, local farmers brought in their tractors and mowed the fields, and King filmed the take-off and landing scenes. King also used the remote Ozark field for the crash scene. Stunt pilot Paul Mantz was covered from all angles by four different camera crews as his B17 made a wheels-up (belly) landing at 110 miles per hour. Mantz also piloted the lead camera ship at Eglin, providing his own B25 with cameras mounted on the tail, the nose, and the side.

After six weeks of location

work, the cast and crew returned to Hollywood to film the interior scenes. In one of the most dramatic and important scenes, Gregory Peck had to take a sergeant's stripes for hitching a ride on a bomber and taking part in a raid. The first time they filmed the scene, Peck expressed a lot of anger and emotion. When Darryl Zanuck saw the rushes, he sent a note to Henry King expressing his displeasure with Peck's performance. King and Peck critiqued the scene together, and Peck realized he had overacted. They went back to the set and did it again, with Peck taking a more sympathetic, soft-edged approach. Both Peck and King knew it was much better underplayed than the way they had originally shot it.

Peck's performance as General Frank Savage earned

him his fourth Oscar nomination. His first win would come twelve years later, for his role as the defense attorney in *To Kill a Mockingbird.*

"You like him or you hate him. He's lousy at a desk job, but he's a hot pilot. You don't meet Frank Savage. You collide with him."
　　　　　—Press ads for *Twelve O'Clock High.*)

Woman of the Year

1942, MGM
Produced by Joseph Mankiewicz
Directed by George Stevens

S·Y·N·O·P·S·I·S

An intellectual political columnist (Katharine Hepburn) falls in love with a sports writer (Spencer Tracy).

Academy Award: Michael Kanin and Ring Lardner, Jr., Screenplay.

Academy Award nomination: Katharine Hepburn, Best Actress.

How do a couple of $300-a-week staff writers start making big money? It helps if they have Katharine Hepburn negotiating the deal.

Ring Lardner, Jr. went to Garson Kanin with a treatment for a screenplay about his father, humorist and short story writer Ring Lardner, and his tempestuous relationship with political columnist Dorothy Thompson. Kanin thought it had potential and asked his brother Michael to help flesh it out. When Katharine Hepburn read it, she wanted it as her next movie, but she knew executives at MGM would refuse to consider it. Ring Lardner, Jr. had been active in organizing the Screenwriter's Guild, and executives at MGM had said he would never work there. Michael Kanin was employed as a $300-a-week writer, and the studio would never trust him with anything as important as a Katharine Hepburn vehicle.

In a bold move, she sent the proposal to MGM without the names of the writers. When Joseph Mankiewicz read it and demanded to know who had written it, she said she couldn't divulge that information. The studio would not commit to the project on the basis of the treatment, so she was given a deadline. Her mystery writers had to come up with sixty script pages by the following Monday. She pitched in and helped them write not sixty but the first one hundred pages. When Louis B. Mayer liked it, she told him she wanted $211,000: $100,000 for her services, $10,000 for her agent, $100,000 for the writers, and an additional $1,000 finders fee for herself. Mayer agreed to her terms, and she gleefully told him that the writers were two men who had never made more than $3,000 on a script.

As her co-star, she wanted a man she had never met but whose work she admired. She wanted Spencer Tracy.

They met for the first time on the steps of the Thalberg building on the MGM lot. In her four-inch high heels, she towered over Tracy. "I'm afraid I'm a little tall for you," she said. Tracy replied, "Don't worry. I'll cut you down to my size." (Joseph Mankiewicz, who was also present, claimed credit for the line. In his version he said to Hepburn, "Don't worry, he'll cut you down to size.")

Spencer Tracy demanded and received top billing over Katharine Hepburn. When Gar-

son Kanin said that Tracy should have allowed the lady to go first, he replied, "This is a movie, chowderhead, not a lifeboat!" He was billed over Hepburn in every one of their movies.

At first the set of *Woman of the Year* was an uncomfortable place to be, as Tracy and Hepburn tested one another. But soon Tracy stopped calling her "That Woman" or "Shorty" and began calling her "Kate." Tracy and Hepburn were about to become one of the greatest screen couples of all time.

While everyone else seemed pleased with the movie, Hepburn hated the ending. In the original script Tess learned to love baseball, and her enthusiasm for the sport eclipsed her husband's. But producer Joseph Mankiewicz and director George Stevens were afraid that the average American housewife was going to hate Tess—who was beautiful, intelligent, competent, and nearly perfect. American women would not want their husbands to compare

them unfavorably to Tess Harding, so Mankiewicz and Stevens added a scene in which she attempts to make breakfast and is totally conquered by the appliances. They said it would allow American wives to relax and turn to their husbands and say, "See, there are things she can't do that I can." Kate called it the worst thing she had ever read, and Lardner and Kanin thought the ending vulgarized their script, but preview audiences loved it and the ending stood.

The chemistry between the stars in this first Tracy/Hepburn film is palpable. Critics were awed by the magic they generated on the screen, a magic that continued through nine subsequent films.

The character of Tess Harding was named after Katharine Hepburn's best friend, Laura Harding.

Wuthering Heights

1939, Samuel Goldwyn/United Artists
Produced by Samuel Goldwyn
Directed by William Wyler

S·Y·N·O·P·S·I·S

A housekeeper (Flora Robson) tells the story of the doomed love between a woman (Merle Oberon) and her foster brother (Laurence Olivier).

Academy Award: Gregg Toland, Black and White Cinematography

Academy Award nominations: Best Picture; William Wyler, Best Director; Laurence Olivier, Best Actor; Geraldine Fitzgerald, Supporting Actress; Ben Hecht, Screenplay; James Basevi, Art Direction; Alfred Newman, Original Music Score.

Imagine the fun of making a movie with two stars who wish they were somewhere else, a director who makes everyone's life miserable with his excessive demands, and a producer who goes behind the director's back to re-shoot the ending, and you may have an idea of the joy cast and crew experienced on the set of *Wuthering Heights.* The most amazing thing was that, in retrospect, they all agreed it was worth it.

Leading lady Merle Oberon was miserable because she had fallen in love with British film mogul Alexander Korda, and Korda was in London while she was in Hollywood. Laurence Olivier was unhappy because his fiancee, an unknown actress named Vivien Leigh, was also far away in London. However, Olivier had a lot more to be unhappy about than just missing his sweetheart.

Wuthering Heights was among his first few experiences in Hollywood, and the early pictures had been disastrous. Olivier hadn't yet learned that acting in movies is a lot different than acting on stage, and he ruined take after take by doing things that would have been terrific on stage, but were just too big for the intimacy of film. Director William Wyler wasn't much help, because he didn't give specific suggestions for improving a performance. After multiple takes on one scene, Olivier confronted the director: "Willie, look. I've done it differently thirty times. Just tell me, what do you want me to do?" Wyler thought for a moment, then replied, "Just be better."

While Olivier was unhappy with Wyler, producer Sam Goldwyn was unhappy with Olivier. Goldwyn, who wanted Ronald Colman or Douglas Fairbanks, Jr. to play Heathcliff, called Olivier "that damned ugly Englishman." When he saw some of the early rushes, he complained that Olivier was "dirty, unkempt, hammy and awful," and he threatened to cancel the production. With Wyler's help, Olivier toned down his performance, and in the process, learned that movie acting is a very specific art.

One of the challenges of the film actor's art is doing a love scene in the intimacy of a sound stage without offending your partner. It's an unfortunate reality of the medium that it can be difficult for an actor to project his voice loudly enough for the microphones without spitting on his partner. When Olivier stared longingly into Merle Oberon's eyes and lovingly murmured his lines, Oberon yelled, "Don't spit on me!" Olivier lost his temper, they argued, and each stalked off the set. They did the scene again after a short break, and this time it was full of emotion. The fact that the emotion wasn't love was irrelevant.

While Oberon had to put up

with unpleasantness in the love scene, her death bed scene was worse. David Niven was having trouble crying on cue, so the prop man gave him a shot of menthol to hide in his handkerchief. For once, Wyler's instructions were specific: "Make your crying face, blink your eyes, squeeze the menthol, bend over the corpse, and heave your shoulders." Niven did exactly as he was instructed, but it didn't come out right. Instead of tears falling from his eyes, he began to sneeze uncontrollably. Merle Oberon, exasperated, leaped out of bed and raced for her dressing room.

When director William Wyler finished editing it, the picture ended with a shot of Heathcliffe's body. Sam Goldwyn complained that a picture of a corpse wasn't an appropriate way to end the movie. Wyler disagreed, and released the cast, but Goldwyn would not be put off.

He assigned an assistant director to film Olivier's stunt double with a girl of approximately the same height and build as Merle Oberon. That famous closing shot of the two lovers superimposed over the clouds was made by a couple of doubles and an assistant director.

Wuthering Heights established Laurence Olivier's credentials as a leading man.

You Can't Take It With You

1938, Columbia
Produced and Directed by Frank Capra

S·Y·N·O·P·S·I·S

The romance of two young lovers (Jean Arthur and James Stewart) is complicated by the antics of the woman's wacky family.

Academy Awards: Best Picture; Frank Capra, Best Director.

Academy Award nominations: Spring Byington, Supporting Actress; Robert Riskin, Screenplay; Joseph Walker, Cinematography; Gene Havlick, Editing; John Livadary, Sound Recording.

In the mid-thirties the chances were slim that the Pulitzer Prize-winning play *You Can't Take It With You* would ever be made into a film. It's authors, George S. Kaufman and Moss Hart, had put a $200,000 price tag on their work, and up to that time no one in Hollywood had ever paid that much money for the right to adapt a play for film. But that was before Frank Capra became angry with Harry Cohn.

Despite the fact that they disagreed often and fought almost constantly, in the late 1930s the Academy Award winning director and the head of Columbia were one of the industry's most successful teams. Everyone in Hollywood knew it was Capra's films that had pulled Columbia out of bankruptcy, and Cohn wasn't happy basking in reflected glory. He was always looking to share credit for Capra's successes. The ten-

sion between the two men grew until, finally, Cohn went too far. The head of Columbia knew that Capra's name on a picture was a strong box office draw, so he released a picture in England and billed it as a Frank Capra film. Not only had Capra not produced or directed it—he had never even seen it. When Capra found out what Cohn had done, he walked out on his contract and filed a lawsuit. Capra's friends told him he was crazy. It could take years to settle the suit, during which time Capra would not be able to work for any other studio. With Columbia's corporate resources, the company could hold out longer than he

could.

For the first year the suit did not go well for Frank Capra. He retained a lawyer who kept filing suit in the wrong city. The suit was thrown out of court in California because Columbia's corporate headquarters were in New York. It was thrown out of court in New York because the infraction occurred in England. Each delay cost Capra time and money.

Finally he arranged for a British lawyer to file suit in London. Columbia's lawyers told Harry Cohn the bad news: Capra had a good chance of winning, and British distributors would probably refuse to book any Columbia films. This was extremely bad news to a small studio constantly teetering on the edge of bankruptcy. Cohn visited Capra at home and asked him to come back at twice his old salary. As an incentive, Cohn bought Capra *You Can't Take It With You.*

The men shook hands, and Frank Capra was once more employed by Columbia studios.

Cohn also gave Capra a large enough budget to hire the best talent in Hollywood. The result was one of the strongest casts Capra ever assembled, including his favorite leading man and lady, James Stewart and Jean Arthur, along with Lionel Barrymore, Spring Byington, and a xylophonist named Dub Taylor.

Taylor's real given name was Walter, but his family started calling him "W," then shortened it to "Dub." Dub realized that there were many more opportunities for actors than xylophonists, so after his successful film debut in *You Can't Take It With You,* he gave up playing the xylophone professionally and appeared in many Westerns throughout the forties. "Dub" wasn't a proper name for a cowboy, so he made Westerns under the name Cannonball Taylor.

Frank Capra was one of the few Hollywood directors who could deal with Jean Arthur, who had left five stage productions because of illness. It was Capra's contention that Arthur had a chronic case of stage fright, and that if you pushed her gently but forcibly in front of the cameras, she would magically blossom into a warm, poised, and confident actress. Capra was so pleased with the combination of Jean Arthur and James Stewart that a year later he teamed them in *Mr. Smith Goes to Washington.*

While a line of dialogue was added explaining why Lionel Barrymore was on crutches, the truth was that his arthritis was slowly crippling him.

Young Mr. Lincoln

1939, 20th Century-Fox
Produced by Kenneth Macgowan
Directed by John Ford

S·Y·N·O·P·S·I·S

Ten years in the life of an awkward Kentucky youth who becomes a lawyer and decides to go into politics.

Academy Award nomination: Lamar Trotti, Original Story.

Henry Fonda didn't think he could play Abraham Lincoln. Fonda had always been an admirer of our sixteenth President, and had read many of the books written about him, but when 20th Century-Fox head Darryl Zanuck asked him to play the role, he refused. Fonda's friends Kenneth Macgowan and Lamar Trotti, the producer and writer of *Young Mr. Lincoln*, put pressure on him, but he refused even their entreaties. However, he couldn't refuse his friends' reasonable request that he do a screen test.

On the morning of the test the makeup department spent more than an hour deepening his eyes, changing his hairline, enlarging his nose, and adding that distinctive wart. They filmed the scene twice, and that afternoon Fonda, Macgowan, and Trotti sat down to watch the test. When Fonda appeared on the screen, all three men gasped. The man they saw on the screen actually seemed to be Abraham Lincoln. Even Fonda was impressed, but only briefly. When he heard his voice coming out of this man who looked like Lincoln, he felt the illusion was ruined. Fonda walked out of the projection room, vowing he'd never play the role.

Several months later Henry Fonda was called into John Ford's office. The two men had never met, but Ford was already a legend, and Fonda was in awe of the director. Ford said that if Fonda thought they were making a movie about a great emancipator, he was wrong. *Young Mr. Lincoln* was a story about a gawky lawyer who rides a mule because he can't afford a horse. Fonda wouldn't be playing a national hero, he'd be playing a real person. Fonda couldn't argue with John Ford, so he agreed to play the young Mr. Lincoln.

During filming, Fonda and Ford worked well together. Unfortunately, you couldn't say the same for Ford and Darryl Zanuck, who didn't like the way Ford paced the picture. Usually a director will shoot more footage than he actually needs, so that if there is a problem in the edit room, he has some options. When the studio head tried to re-edit the picture, he was stymied. Ford had made only the shots he needed, which meant that if Zanuck wanted to make major changes, he would have to call back the cast and crew for expensive retakes. Zanuck acquiesced, and Ford edited the picture his way.

There was one scene both John Ford and Henry Fonda liked but that Darryl Zanuck insisted

on cutting. Fonda stops his mule outside a theater and pauses to read a poster advertising a production of *Hamlet*, starring the Booth family. Lincoln wants to attend but doesn't have the money. A young boy, a member of the famous family of thespians, walks out of the theater and looks condescendingly at the shabbily dressed man on a mule.

Of course, he was supposed to be the young John Wilkes Booth, many years before he would end Lincoln's life at Ford's Theater.

There were a few future TV stars scattered among the supporting cast of *Young Mr. Lincoln*. Stephen A. Douglas was played by Milburn Stone, who would later enjoy a long run as Doc on *Gunsmoke*. Jack Kelly, who was just ten years old when he appeared in *Young Mr. Lincoln*, would later be one of the stars of TV's *Maverick*.

It rained on the day John Ford planned to film the closing image of Henry Fonda walking off into the distance. Rather than wait for better weather, Ford incorporated the rain into the shot.

Bibliography

Arce, Hector. *Gary Cooper: An Intimate Biography*, New York: Morrow, 1979.

Astaire, Fred. *Steps in Time: An Autobiography*, New York: Harper & Brothers, 1959.

Behlmer, Rudy. *America's Favorite Movies Behind the Scenes*, New York: Frederick Ungar Publishing Co., 1982.

Behlmer, Rudy. *Inside Warner Brothers 1935-1951*, New York: Viking Press, 1985.

Behlmer, Rudy. *Memo From David O. Selznick*, New York: Viking Press, 1972.

Berg, Scott. *Goldwyn: A Biography*, New York, Knopf, 1989.

Boller, Paul F. and Davis, Ronald L. *Hollywood Anecdotes*, New York: William Morrow and Co., 1987.

Brooks, Tim. *The Complete Directory to Prime Time TV Stars*, New York: Ballantine Books, 1987.

Cagney, James. *Cagney on Cagney*, Garden City, New York: Doubleday, 1976.

Canutt, Yakima and Drake, Oliver. *Stunt Man: The Autobiography of Yakima Canutt*, New York: Walker Publishing Co., 1979.

Capra, Frank. *The Name Above the Title*, New York: Macmillan Co., 1971.

Carey, Gary. *All the Stars in Heaven*, New York: E.P. Dutton, 1981.

Clarens, Carlos, *An Illustrated History of the Horror Film*, New York: Capricorn Books, 1967.

Dickens, Homer. *The Films of Ginger Rogers*, Secaucus, N.J.: Citadel Press, 1980.

Davidson, Bill. *Spencer Tracy: Tragic Idol*, New York: E.P. Dutton, 1987.

Eames, John Douglas. *The MGM Story*, New York: Crown Publishers, 1982.

Edwards, Anne. *A Remarkable Woman: A Biography of Katharine Hepburn*, New York: William Morrow and Company, 1985.

Edwards, Anne. *Judy Garland*, New York: Simon and Schuster, 1974.

Edwards, Anne. *Shirley Temple: American Princess*, New York: William Morrow and Company, 1988.

Eels, George. *Robert Mitchum*, Franklin Watts, New York, 1984.

Everson, William K. *The Detective in Film*, Secaucus, New Jersey: Citadel Press, 1972.

Eyles, Allen. *James Stewart*, New York: Stein & Day, 1984.

Fonda, Henry. *Fonda: My Life*, as told to Howard Teichmann, New York: New American Library, 1981.

Fontaine, Joan. *No Bed of Roses*, New York: Morrow, 1978.

Ford, Dan. *Pappy: The Life of John Ford*, Englewood Cliffs, N.J.: Prentice Hall, 1979.

Fordin, Hugh. *The World of Entertainment!*, Garden City, New York: Doubleday and Co., 1975.

Frank, Gerold. *Judy*, New York: Harper & Row, 1975.

Freedland, Michael. *Cagney: A Biography*, New York: Stein and Day, 1976.

Geist, Kenneth L. *Pictures Will Talk, The Life and Films of Joseph Mankiewicz*, New York: Charles Scribner's Sons, 1978.

Guiles, Fred Lawrence. *Legend, The Life and Death of Marilyn Monroe*, New York: Stein and Day, 1984.

Gussow, Mel. *Don't Say Yes Until I Finish Talking*, Garden City, New York: Doubleday, 1971.

Harmetz, Aljean. *The Making of the Wizard of Oz*, New York: Alfred A. Knopf, 1977.

Hardy, Phil. *The Encyclopedia of Horror Movies*, New York: Harper & Row, 1986.

Harris, Warren G. *Cary Grant: A Touch of Elegance*, New York: Doubleday, 1987.

Haver, Ronald. *David O. Selznick's Hollywood*, New York: Bonanza Books, 1980.

Hingham, Charles and Moseley, Roy. *Cary Grant: The Lonley Heart*, New York: Harcourt Brace Jovanovich, 1989.

Hingham, Charles. *Charles Laughton: An Intimate Biography*, Garden City, New York: Doubleday, 1976.

Hirschhorn, Clive. *The Warner Brothers Story*, New York: Crown Publishers, 1979.

Jewell, Richard B. and Harbin, Vernon. *The RKO Story*, New York: Crown Publishers, 1982.

Kael, Pauline, Mankiewicz, Herman, and Welles, Orson. *The Citizen Kane Book*, Boston: Little, 1971.

Katz, Ephraim. *The Film Encyclopedia*, New York: Putnam Publishing Group, 1979.

Kobler, John. *Damned in Paradise, The Life of John Barrymore*, New York: Athenaeum, 1977.

Kotsilibas-Davis, James. *The Barrymores: The Royal Family in Hollywood*, New York: Crown Publishers, 1981.

McGilligan, Pat. *Backstory*, Berkeley and Los Angeles: University of California Press, 1986.

Maltin, Leonard. *TV Movies*, New York: New American Library, 1982.

Marx, Arthur. *Goldwyn, A Biography of the Man Behind the Myth*, New York: Norton, 1976.

Milland, Ray. *Wild-Eyed In Babylon*, New York: William Morrow & Co., 1974.

Moore, Darrell. *The Best, Worst, and Most Unusual: Horror Films*, New York: Beekman House, 1983.

Mosley, Leonard. *Zanuck: the Rise and Fall of Hollywood's Last Tycoon*, Boston: Little, Brown and Co., 1971.

Ott, Frederick W. *The Films of Carole Lombard*, Secaucus, New Jersey: Citadel Press, 1972.

Russell, Rosalind. *Life is a Banquet*, New York: Random House, 1971.

Shepherd, Donald and Slatzer, Dave Grayson. *Duke: The Life and Times of John Wayne*, Garden City, New York: Doubleday and Co., 1984.

Shipman, David. *The Great Movie Stars, The Golden Years*, New York: Plenum Publishing, 1979.

Sikov, Ed. *Screwball: Hollywood's Madcap Romantic Comedies*, New York: Crown Publishers, 1989.

Sinclair, Andrew. *John Ford*, New York: The Dial Press, 1979.

Spoto, Donald. *The Dark Side of Genius: The Life of Alfred Hitchcock*, New York: Ballantine Books, 1983.

Taylor, Al and Roy, Sue. *Making a Monster*, New York: Crown Publishers, Inc., 1980.

Tierney, Gene. *Self Portrait*, New York: Wyden Books, 1978.

Thomas, Bob. *King Cohn*, New York: Putnam, 1967.

Thomas, Bob. *Selznick*, Garden City, New York: Doubleday & Co., 1970.

Thomas, Tony, and Solomon, Aubrey. *The Films of Twentieth Century Fox*, Secaucus, New Jersey: Citadel Press, 1985.

Wiley, Mason and Bona, Damien. *Inside Oscar: The Unofficial History of the Academy Awards*, New York: Ballantine Books, 1986.

Wood, Tom. *The Bright Side of Billy Wilder, Primarily*, Garden City: Doubleday & Co., 1969.

Zierold, Norman J. *The Child Stars*, New York: Coward-McCann, Inc., 1965.

Zolotow, Maurice. *Billy Wilder in Hollywood*, New York: G.P. Putnam's Sons, 1977.